Foundations of
Criminal Investigation

Foundations of
Criminal Investigation

Frank Morn

Carolina Academic Press
Durham, North Carolina

Library of Congress Cataloging-in-Publication Data

Morn, Frank, 1937–
    Foundations of criminal investigation / Frank Morn.
        p.   cm.
    Includes bibliographical references
    ISBN 0-89089-874-X
    1. Criminal investigation. 2. Forensic sciences. I. Title.
HV8073.M7824 1999
363.25—dc21   99-28283
                                                          CIP

Carolina Academic Press
700 Kent Street
Durham, North Carolina 27701
Telephone (919) 489-7486
Fax (919) 493-5668
E-mail: cap@cap-press.com
www.cap-press.com

Printed in the United States of America

Contents

SPECIFIC CRIMES INVESTIGATION

Foundations of
Criminal Investigation

INTRODUCTION

Chapter 1

Scientific Method and the Criminal Investigative Process[1]

Introduction

The scientific method is a process and procedure used to find and analyze information. The purpose of "pure" or theoretical research is to develop and test theories. When possible, this method is used to predict actions and interactions in the world as well.

"Applied" researchers, on the other hand, are less concerned with theory and are more interested in current problems and how their work can be used in practical ways. Both types of researchers are important in trying to understand and explain the complicated world and universe.

Although "science" seems to be an operative word here, the process of science is not monopolized by the various disciplines of the so-called "hard sciences." Instead, all seekers of information, all investigators, may profit from using a systematic approach. Journalists, historians, and a variety of social scientists use a variation of the scientific method, as do criminal investigators. Criminal investigators, of course, use methods that are much more applied than theoretical. That is not to say that the urge for the theoretical problem solver is not there; witness the popularity of the various fictional detectives and mystery writers in Anglo-American literature. Sherlock Holmes, the private armchair theoretician, and Inspector Lastrade, the public policeman caught up in the more mundane aspects of investigation, illustrate the point.

Consideration of research methods does raise a question that is more pressing in the world of academic criminal investigators than it is perhaps for other methodologists; i.e., is investigation/research an "art" or a "science"? Perhaps the question is a bit academic, but its answer is important. Because if investigation is an art, very little might be taught. Just like most crime is committed by a few people, much of the successful criminal inves-

---

1. Much of what follows I owe to James W. Osterburg's "The Investigative Process," in the *Journal of Criminal Law, Criminology and Police Science*, vol. 59, no. 1 (1968), pp. 152–158; and "The Scientific Method and Criminal Investigation," in the *Journal of Police Science and Administration*, vol. 9, no. 2 (1981), pp. 135–142.

MacNelly's view

tigation is done by a few investigators from a large pool. In short, a few stars do most of the successful work. One study indicated that twelve percent of the detectives did fifty percent of the arrests. One-fifth of the detectives studied affected no arrests at all. Teaching the investigative process, therefore, will likely fall on deaf ears. On the other hand, if investigation is a science, its methods could be taught and successful investigators might be made rather than just born. Indeed investigation/research is both an art and a science. A small number of investigators/researchers are born to do the work. All they need are the fundamentals to get started and the means to discover their own innate talents.

All researchers—academic, scientific, or criminal investigators—must make four assumptions described by the words determinism, objectivity, relativism, and skepticism.

Determinism means that one assumes that there is a fact or truth "out there" and it can be discovered. Such a notion can be seen in the popular idea of the "six degrees of separation." In short, this means that anything can be known within six phone calls. Of course, a rational person knows there are many undiscoverable facts out there that are irretrievably lost. Nonetheless, one must assume or act as if that is not the case, as such a view fuels the investigation.

a locard exchange

Objectivity has to do with the researcher's prejudices. We all have biases, and by merely being on the scene, a crime scene for example, we change it. Investigators need to be aware of their own biases and work to control them as much as possible. Natural scientists have laboratories, or controlled environments, in which to minimize any bias. Social scientists have concocted techniques, such as random sampling, to do likewise. Professional standards of ethics guide others, such as journalists, to control their biases. Objectivity is particularly important for criminal investigators when issues of racism, sexism, and classism arise.

Relativism means that facts have meaning and importance but they may not have equal value. There are so many possible pieces of information that it is critical to have a means to allow more important pieces to emerge. One way to look at relativism is the notion of Occum's Razor or the Law of Parsimony. Simply put, this principle suggests that one should do the simplest thing first. In a jigsaw puzzle, for example, one finds border and corner pieces first, and then assembles the patterns and colors. Doing the easiest pieces first paves the way for accomplishing more difficult and abstract ones. It is like an athlete, perhaps, stretching and warming up before the start of the contest.

Skepticism means that one must look at information and sources of information with some "healthy doubt." Information and sources must be tested for reliability. In fact, the investigative process is largely testing and retesting propositions and positions that one has uncovered.

The Scientific Method

The scientific method is made up of four distinct but equally important steps: (1) the determination of a problem, (2) the collection of information, (3) the analysis of information, and (4) the presentation of information.

Determination of a Problem

In any investigative endeavor it is important to frame the project in a problematic way. For example, to study the causes of the Civil War takes on new meaning and momentum if one addresses the issue of slavery (or economics, or nationalism, or conflicting cultures, or religion) as the cause of the conflict. By doing this, one may create a hypothesis or tentative answer to be proved or disproved. Such an exercise gives direction to the investigation. There is a danger, of course, that one sets up a problem or hypothesis and then looks only for information to support that position. To safeguard oneself from such a pitfall, the investigator should think of these hypotheses as only tentative, as ideas subject to change as information is objectively gathered.

For criminal investigators this stage is particularly important. At first glance this would not seem apparent. After all, that dead body is a dead body, or that fire is a fire. What is problematic about that? Therefore, corpus delicti is useful here.

Corpus delicti, in the law, is "the body of the crime," the elements that make up the criminal law. More appropriately for the criminal investigator, it is all of the elements of the crime. In other words, "has a crime been committed?"

Back to the dead body. There are at least four causes of death: natural causes, accident, suicide and homicide. Clearly in the latter two cases the investigator has a jurisdictional responsibility; there is a legitimate problem. In the earlier two cases, the role of the criminal investigator is not as clear or self-evident. Fires may start by accident, nature, or arson. In every criminal investigation a corpus delicti must be established before the legitimate research goes on. Certainly such a quest seems self-evident and agreeable. But in some circumstances, as in a rape investigation, corpus delicti may become controversial as investigators are occasionally accused of not believing the victim.

Collection of Information

The second commonly accepted, and perhaps the most interesting, step in the scientific methodology is collecting the data or facts. The desire is to reduce ambiguity and come as close to certainty as possible. This is true of the criminal investigative process as well. There will always be some constraints in obtaining information. For example, that historian working on the causes of the Civil War will not be able to talk to slaves or Presidents Abraham Lincoln or Jefferson Davis. An archeologist of early Babylonian cultures may not be able to go into Iraq. Furthermore, there are hard facts, or pieces of information that have a direct link to a project in which you are working. There may be soft facts— those where the linkage is weak but can be made by inference. Every researcher has to do the best he or she can within certain constraints.

Clearly the criminal investigator faces obstacles as well. For example, the United States Supreme Court has placed restraints on search and seizure practices. Warrants must be obtained. Inappropriate interrogations may "taint" evidence or information and make them inadmissible in court. The jurisprudential doctrine of the "Fruit of the Poisoned Tree" stipulates that good information (fruit) obtained inappropriately becomes poisoned and bad.[2]

---

2. Jack Call, "Constitutional Limitations on Police Investigations," in James N. Gilbert, *Criminal Investigation: Essays and Cases* (Columbus, OH: Merrill Publishing Company, 1990), pp. 55–75.

There may be bureaucratic restraints as well. For example, investigators might have to work on several cases at once or have limited resources due to a crime wave.[3]

The collection of facts may be guided by one of four research "strategies." Basically, these strategies can be found in all research/investigative activities, and are described by the words historical, observational, survey, and experimental.

Historical research, aside from historians doing historical studies themselves, places the discipline and research in a historical context. For example, a sociologist studying current race relations would want to study past race riots.

Observational research entails going out and looking at that which one wants to study. A student of educational psychology, for example, might want to observe the interaction of students in a classroom. An anthropologist might want to watch tribal relations in a jungle community in the Amazon.

Survey research is the process of asking questions and obtaining answers from people and other sources. People might be asked their voting preferences and patterns in exit polls. In various self-reporting crime surveys, people might be asked if they had been a victim of a crime and whether they reported it to the police.

Experimental research uses the laboratory, with all of its scientific paraphernalia in which to ask and test questions. The search for the causes and cures of a disease would take place in the lab.

All of these strategies are respectable ways of collecting facts. Indeed, some researchers may use all four. Criminal investigation, as a research method, certainly uses all four; but like many fact-seeking endeavors, it has an emphasis. These strategies are listed below according to their importance to the criminal investigator.

1. *Historical*, because by the time an investigator arrives at the scene all crimes have become historical events.
2. *Survey*, because a major source of information in these historical events will be gained by questioning, interviewing, and interrogating people.
3. *Observational*, because scenes, suspects, and circumstances will be closely scrutinized. Observational strategies would be even more important in undercover and surveillance activities.

---

3. See David M. Jones, "Public Administration Theory and the Study of Criminal Investigation," in James N. Gilbert, *Criminal Investigation: Essays and Cases* (Columbus, OH: Merrill Publishing Company, 1990), pp. 117–127; and James R. Farris, "Managing for Investigative Productivity," in Gilbert, pp. 129–135.

| 4. *Experimental*, because physical evidence and forensic science has become increasingly important in criminal investigation, but the ordinary investigator would relegate this to the expert.

All of these strategies, as for many scientific methodologies, may be used on the same project but they are not all equally important for criminal investigation.[4]

There are several "sources" of information used in the collection of facts. Again these are important for any researcher/investigator, but here they are discussed in terms of the criminal investigator.

People are a major source of information; they may be a vexing source as well. For example, both the victim and the offender are primary sources of information. Many investigators may argue that the victim's and offender's testimonies to any event have particular strength. This is true, but there are some pitfalls as well. A victim of a crime has been traumatized by the event; being a victim would be a surprising and intimidating experience. Consequently, a victim's observation and recollection, while important, might be faulty and incomplete. A suspected or accused offender has a vested interest in appearing innocent. There is a "song of the streets" in most police circles, and that song is that "everyone lies." This may not be true for the general public, but it certainly is truer for offenders. Other witnesses may include "direct" and "indirect" witnesses. Direct witnesses are those who saw the criminal-victim encounter but were not personally involved. A variety of elements, discussed in later chapters, will undermine the reliability of these witnesses as well. Indirect witnesses are those who did not see the event but because of living or working patterns they were in the vicinity of the crime. Informants are people, many of whom are petty criminals themselves, who for a variety of personal and pecuniary reasons become sources of information to the investigator. A host of ethical problems, discussed in a later chapter, surround this information source. Significant others, such as patrol officers, other detectives working on similar cases, supervisors in charge of resources, and a variety of academic and scientific experts, may be important sources of information in any inquiry.

Documents are another important source of information in any research work. The historian rummages through manuscript collections to find diaries and letters of those who lived in the past. A sociologist may study census data while a political scientist reads congressional reports. An arche-

---

4. Indeed some would argue for "futures" research as well. William L. Tafoya, "Futures Research Implications for Criminal Investigations," in Gilbert, pp. 197–218.

ologist studies ancient languages and texts. The criminal investigator must use a host of documents as well. For example, "field reports" from crime scene investigators detailing the sketch of the scene, photographs, interviews of witnesses, and lab conclusions are important documents that give direction to the investigation. Various in-house sources such as "Modus Operandi" and "Known Offenders" files are constant references.

Personal Experience is another source of information. One's memory and past experience form an "occupational wisdom" that allows for intuitive breakthroughs in research and investigation. The discovery of a tomb in Egypt may appear to be serendipity; but generally it is due to years of ground work.

Organizational Setting is another source of information. Studying the Supreme Court becomes more manageable with the support of those who are in charge of that court. The work of academic professors is expedited by release time and funding from their universities. This is specially true of the criminal investigator. Resources, in terms of money, personnel, and time, shape the investigative process. For example, as the rise of the "case disposition guides" would suggest the amount of time and effort expended on a case might vary depending upon police administrators.

Science — here meaning the so-called hard or natural sciences — has provided major advances in investigative practices. For example, the invention and development of the computer has touched such investigators as historians, political scientists, and sociologists. New findings in genetics, for example, may reshape how psychologists think about homosexuality. Developments in meteorology, botany, and biology may impact the archaeological study of the rise and fall of ancient cultures. The criminal investigator has increasingly benefitted from advances in science. Physical evidence, from minute drops of blood and semen to fibers and hair, can be examined by scientists. The discovery of DNA and the development of so-called "genetic fingerprinting" have revolutionized personal and specific identification of persons using minute samples of body fluids.

When collecting information, keep in mind that the standing or weight of any particular piece of information that is gathered depends upon four principals: whether or not the information is germane, its reliability, its completeness, and its consistency.

(1)*Germane* brings to mind whether or not the data, facts, or evidence are relevant and pertinent to the task at hand. In the discovery and development of facts, many pieces of information do not seem important and related. The relevance of the information may not become evident until subsequent research reveals its importance. There is the dual danger of not collecting the information only to discover later how important it is, and, conversely, over-collecting data. How many college students researching a term paper in a panic rush back to the library in hopes of finding something they remember reading earlier but failed to note? And as they write their research paper they find that lost information indispensable. Or how many students find that in their packet of 3-by-5-inch research cards one-half never make it into the body of their research paper? Of course, this problem confronts all researchers, and criminal investigators are no exception. For example, that discarded match-book cover near a crime scene at first seems irrelevant but later looms large in tying a particular person to that scene.

2. _Reliability_ asks if the method of inquiry is sound. If another investigator gathers information from the scene and uses the same methods, will his or her results be the same? Is the data real or fabricated? The data may be very germane to the investigation, but is it honest? In history, for example, a series of papers by German Chancellor Adolph Hitler were "discovered." After creating quite a stir in scholarly circles, the papers were found to be forgeries. Almost every academic and scientific discipline has such horror stories. Of course, criminal investigators have similar problems. Even the best of people might become unreliable witnesses. Trauma as well as ordinary inattentiveness and forgetfulness tend to make many law abiding people bad sources of information. By definition, almost all criminals are deceptive and ready to lie in order to avoid arrest and prosecution.

3. _Completeness or sufficiency_ to whether the information validates what is already known. Does it reduce ambiguity and the need for inferential interpretation? All researchers/investigators want clean, causal lines linking A to B to C. In short, they want a tidy project. The stronger these links the firmer the conclusions. On the other hand, the weaker the links are the more uncertain the conclusions. In reality, of course, such completeness and finality can rarely be achieved. Criminal investigators have additional work and bureaucratic pressures that make the search for completeness difficult.

4. _Consistency_ addresses the notion of common sense. Is this data, evidence, or story appropriate? Do they fall within the parameters of "normalcy." Of course, there must be room for the extraordinary, the sensational new discovery. But, given conventional wisdom, the information should not be too preposterous. Criminal investigators are often confronted with the problem of consistency. On one hand, the information is simple and clear-cut. For example, an ordinary residency with spent gun cartridge casings is inconsistent. On the other hand, to find such data at a gun club would not be inconsistent. Additionally, an ordinary person being questioned who is acting extremely nervous seems inconsistent and suggestive of complicity. Conversely, a person who is known to be nervous and who acts nervous seems normal. But criminal events and actors are not so easily explained. In other words, even a normal and innocent person should

be nervous under accusation and interrogation. Whereas an experienced criminal might appear confident and unruffled.

Analysis of Information

One may not cleanly break off the collection of information. As new thinking and analysis of the problem occurs, the investigator might feel compelled to do further research. Furthermore, the collection of new information is exciting and interesting and many researchers find it difficult to get to the more difficult stage of analysis. Nonetheless, analysis of the accumulated facts against the backdrop of earlier problems or hypotheses must occur. Analysis will be aided if several things are kept in mind.

One of the first things to do in the analysis of the facts is to _arrange_ them into patterns or to give apparent nonsense some sensible meaning. Of course the standard, more established scientific way is to classify the facts. For generations natural scientists have been creating vast classification systems, such as phylum of animals or a periodic chart of chemical elements. Historians have the principles of chronology to bring order out of the seeming disorder of facts. Clearly Occum's Razor or the Law of Parsimony is relevant here. Analysis becomes easier if the simplest things are done first; the very process of breaking ground for what is to follow.

Validity is another important issue in the investigative process. Basically, validity is the correspondence between the collected information and the real world. In sociological and anthropological studies, for example, the presence of the researcher may shape the conduct of the people being observed. A tribe or group of people might act or answer questions differently than if the observers had not been there. This would be a problem of "internal validity." The similarity to criminal investigation is obvious. A witness or a suspect to a crime might change his story or behavior because of the presence of the police officer. "External validity," on the other hand, has to do with the generalizations one may make from data. Does this collected sample of information reflect the larger picture? By asking doctors and lawyers a set of questions can we believe that the rest of the community agrees? Serial killer profiling by talking to several serial killers and creating a social and psychological profile of them to better capture those who are still active is an example of striving for external validity in criminal investigation.

Another thing to be aware of is *intuition.* Simply defined, intuition is the "blinding breakthrough"; the transition from not knowing to knowing. Although intuition is not magic, it is almost magical. In order to achieve this intuitive insight, several steps or prerequisites are needed.

1. One's mind must be steeped in the details and the facts of the investigative project.

2. Within reason one must be freed from competing interests and worries.
3. One should be free from distractions and interruptions.
4. One should be free from mental and physical fatigue.
5. One should have periods of rest or diversion away from the conscious concentration on the problem.
6. One should get intellectual stimulation from colleagues to fertilize his or her own imagination and test hypotheses.
7. One should have access to facilities for recording fleeting intuitive thoughts as they arise.

The story of Sir Isaac Newton being hit on the head by an apple falling from a tree and his sudden understanding of the laws of gravity illustrate the intuitive process. Ancient Greek philosopher-scientists running through the streets of Athens partially clad shouting "Eureka, I've found it" is another. That is why, perhaps, that in higher education the "great researchers" are given large grants and small teaching assignments. This might be possible, in some Sherlock Holmesian way, for criminal investigators as well. But modern day police/detective bureaucracies are such that the luxury of intuition is rare.

Methodological *orientations* at this point also impact the analysis of data. Inductive analysis or "a posteriori" process, goes from empirical facts or particulars to general principles. Experience and experimentation are the important elements behind this form of analysis. Accumulated data, such as numbers, observations, and historical events, leads one to make a general conclusion. In the past this empiricism was difficult because enormous numbers of particular facts were necessary to remove doubt from the conclusions. Probabilities rather than certainties were likely. Laws of statistics and probability and sampling helped the analysis somewhat. Of course, the advent of computers and their power has made induction more attractive.

Deductive analysis begins with a generalization or premise and goes to a particular conclusion, thus the "a priori" process goes from cause to effect. Theory becomes a major guide to this analytical tool. Aristotle's syllogisms are a part of such logic. A major premise or theory is known. A minor premise is stated. Then a conclusion might be drawn.

Major premise	$A = B$
Minor premise	$B = C$
Conclusion	$A = C$

Of course, one must be careful of the major premise; for example:

Major premise	All birds fly
Minor premise	Penguins are birds
Conclusion	Penguins can fly

This syllogism flies (pardon the pun) in the face of empirical observation because, in fact, penguins do not fly. However, the predictive power of the syllogism indicates, perhaps, that penguins did at one time fly and evolution and adaptation to new environments and conditions robbed them of such ability.

Finally in this analysis phase, as the data begin to take shape and meaning it is time to test and/or revise the original hypotheses established earlier. The researchers might, indeed, find themselves going back to the beginning and starting the process all over using a new hypothesis.

Presentation of Information

The presentation of one's research and investigations is as critical as all the previous steps. Work needs to be shared with others, peers, and critical public to advance the state of the science, discipline, or activity. Scientists need to report their work to provide others with an opportunity to replicate and test its validity. Papers presented at conferences and in peer reviewed journals are common devices for presentation. Scholarly books are another way to report years of investigation and research. Criminal investigators also need to present the findings of their inquiries. Reports are filled out and files are compiled for other persons in the change of investigation. For example, a crime scene investigator or patrol officer must create a field report that is used by subsequent plainclothes detectives. These detectives, in turn, must prepare documents for their supervisors and other investigators who might come on the scene. Finally, and most importantly, the investigative case file must go to the prosecutor for a decision on further action. A prosecutor might "nols-pros" (short for *nolle prosequi* or no prosecution), the refusal to prosecute based on inadequacies of the case file or previous investigation. If the case is prosecutable then the detective will likely be called upon to present the findings in a public forum, the courtroom. In short, the presentation of one's data in any research/investigative activity will reflect past methodological skill and future outcomes of the research or case.

The Good Investigator

The discussion above was designed to show, in an admittedly simplistic overview, the scientific method and its close relationship to the criminal investigative process. Two final points need to be made.

First, the investigator—contrary to natural inclination, perhaps—must appreciate the context within which his work is carried out. Organizational and financial resources are important. The "mission" of the organization, for example, might shape research efforts. The work of an academic researcher is affected by the kind of institution of higher education in which she works. The expectations and support of a research university is considerably different than those found at a teaching college. Pressures for tenure, and whether research or teaching is valued more highly, shapes the quality and quantity of the investigator's activity. Of course, these factors are similar in criminal investigative units as well. Is it a large organization in which detectives are broken down into specialties such as homicide, bunco, and robbery? Or is it a small one in which the detective is required to take on any crime no matter what its nature?

There is a distinct difference between federal criminal investigators and local ones as well.[5] Broadly speaking, the federal police have a clear single-purposed mandate: fight and investigate crime. Local police have to do many diverse tasks such as patrol the streets, prevent disorder, and provide a variety of social services. But to be more specific, let's look at the differences in activities between a detective at the Federal Bureau of Investigation (FBI) and the typical local police detective.

FBI	LOCAL
1. Deals largely with organized crime	1. Deals with personal crime
2. Suspects are less likely to know about the investigation and flee	2. Suspects are more likely to flee
3. Work enviroment is orderly	3. Work evironment is less orderly
4. Staid, regulated work	4. More open-ended work
5. Predictable work hours	5. Open work hours
6. Less dangerous	6. More dangerous
7. Crimes are old and stale	7. Crimes are fresh
8. Deals with a limited number of crimes	8. Deals with a large number of crimes

Second, there are several personal qualities that are hallmarks of the "good investigator." Investigators, as defined here, includes students, academicians, scientists, and detectives. These qualities are:

1. *Perseverance and patience,* or the ability to stick to a project through the good times and the bad. To stay with it, given other demands and pressures, when apparent dead ends have been reached. That is not to say, however, that there is not a time to let

---

5. See James Q. Wilson, *The Investigators* (New York: Basic Books, 1978).

go and end a project. But it is easier, sometimes, to give up than to hang on; thus, perseverance marks the good investigator.

2. *Thoroughness*, or attention to the details. "The Devil (or is it The Divine?) is in the detail." In all large discoveries, the answers are in the small details. The problems with details are that they are generally small and tedious, and they are easily overlooked by the fatigued, hurried, or lazy. "Competent craftsmen," experienced investigators, get in the habit of taking intelligent short-cuts and in the process they miss important evidence.

3. *Curiosity* may have killed the cat, but it is the lifeblood of the researcher/investigator. The drive to know will be the means for a successful trip in investigations. An investigator who is bored or simply does not care is doomed from the start.

4. *Literacy*, or the ability to communicate, through writing and talking, is important in all research. It is a shame that some fields and some investigations have become so arcane that the workers can speak only to themselves; they frequently need "popularizers" to translate their knowledge to the wider public. Since criminal investigators deal with people and report writing so often, it is important to develop the literacy attribute. In fact, in policing in general and in investigations in particular "The Gift of Gab" should replace the "Gift of Grab."

5. *Intelligence*, or the general knowledge of life and people beyond the specific occupation. Often it is the insight or nuance coming from other areas of knowledge that allows a person to see and appreciate the complex and interrelated aspects of the investigation.

6. *Sensitivity*, or the appreciation and respect of other people and fields of knowledge. A student of primitive peoples would ill-serve the investigation if they had a distaste or dislike for that culture and some of its practices. Since the police and criminal investigators often work among racial and ethnic groups, it would be a poor investigation if the officers were racist. A sexist officer might ruin a rape investigation.

7. *Honesty*, or conducting the research/investigation in ethical ways. Many projects, especially those on human beings, have ethical restrictions. Issues of coercion, invasion of privacy, and moral turpitude face many researchers. Criminal investigators, faced with bureaucratic and popular pressures to produce, have enormous temptations to "fight fire with fire" and let the ends justify the means. A growing body of literature worldwide indicates that the police in general believe that their work cannot be done by the book.

8. *Courage*, or the moral and physical fortitude to see and tell the truth despite the repercussions. Criminal investigators, especially those in vice detection, see corruption all around. For years the FBI stayed away from drug enforcement simply because of the possible corrupting influence upon its agents.
9. *Technical know-how*, or understanding the processes of investigation.

The purpose of this chapter was to show the overall investigative method and how it is similar to research investigation. There will always be a few stars investigators, but most will be adequately trained people who follow a clear-cut established process. The process is easily learned and is the focus of the rest of this book. Of course, the emphasis is on the process as it relates specifically to the criminal investigator. But it is hoped that the reader appreciates that the processes used by the criminal investigator are in the tradition of all investigators.

Chapter 2

History of Criminal Investigation

Introduction

To appreciate the nature and extent of criminal investigations today the student needs to see the process, procedure, and profession in a historical context. To do so one needs to look to Europe and the developments there.

Of course, there have always been investigations and investigators in the past, but—particularly in Anglo-Saxon history—much of these were left to private persons. Government was slow to take on this expansion of power. When it did, it was frequently within a narrow area. Those earliest governments that did so, did it in the context of a police state.

Tsarist Russia set up an investigative force very early. In the sixteenth century, as the national state was being created by aggressive and ruthless leaders, Ivan the Terrible established the oprichnina, an elite guard whose job it was to spy and eliminate political criminals. Subsequent tsars— changing the name but not the mission—established similar police that specialized in political criminals. Peter the Great's Preobrazhensky office was particularly ruthless in putting down resistance to the tsar's westernizing reforms in seventeenth century. Catherine the Great did much the same in the eighteenth century. Throughout the nineteenth century similar devices, such as the Third Section and Okhrana, grew and expanded by spying on the intelligencia.[1] When the Soviet Revolution occurred these Tsarist tools were replaced by Communistic ones with a variety of names like the NKVD, Cheka, MVD and KGB. The purposes remained the same, investigators were agents of the state protecting the ruling elites against treasonous upstarts.

In France similar developments occurred after the creation of the police in the seventeenth century. But it was after the Revolution and the rise of Napoleon Bonaparte that the modern police state was established under the Minister of Interior, Joseph Fouchè. While Napoleon was off trying to conquer the world, Fouchè subdued France. He built a vast intelligence empire with agents infiltrating groups, spying on ordinary citizens, tor-

---

1. Marc Raeff, *The Well-Ordered Police State: Social and Institutional Changes Through Law in the Germanies and Russia, 1600-1800* (New Haven, CT: Yale University Press, 1983), pp. 181–250; and Sidney Monas, *The Third Section: Police and Society Under Nicholas I* (Cambridge, MA: Harvard University Press, 1961).

turing suspects under interrogation, and censuring the media. His secret service, the Sureté, had little time for ordinary crime unless it was disruptive to the ruling elites. One criminal was an embarrassment.

Eugene Vidocq was one of those marvelous characters in history who illustrate many points. First, he was an extraordinary criminal and escape artist. His knowledge of the Parisian underworld was great. However, he tired of crime and negotiated his freedom with the Sureté by becoming an informant. This arrangement grew to the extent that he eventually joined and achieved a high place in the organization leading to the expectation that "It takes a thief to catch a thief."[2]

Emanating from both Russia and France two mindsets emerged. Early detectives were spies for the state and at best they were crooked in order to be successful. To a degree England proved the point.

With rare exception ancient and medieval England kept law enforcement and crime detection in the hands of the citizenry. The monarch's power, most notably in the sheriff system, was limited and distrusted. In the popular mythology of a "robber-hero" (Robin Hood) the villain was the sheriff. As late as the seventeenth century royal experiments in policing were slight. Highway banditry became such a problem that a Highwayman Act was enacted in 1692. This law encouraged citizens to help authorities apprehend and convict a group of criminals who were on the brink of becoming heroes to the masses by offering financial rewards. A group of thief takers emerged who made a career of capturing crooks for the "blood money." The most famous was Jonathan Wild. He soon amassed a fortune by capturing criminals and collecting rewards. More often, however, he was an *agent provocateur* encouraging people to commit crime only to turn around and arrest them. He was less of a thief taker and more a thief maker. In addition, he acted as a go-between. In this process, rather than arresting a felon, Wild found the crook and exacted part of the stolen goods, some to return to the victim and some for himself. Shortly he had a thriving fencing operation. When he was eventually found out, this early private detective was tried, convicted, and sentenced to death. On his march from Newgate Prison to Tyburn Tree, the place of execution, thousands of people jeered obscenities and pelted him with garbage. In the audience watching the execution was future magistrate, Henry Fielding.[3]

Henry Fielding and his brother after him were judges at the Bow Street court in London. Henry Fielding was concerned with the growing crime and

2. Philip John Stead, *The Police of France* (New York: Macmillian, 1983) and Samuel Edwards, *The Vidocq Dossier: The Story of the World's First Detective* (Boston: Houghton-Mifflin, 1977).

3. David Nokes, ed., Henry Fielding, *Jonathan Wild* (New York: Penguin Books, 1982).

disorder on the streets of the city and in his court. He created a number of subordinates, known as the Bow Street Runners, to provide legal services to the court. They would keep order in the court, bring in felons, protect witnesses, and chase down bail jumpers. Although they were limited to the Bow Street jurisdiction they found excuse to exceed it. Furthermore, other judges followed suit. Soon, the Bow Street Runners outgrew their original mission and acted very much like a police system but they were under the direction of the judiciary. They were more a precursor to the police than an investigative unit that had to follow the establishment of the bobbies.[4]

Crime remained a problem in urban London and, increasingly, disorder became an issue. Sir Robert Peel, the home secretary, responded with the creation of the London Metropolitan Police in 1829. This modern police had uniformed, disciplined, salaried personnel guided by a preventive mission. Patrol became the backbone of this new police. Conspicuously absent were detectives. Too many negative models, from Russia and France, were visible and the bobbie system for the first decade had no detectives. It was not until the Chartists, a workers' movement demanding more representation in Parliament which was seen as radical, that the police established an investigative force to infiltrate and eliminate these groups.[5]

Consequently, as America — the country and its police — was being founded most models of policing and investigation assumed frightening and foreign proportions.

America

Colonial Era

For much of American history there was no modern police or detective organization. Throughout colonial America much of such activity was done according to Old World models, especially those from medieval England. Largely American citizens were in charge of their own investigations. There was a constable/night watch system. During the daytime constables, elected from the citizenry, would offer some police/detective work, but with rare exception they were incompetent and halfhearted. Some former constables, taking a liking to the work, provided investigative services in

---

4. T.A. Critchley, *A History of Police in England and Wales* (Montclair, NJ: Patterson Smith, 1972).

5. Wilber R. Miller, *Cops and Bobbies: Police Authority in New York and London, 1830-1870* (Chicago, IL: University of Chicago Press, 1973).

a private capacity after their official obligations expired. Even into the period of building the new nation, there was little reform.[6]

Nineteenth Century

One crime proved the inadequacies of the old system and introduced another source in the development of investigations. In July 1841, a young woman in New York City by the name of Mary Rogers disappeared. Shortly after, her nude body was found in the North River [later renamed the Hudson River]. All kinds of suspects emerged, from youth gangs, abortionists, to former boyfriends. However, the constable/night watch could make no arrests. In the meantime, James Gordon Bennett's newly established newspaper, the *New York Herald,* began investigative reporting as they criticized the police, suggested suspects, and kept the case before the public. One reporter, Edgar Allen Poe, was particularly active and even published a book based on the case. In *The Mystery of Marie Rogêt,* Poe suggested a solution that has lasted for one hundred and fifty years. In addition, he became a pioneer of a new genre, the detective puzzle. Furthermore, this case — and Poe's fictional solution — prompted the mayor of New York City to found a modern police system similar to that of the bobbies of London. Enough timidity still existed and detectives were nonexistent in these formative years. But, clearly in the emerging world of criminal investigations, representatives of the media were going to have an impact.[7]

When the modern police were created in the 1840s and 1850s detectives were not part of the program. The role of the police was to prevent crime and disorder. Ordinary patrol officers, being familiar to the area and the first on any crime scene, were likely to be the better crime investigators. Fuller development of police detectives would have to await the post-Civil War era.

Actually, some of the earliest developments of criminal investigation in America came from the Pinkerton detectives. Allan Pinkerton was a refugee from the English persecutions of the Chartists. He settled in Illinois in the 1840s and eventually ended up in Chicago. In the 1850s he was a deputy sheriff in Cook County and a postal inspector for Chicago when a group of railroad leaders approached him in 1855 to establish a railroad police, called the Northwest Police Agency. His main job, and later the main activity of his growing body of assistants called "operatives," was to pose as a customer on a railroad car and spy on the conductor.

6. Douglas Greenberg, *Crime and Law Enforcement in the Colony of New York* (Ithaca, NY: Cornell University Press, 1976).

7. James Richardson, *The New York Police: Colonial Times to 1901* (New York: Oxford University Press, 1970).

Allan Pinkerton (second seated figure from left) and secret service officers in Cumberland, Virginia, May 14, 1862.

Soon, a virtual army of spies were going through the country exposing dishonest employees. One operative heard rumors that the newly elected president, Abraham Lincoln, was to be murdered on his trip from Illinois to Washington. Somewhere in Baltimore, as there was a transfer of trains, he would be killed. Pinkerton rushed to President Lincoln with the story. Some New York police officers hearing similar rumors corroborated the story and Lincoln was spirited safely through the hostile city only to die four years later at the hands of an assassin.

After the Civil War began, the generals needed an intelligence service. When George McClellan took over the Union troops he hired Pinkerton to head up the newly formed Secret Service. Agents went throughout the South gathering information on troop strength and movements while others stayed behind to find Confederate spies in Washington. Other wartime crimes, such as government and business corruption, were investigated by the Pinkertons until McClellan lost his job. Pinkerton returned to Chicago to continue offering policing to the railroads.[8]

Throughout the remainder of the century, the Pinkerton Agency expanded in offices and obligations. Being a railroad police soon involved them

---

8. Frank Morn, *"The Eye That Never Sleeps": A History of the Pinkerton National Detective Agency,* (Bloomington, IN: Indiana University Press, 1982).

in chasing the numerous bandit gangs such as the Renos, James brothers, the Daltons, the Younger brothers, and Butch Cassidy. In addition, the Jewelers Security Alliance and the American Bankers Association retained them to chase thieves and burglars. As workers began to organize into unions, the Pinkertons got involved by providing spies who infiltrated the unions and guards to protect property from strikers. As nineteenth century detectives, the Pinkertons originated many of the procedures of the modern day investigators. Ideas on surveillance, identification, management, accountability, and managerial honesty emanate from the Pinkerton organization.

The modern local police were slow to develop a detective operation. Such activity could be done well enough by the patrol officers. Before the Civil war, only a few officers became detectives. After the war more and more detectives emerged in the local police. This was for several reasons. First, the Civil War ushered in a crime wave and having a preventive patrol to maintain order was just not enough. After all, the post-Civil War era started with a sensational murder, the assassination of President Abraham Lincoln. Second, the work of the Pinkertons, especially after Allan Pinkerton started writing about his cases and adventures, stimulated the industry. Third, even though segments of society and the law were against it, vice became an important part of society. Red light districts emerged, particularly in the large cities. These geographical segments of the urban landscape were marked with brothels, saloons, and gambling dens. Corrupt city bosses and police chiefs controlled and protected these places for a fee. On occasion uniformed officers acted as "bag men," those who picked up the bribes. But it was more discrete to have plainclothes people do this. Fourth, after the creation of the modern police, with more personnel more intensively involved in the neighborhoods, more arrests occurred. But the courts could not keep up and many of those arrested were quickly returned to the streets. Consequently, police officers saw that they needed to administer street justice, which ended up as beatings and brutality. Although, to a degree, patrol officers administered street justice, it was more discrete to have plainly dressed personnel act as thugs.[9] Fifth, criminal identification became easier with the introduction of anthropometry, or the Bertillon system. In theory this system was based on measurements of numerous features of a suspect. It was believed that if enough key measurements were taken of an individual that no other person could match them. Subsequently, the Criminal Identification Bureau was established in Chicago in 1884. Sixth, there had been some modest gains by the federal police. Postal inspectors had always been important in finding dishonest employ-

9. Samuel Walker, *A Critical History of Police Reform: The Emergence of Professionalism* (Lexington: Lexington, 1977).

ees and other mail thieves. More importantly, after the Civil War the Secret Service, the military intelligence system of the war, became active due to a wave of counterfeiting. Throughout the remainder of the century, the Secret Service was important in the war on counterfeiters. Seventh, popular literature had some impact as well. The number of crime reporters grew and were as knowledgeable about the underworld and the criminal justice system as most detectives. Their investigations and stories filled the newspapers and educated the public. Several famous detectives, like Allan Pinkerton, wrote books about their exploits. For example, Pinkerton between 1874 and 1884 wrote more than a dozen books about his cases and became the father of the "true detective" genre. Mark Twain's *Puddin' Head Wilson* introduced the reading public to the idea of fingerprints as a means of identification. Eighth, science was having some impact upon criminal investigation. Besides the rise of the Bertillon system other advances in science were appearing. For example, in France and Germany some scientists noted identifying striations on slugs taken from bodies.[10] However, further development of ballistics would have to await the twentieth century. By the turn of the century, a means of distinguishing animal from human blood was attained. In addition, blood was placed into four distinct groups, A, B, AB, and O. Finally, a few sensational characters appeared on the scene as detectives. In Chicago, John Bonfield dominated policing throughout the 1880s. In New York City, Thomas Byrnes became chief of detectives and later was promoted to chief of police. In 1886 Byrnes published *Professional Criminals*; it was mostly his rogues gallery, but the book contained some interesting discussions of criminal investigation. Later he was caught up in revelations of a scandal and was sent to prison. In fact, those scandals in New York and general dissatisfaction among the police chiefs across the country over their lack of control over their subordinates led to reform.

Twentieth Century

Progressive Era, 1900–1920

As early as 1892 several police chiefs met at the Columbian Exposition World's Fair in Chicago to discuss the plight of policing in America. A new organization, the International Association of Chiefs of Police, resulted.

High on their agenda was the professionalization of the police. Beginning in the early twentieth century, these ""professionalizers"—people like Richard Sylvester and August Vollmer, to name a few—sought to

10. Jurgen Thorwald, *The Marks of Cain* (London: Thames and Hudson, 1969).

reform the police. Reform was to be done in several ways. First, the chief was assured power over subordinates such as captains. The position of chief was less political and was protected from the whims of city bosses. Second, the quality of personnel was based on merit hiring and promotion, thus politics in hiring and promotion was removed. Third, officers were supposed to be trained, and August Vollmer created a training academy for his police department in Berkeley, California. Soon, the notion of police academies spread throughout the nation. Fourth, the emphasis of policing was rearranged. The purpose of the Peel revolution was to create a preventive police. Patrol was to be the backbone of policing. Order, maintenance, and social service took precedence over crime fighting. The "professionalizers" emphasized crime fighting as a major mission and bolstered the development of detectives and the detection process. Fifth, the advent of dactyloscopy or fingerprints gave investigation impetus and the "professionalizers" were in the forefront of adopting this new science.[11]

In addition, during the Progressive era the federal police grew. By the turn of the century the Secret Service remained largely concerned with counterfeiters. After three presidential assassinations (Abraham Lincoln in 1865, James A. Garfield in 1882, and William McKinley in 1901), the role of the Secret Service was expanded. Vice President Theodore Roosevelt, a former police commissioner of New York City, became president upon the murder of McKinley and presidential protection by the Secret Service soon followed. Roosevelt angered Congress by using the Secret Service — agents like William Burns, who later formed a famous private detective agency and headed the Bureau of Investigation — to spy and investigate the misdoings of congressmen. A law was passed forbidding this practice, and in 1908 Roosevelt simply created another organization in the Justice Department to do so — the Bureau of Investigation. Due to fears over radical aliens, coast guards and border patrols became a part of the Immigration and Naturalization Service. Passage of the Harrison Drug Act in 1914 and the Volstead Act in 1920 promised to expand the power of the federal police.[12]

Crime Control Decades, 1920–1960

The professionalizing movement expanded throughout 1920-1960. August Vollmer's police academy idea became prevalent. Vollmer, as chief of the Berkeley, California, police department used a nearby college, the University of California, to further promote academic police studies. Besides

---

11. Samuel Walker, *Popular Justice: A History of American Criminal Justice* (New York: Oxford University Press, 1980).
12. Sanford Unger, *FBI* (Boston: Little, Brown, 1971).

J. Edgar Hoover, 1935.

administration, investigations were highlighted as part of this new academic component. Paul L. Kirk, a biochemist and founding member of this "School of Criminology," coined the word criminalistics and wrote a classic textbook, *Crime Investigation: Physical Evidence and the Police Laboratory.*[13]

The bureau of investigation had little to do in the first decades of its existence. Leadership and personnel were not of the highest quality and a scandal occurred in the early 1920s. J. Edgar Hoover took over in 1924 and began to reform the organization. Higher hiring standards were instituted for personnel. The largest employment pool was from the ranks of lawyers and accountants. In the 1930s the number of federal crimes increased. Bank robbery, kidnaping, and Communists soon became an FBI (as it was officially named in 1935) preoccupation. In 1932, a crime laboratory was opened. Three years later, a National Academy was started. The collection of crime statistics began and led to the issuing of the Uni-

13. Gene E. Carte and Elaine H. Carte, *Police Reform in the United States: The Era of August Vollmer* (Berkeley: University of California Press, 1975). Also see Frank Morn, *Academic Politics and the History of Criminal Justice Education* (Westport, CT: Greenwood Press, 1995).

form Crime Report. Famous gangsters, such as Pretty Boy Floyd, Bonnie and Clyde, and John Dillinger, cast the FBI in heroic roles. Popular media and entertainment industries, such as the radio and motion pictures, soon popularized Hoover and his men.[14]

Other agencies expanded their role as well. The Internal Revenue Service chased income tax evaders. Some famous gangsters, like Al Capone, ended up going to jail for tax evasion rather than other crimes. Prohibition agents, under such leaders as Eliot Ness, were active in the 1920s but a shift occurred after repeal. Harry Anslinger's agents in the Federal Bureau of Narcotics became more active particularly after the passage of the Marijuana Act in 1937. With the advent of World War II and the Cold War, concerns turned to organized crime and Communists.

Modern Era, 1960s and Beyond

The 1960s had a profound impact upon America and the criminal justice system. Ordinary crime increased at tremendous rates. Spectacular crime, such as assassinations and mass murders, also challenged the system. Public disorder in the form of racial riots and student civil disobedience further shook the system. Concern over radical student and racial groups stimulated the FBI. In 1956, COINTELPRO (Counter Intelligence Program) was started and was expanded in the 1960s. The Socialist Workers Party, Students For A Democratic Society, the Black Panthers, to name a few, became the focus of the FBI.[15]

The Due Process Revolution occurred in which the Supreme Court, under the leadership of Earl Warren, made decisions that addressed police work. Some of these had a direct relationship to investigations. Decisions on search and interrogation, such as *Mapp v. Ohio* (1961), *Escobido v. Illinois* (1964) and *Miranda v. Arizona* (1966), promised to make the work of detectives more accountable and difficult.[16]

Development of criminal justice as an academic discipline promised to bring research and education to bear on the problems of crime and criminal justice in America beginning in the 1970s. Throughout the 1970s, the Law Enforcement Assistance Administration (LEAA) allocated millions of dollars to local police agencies to become more efficient. A crime fighting and investigating hardware industry was started. Law Enforcement Educational Programs (LEEP) sent thousands of dollars to colleges and universities to set up academic criminal justice programs. The drug wars of the 1980s greatly expanded the role of the Drug Enforcement Administration

---

14. Ibid.

15. David J. Garrow, *The FBI and Martin Luther King, Jr.* (New York: Penguin Books, 1981).

16. Archibald Cox, *The Warren Court*, (Cambridge: Harvard University Press, 1968).

(DEA) and the FBI. The division of Alcohol, Tobacco, and Firearms (ATF) took on new importance as guns, arson, and explosions became a greater threat in the 1980s and 1990s.

Perhaps the biggest advance for investigations in the modern era has come from two sources. First, there was the advent of genetic fingerprinting due to DNA.[17] Deoxyribonucleic acid is the building block of all life—a genetic material found identically in every cell of an individual that determines everything, from the mundane to the monumental, about a life form. DNA is unique to each individual, with the chance of duplication with another individual being estimated at between 30 and 100 billion to 1. The pioneering work of Alec Jefferys in genetic fingerprinting at Leichester University in England helped convict a rapist killer in 1987.[18] That same year Tommie Lee Andrews was convicted of several rapes in Orlando, Florida, due to DNA evidence. The Andrews case was the first use of DNA evidence in the United States. The following year on December 15, 1988, the FBI laboratory began offering DNA analysis.

Computers and information management have been important to investigations as well.[19] Of course, computer crime has increased at alarming rates. Initially these "hackers" had considerable more skill than most detective units. Money theft using computers was the largest problem. But other problems were theft of information from computers, damage to software, alteration of data, and theft of services. Computers have become useful to investigators in many ways. First, on the most elemental level, they have been used as word processors replacing the typewriter. Second, they have been used to store vast amounts of information. Data banks of missing persons, stolen guns, and repeat offenders are kept. Third, they are an analytical tool to manipulate data. For example, the automated fingerprint system (AFIS) can rapidly sort through thousands of fingerprints, a process that would take an individual several months. Crimes analysis units might also create more detailed and reliable maps of crime patterns in their community.

Clearly, advances in science in the mid-20th century have revolutionized criminal investigations.

Conclusion

History has valuable lessons for understanding criminal investigation. On one hand, there is a history of suspicion toward detection. In those

---

17. This will be explored more fully in a later chapter.
18. Joseph Wambaugh, *The Blooding* (New York: Bantam Books, 1989).
19. See Bruce Sterling, *The Hacker Crackdown, Law and Disorder on the Electronic Frontier* (New York: Bantam Books, 1992).

countries labeled police states, the investigators play a major role in discovering and destroying enemies of the state. Even in more democratic
settings, there is the belief that daily dealings with the lowest of society
somehow taints the investigator, particularly among groups who feel
oppressed, as the detective is looked upon with fear. On the other hand,
rising crime problems need to be met. One way to do so is to keep the
police efficient but responsible to the people. At first, those most in need
of detective services simply hired private detectives. Next, the sharpest
development was on the local levels. It was not until the twentieth century that the federal agencies began and maintained momentum in detection. Such development was connected to the wider society's faith and
acceptance of the role of government. Particularly after the Progressive
era, Americans expected more in terms of police power to come from the
federal government. Certainly, one way to control this instrument of government was to minimize corruption and maximize efficiency, which was
best done by using a scientific methodology, such as the investigative
process.

INVESTIGATIVE
PROCESS

Chapter 3

Preliminary Investigations

Introduction

General Connections

In any investigative process the beginning is generally more important than any other stage. Every investigative exercise, such as a college student fulfilling a class research requirement, an academic professor conducting a major project, or a criminal investigator working on a crime scene, the beginning sets the dimensions of later success or failure. Preliminary stages are important across the world of research in additional ways.

The *Discovery and Detail stage* is when the greatest excitement and newness of information occurs. Levels of learning, if not its subtlety, occurs at this time. In that excitement, however, some of the detail may be overlooked, and in the last analysis, it is the detail that may loom large later.

In the *Destroy and Distort* stage the likelihood of disrupting reality by the intrusions of the investigator are now a problem. Simply the handling of the facts, the evidence, the observation may alter it. Not just ones biases — which, of course are always a problem — but the mere presence of the investigator changes things.

The *Chaos and Control* stage is when information discovered and distorted also most likely will lack meaning; it will appear unconnected and unreliable. The investigator must bring some sort of control to the otherwise chaotic data. Of course, the personal bias or prejudice of the investigator needs to be controlled at this time.

These three stages, or connections to all researchers, are true for the criminal investigator, as well.

Definitions

Generally speaking when the phrase "preliminary investigations" is raised in criminal investigations, it refers to the series of activities going on at the crime scene. But the crime scene itself takes on several meanings that must be kept in mind.

Obviously, the crime scene is the *immediate* area in which a crime has been committed. This "hot scene" is the room in which the body was found, the automobile in which the rape occurred, the apartment foyer where the robber sprung for his victim, and the place of origin where the arsonist struck the fire. Of course, the importance of this form of crime scene is obvious.

Adjacent areas may be equally important. To appreciate these "warm scenes" the reader must understand the nature of most criminal/victim encounters. Generally speaking most criminals go through three stages in any criminal event. Like any first year college English essay there is a beginning, middle and end. Depending upon experience and preparation, the typical criminal will experience anxiety which will be useful to the investigator. For example, as the criminal approaches the criminal event itself there will be high levels of excitement and doubt. Therefore, the criminal's path of entry to the hot scene will have evidence left due to carelessness and preoccupation. We might call this "entrance-itis." While on the hot scene the criminal will be transferring his own anxiety to the victim by threats, intimidation and quickened pace. Then as the offender, or "perp" for perpetrator in police language, leaves the scene there is a relaxation over successfully doing the deed and excitement in the escape. At this stage evidence might be left due to what we might call "exit-itis." Consequently, the "warm scene" are these areas adjacent to the central or "hot scene." Not the room where the body was found but the hallways and entry ways leading to the body are critical to discover and cultivate. An investigator should find out as soon as possible any witnesses perception of where the offender came from or exited.

There are some additional things to keep in mind when defining the nature of a crime scene. Less obvious than those described above are those crimes in which there might be multiple crime scenes. For example, an offender might break into an apartment, kidnap a young woman and carry her away, rape her at some distance, kill her at still another place, and dump her body even elsewhere. In such a case there four or five possible crime scenes or places of potential information. Or a person was murdered at one place and their body was transported to another place. In this case part of the crime scene investigation would be the determination of other likely scenes.

Finally, there is always the possibility that there might be some controversy over the nature and even location of the crime scene. Take the assassination of President John F. Kennedy in Dallas, Texas in 1963. Obviously, since he was killed over a considerable distance, the automobile in which he was riding becomes an important source of information, particularly when it comes to bullet slugs. Then, there was the building from which the assassin fired the shots. These two places are important and there is little debate. But many witnesses and investigators feel there were other shots, that the president was caught in a cross-fire. If true this means that

another crimes scene or scenes—be they on the "grassy knoll" or not—
need to be investigated. In such a case, the crime scene itself becomes a
major concern of the preliminary investigations.

Importance

The preliminary or crime scene investigation is of critical practical and
academic importance for the following reasons.

Solvability. Many cases simply solve themselves. For example, a battered woman, with smoking gun in hand, standing over the dead body of
an abusive husband presents a case pretty much solved; it has high solvability. Other cases, those of a more puzzling nature, will have solvability depending upon many factors. The quick arrival of the uniformed police,
after that had been notified of the crisis, to the scene of the crime. This is
called "response time." But clearly the work done at this time, at the preliminary investigation, will impact upon the possibility of solvability and
clearance. A job poorly done here impedes subsequent investigations.

Evidence. Four types of evidence will confront the preliminary investigator. Of significant importance is *corpus delicti.* On one level, this is evidence that indeed a crime has been committed. All kinds of strange things
may happen but they do not fall within the area of criminal justice. An
explosion and accompanying fire, for instance, may be the work of a terrorist group or a faulty gas line. But there is another way to view the importance of corpus delicti and that has to do with issues of jurisdiction. First,
there is the matter of geography: does this crime fall within my jurisdictional
powers? This body on the road is one half mile beyond the city limits. Of
course, proper authorities must be notified but what share of the investigation might I lay claim to since it is outside my territory? Second, there
is the matter of agency responsibility. A crime has been committed and it
is within the jurisdiction of my police powers but the state or federal authorities will come in and take over. Let us illustrate, not only corpus delicti but
the multiplicity of policing agencies in America with a hypothetical.

Juan Ortiz, a bright young Mexican student at State College, received
a low power rifle in the mail from his parents in Darango. It was to be
used for target practice and small game hunting in the fields near the college town. It was discovered by post office personnel and the (1) University police, (2) Town police, (3) State Agency for Gun Control, (4) Postal
Inspectors, (5) Alcohol, Tobacco and Firearms agency, (6) Customs, and
(7) F.B.I. came a knocking on the door of the hapless student. In short,
who actually and ultimately had corpus delicti jurisdiction here?

Other forms of evidence will likely be discovered at this stage. One will
be *associative evidence*, or that information that links a person not on the
scene to having been on that scene earlier. There might be *trace evidence*

as well. Trace evidence raises some interesting new problems. On one level, trace evidence is minute or particularly small pieces of information such as a thread of fiber or hair strand or dusty dirt. On another level it raises the issue of relevancy. Is this piece of information related to this case? The answer predisposes the investigator to one of two investigative strategies. This evidence does not seem to be important right now but it may become so later. Therefore, I should collect it, some might call it over collect, and risk the resultant clutter. Or I might decide to not collect it and risk its loss to the investigation. Finally, there is *indicative evidence.* This evidence may appear to be normal things but indicate time lapse. For example, numerous newspapers on the front porch or mail in the letter box indicate considerable time has gone by. Dead pet gold fish floating on the surface of the aquarium, excessive dog excrement in the house might be some other indications to help conceptualize the scene.

Due Process Revolution. The United States Supreme Court has placed obstacles to optimal efficiency in the way of criminal justice in general, the police in particular, and the criminal investigator in most particular, in carrying out their job. There is a reason for this and it may be called the Frankenstein Syndrome. The agencies of criminal justice are artificial; they were created by society against many historical counter forces. Detectives were created sometime after the setting up of the police in the nineteenth century. These agencies were created for good reason, but there remained always a fear that if left alone—unencumbered and unobstructed—that they would turn on and destroy the larger society. Just like Dr. Frankenstein created life for good reasons, that life became monstrous and turned upon the creator and destroyed him. To safeguard society that monster had to be destroyed or controlled.

America does not want a gangster state, but it does not want a police state either. The Supreme Court tries to strike the balance, giving the police considerable power but at the same time safeguarding against any abuse of that power. Almost every session of the Supreme Court addresses issues of police practice particularly in the area of search and seizure and interrogation. Robbed of the opportunity for optimal efficiency through overbearing tactics the police must be more efficient in gathering evidence and witnesses at this preliminary stage of investigation.

People. Another important aspect of the preliminary investigation is that it highlights the roles of various people. A variety of people will be apart of the crime scene. First, the uniformed beat officer will be on the scene. Indeed, a primary figure in the preliminary investigation will be the uniformed branch of the police. A strong sense of territoriality might develop as these officers resent any intrusions from outsiders. What they do, and how they do it, will effect the outcome of the investigation. Beat officers will soon be joined by "officers of rank" such as sergeants and lieutenants. Second, a group of experts will shortly arrive. In larger departments there might be specialized crime scene investigators who will come in and take over, there might be officers from forensics such as evidence technicians and morgue investigators with their special skills, and finally there are the plain clothes detectives who will take over the process. Third, the press might be hovering around with critical questions, eyes and pens. Fourth, numerous onlookers linger around the scene and need to be controlled. Finally, witnesses and victims need to be taken care of so that their health and information does not become jeopardized. In short, the crime scene becomes a dramatic presentation in which bureaucratic relationships and operational skills are openly on display.[1]

Crime Scene Investigation

There are three critical steps in any crime scene investigation. Many of the comments that follow must be understood to be happening at the same time but for organizational reasons they will be set forth in discrete categories.[2]

Initial Steps

There are three important considerations or steps an officer must consider when coming upon a crime scene; they are caution, care and control, the "three C's."

First, there is *caution.* Because of the possibility of the perpetrator still being on the scene the officer should exercise caution for personal safety. But, beyond that, the officer needs to be cautious about the evidence on the scene. By just being there the officer heightens the chance of changing and destroying the purity of the scene. A walk through of the scene, a procedural necessity where special care should be taken not to touch anything, can not help but alter the scene.

Second, *care* should be taken. Presumably, in the cautious approach officers have taken care of themselves. Now it is important to care for the victim. First aid and subsequent medical attention must be arranged. If the

---

1. For a thoughtful sociological approach to this topic see William B. Sanders, *Detective Work: A Study of Criminal Investigations* (New York: The Free Press, 1979). Also R.V. Ericson, *Making Crime: A Study of Detective Work* (Toronto, Canada: Butterworth, 1981).

2. For an overview see Barry Fischer, A. Svensson and O. Wendel, *Techniques of Crime Scene Investigation,* 4th ed. (New York: Elsevier, 1987).

victim is about to die then care is needed to obtain dying declarations, a form of admissible hearsay evidence. Finally, care of evidence is needed. For example, a gun lying on the ground must be spotted and secured so that it does not disappear into the assembling crowd.

Third, there is the need to *control* the scene. An officer needs to protect the scene or at least minimize contamination. Special barriers or territorial lines with special colored tape need to announce that this an official crime scene. Control of people such as witnesses at the scene must occur. Witnesses are distraught and very susceptible to suggestions so it is necessary to separate them out and maintain their purity. One witness's story might be altered and elaborated by over hearing the talk of others.

Secondary Steps

There are numerous steps that might occur at this stage of the preliminary investigation.

First, a *sketch* or drawing of the crime scene should be done. In this modern day with all of its sophisticated technology one might question the use of this old-fashion devise. But it should be seriously considered in any crime scene investigation. The purpose of the sketch is to:

1. render a relatively uncluttered picture of the crime scene, to allow officers to "see the forest rather than the trees";
2. to give perspective, to allow officers to have a "bird's eye view" of the scene;
3. pass on to subsequent investigators a blueprint so they may place evidence on the scene much later in the investigation.

This sketch may take two forms: a rough on-the-scene sketch which makes no pretention of artistic merit and accuracy, and a later more finished drawing with symbols and legends and scales that inform further investigations and be used in the court of law as an exhibit or aid in testimony. In the latter case precautions must be taken to assure its authenticity. This is done by making sure that the original sketcher either produced the finished drawing or at least swore to its reliability and accuracy.

Basically, there are two types of sketches, the coordinate and cross-projection; their use will depend upon the nature and complexity of the scene. In either case the principle of triangulation will be used. Triangulation is the use of two or more baselines from which measurements allow objects to be placed in the sketch. The purpose of the sketch is to present a relatively uncluttered picture of the scene—detail is being sacrificed in the name of perspective—and too many lines will merely contribute to complexity and confusion. So as the sketch is progressing an important decision on the number of baselines to be used is essential.

The simplest sketch would be the coordinate. In this case it would be a birds-eye view of the scene which in effect allows the viewer to see the floor plan of the crime scene.

Example of a Coordinate Sketch

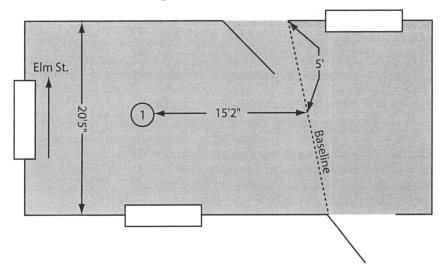

The placement of the evidence would be shown. In addition, base lines would triangulate and allow the sketcher to measure placement of key evidence. These baselines should start at fixed points—a corner of a room, a fire place, or window siding sash. Using movable objects as terminal points would be self defeating and frustrating because these features can be move about over time. As to the number of baselines simplicity should be kept in mind. KISS or "Keep it simple sketcher" should be the motto. Of course, a minimum of two seems to be necessary to triangulate. Beyond that, however, is dependent upon the quantity of evidence needing to be placed on the sketch. But it must be remembered that the purpose of the sketch is to reduce complexity. A sketch with too many baselines becomes cluttered with the measurements. A good working number might be between two and six.

In many scenes there are pieces of information present but not on the floor. A bullet hole in the window, a smear of blood on the wall, a door that has tool marks, are examples. A simple coordinate sketch would not adequately show these items. Instead, another type of sketch is needed, the cross-projection. This drawing is basically like the coordinate but to capture the walls one additional thing needs to be done. The cross-projection sketch resembles a box with the sides folded down. The base of the box would be treated as in a coordinate sketch, and each side likewise would be given its own coordinate rendition. Now that bullet hole or blood stain can be shown as so many feet from the floor and from the nearest wall.

Of course, the point of these sketches is to allow the investigators to recreate the scene long after it has been returned to the public.

For sketches of outside scenes the drawer should look for the more fixed items of landscape—an old tree, rock formation or building—and draw base lines from them. Because of the possible vast nature of outside scenes more triangulation lines may need to be used.[3]

Example of a Cross-Projection Sketch

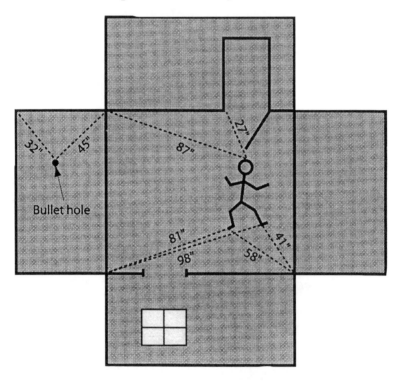

Second, *photography* is an important step at this point. Its purpose is to sacrifice perspective to capture the clutter and detail. The rule of thumb here is to "burn film" or take a lot of pictures. In the past, a standard 35mm camera giving black and white pictures was sufficient. Increasingly this has given way to color film to catch the nuance of color on the scene. Two basic approaches are necessary here:

---

3. J.W. Sullivan, "Techniques and General Rules for Sketching," *FBI Law Enforcement Bulletin* (November 1978), pp. 10–12.

1. First, the focal point of the crime scene needs to be photographed thoroughly. At a death scene the body needs to be recorded at every angle and height. Any wounds on the body need to be filmed as well. Bite marks, ligatures, bullet holes, knife slashes and contusions are only a few of the possible wounds needing to be recorded on film. Not only bodies, however, might be the focal point. A safe that has been broken in to or a window that has been smashed are other examples of focal points in a crime scene investigation.

2. Second, a panorama needs to be created. In this way the entire scene needs to be photographed. One common way to achieve this perspectives is for the photographer to stand at a predetermined fixed point and then turn in a circular way taking pictures that overlap with each other. The product will be a vast array of photographs like jigsaw puzzles needing to be put together. Another way is called "painting with light." A wide angle shot is taken with the shudder open and several flashes from different areas go off giving a wide exposure.

Photographs are the trees; the sketch is the forest. The detailed complexity of the photograph, which is a benefit in of itself, is held in check by the sketch.[4]

Of course, there are other forms of investigative photography that should be kept in mind. They are:

1. Surveillance photography, in which the identity and behavior of suspects is established;
2. Aerial photography for extensive out of doors areas;
3. Laboratory photography done by expensive and delicate equipment in the crime lab. X-ray and infrared technology is frequently used;
4. Night photography; and
5. Mug shot picture taking.

Third, a *search* is important at this time. Presumably a decision has already been made that a search is necessary. That is not always a given. In some cases, in which the scene is very small and the case has already solved itself, a search might not seem as important. Once it has been determined that a search will be instigated, however, four further decisions need to be addressed. They are: when to conduct it, the boundaries of the search, the pattern of the search, and its duration.

---

4. See J. Duckworth, *Forensic Photography* (Springfield, IL: Charles C. Thomas, 1983).

1. *When* to carry out a search. Recent U.S. Supreme Court decisions have made it necessary to obtain a warrant to conduct a crime scene search once it has been secured. Police attempts at getting a "murder scene exception" to the Fourth Amendment's warrant requirement have failed.[1] A "consent to search" form may have to be signed by someone who has legal control over the area—a landlord or roommate or relative, for example—but such permission is more easily obtained than a warrant, which will be discusses in a subsequent chapter. Other conditions influence when a search will begin. For example, inclement weather or darkness might delay the beginning of a search. The particular sensation of the crime might determine the search schedule. A young girl kidnaped in the middle of a wintry night might compel the beginnings of a search in spite of the conditions. When TWA Flight 800 went down in the summer of 1996 with 230 passengers and crew lost, in spite of the horrendous conditions the public demanded an immediate and undaunted search.

2. *Boundaries* of the search are important as well. Some crimes draw their own boundaries easily; the single room of the murder, or car in which occurred a rape, for example, might establish the parameters of the search. But it must be remembered that the hot scene might not be the most productive place for evidence. Warm, or adjacent, scenes need to be determined and the search should somehow encompass them. Other scenes, however, might have an expansiveness that demands some limits to be set. The parents of a child kidnaped and taken into a forest preserve or national park might justifiably expect a search of considerable magnitude. The search for bodies to be recovered from soil or watery graves will be discussed in a later chapter.

3. *Patterns* the search should take are another important decision. The scope of the area to be covered and the availability of personnel might shape this decision. There are three basic search patterns.

Spiral patterned searches are the simplest. The spiral approach is best for relatively small search areas and where there are few personnel on the scene. The person conducting a spiral search simply starts at a fixed point—either at the focal point of the crime or at the outer boundary of the search area—and searches in a circular pattern.

Strip search patterns would be a higher level of thoroughness. In this search style the searchers—any where from two to twenty-two—simply conduct a search in tandem of predetermined lanes. They march together from one boundary of the search area, combing their lane, until they reach another border, then they come back in different but parallel lanes. This is done until the entire search area has been covered.

---

1. *Filippo v. West Virginia* (1999).

Drawing of a Spiral Search Pattern

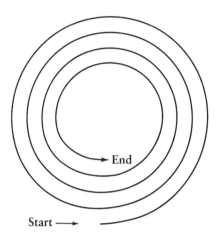

Drawing of a Strip Search Pattern

Drawing of a Grid Search Pattern

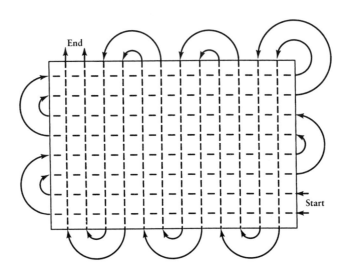

Drawing of the Zone Search Pattern

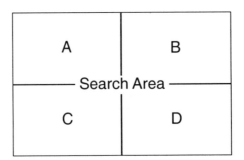

Drawing of a Wheel Search Pattern

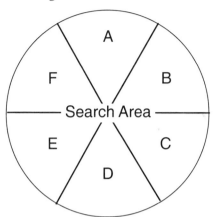

Grid searches are the same as a strip but in the name of thoroughness when the searchers finish the initial lane scheme they then turn and do the same thing but this time against the grain of the earlier strip pattern. In this way the searchers go over the same terrain but from a different angle in hopes of finding some evidence that they might have missed on the first occasion.

Zone patterns might be necessary if the geographical size of the search is very large. This pattern simply takes a very large area and breaks it down into smaller units. These smaller areas now can be searched by spiral, strip or grid patterns. In fact, the zones—depending upon their closeness to the hot scene and the number of personnel available for the search—may have a mix of patterns. For example, those zones around the focal point might have grid searches, Those further away or on the outer margins of the search area might get a variety of strip or spiral patterns.

Wheel or pie patterns are another variation of the zone concept. This choice might be dictated by the lay-out of the land. There might be a mountain or a lake within the search area that requires special consideration. These pattern boundaries are circular with search areas resembling slices of a pie or spokes of a wheel radiating out from the center. The central part of this type of pattern would be the hot scene.

The point here is that any search should be a product of thoughtful decision making and not left to chance.

4. Duration of the search is an important consideration, as well. Just how long should a search go on? It must be hoped and expected that it will continue until all relevant information or missing persons are found. But the economics of time and resources, and the knowledge that even

though one hopes to find everything much will never be recovered, pressures officers to draw the limits of the search. The more sensational the crime, the more likely the search will last longer. In addition, the productivity of the search might shape duration. For example, if a lot of evidence has been recovered there might be a temptation to be satisfied and bring the search to closure. On the other hand, the absence of meaningful information might either drive searchers on or frustrate them. Certainly the search, no matter what has been found, must eventually be ended.[5]

Documentation is another critical part of the secondary steps in the crime scene investigation. It might be thought of in three ways: note taking, care of evidence, and considerations for the crime lab.

1. *Note taking* is critical to any investigative process. Memory is fragile and the need to recall during the investigation and at the later stages of adjudication is critical. An investigator working on a lengthy case or one who must leave the investigation because of vacation time, transfer, or the press of other cases needs to be able to pass on to others critical information. *Res Gestae* —Latin for "things done" but more particularly in the law it means "material facts" —allows the criminal investigator to get by the hearsay restrictions in the court. Evidence, particularly witness statements might be excluded from the court under hearsay provisions, but by being written down and documented they have greater weight and admissibility. In addition, it allows the officer to refresh the memory prior to and upon the witness stand.

2. *Care of evidence* is another part of the documentation process. For example, all physical evidence must be carefully identified. The artifact itself should be permanently marked but in such a way that it does not destroy or undermine its later admissibility in court. In addition, once appropriately packaged there should be labeling of the evidence: what it is, where it was found, when it was recovered, and who discovered it.

This brings us to the *chain of custody*. This is a bureaucratic device to keep officers from being careless with evidence and to place blame if evidence is lost, altered or damaged. Every piece of evidence, once it has been collected by a crime scene investigator, begins a hazardous journey. It might go from the investigator on the scene to an evidence technical, to the crime lab, to the plain clothes detectives, to a storage place, to the prosecutor. At each stage it might get lost or be changed. Every officer handling the evidence must document personal responsibility by placing their name on a form or section of the evidence package that accompanies the object. Thus, all directly involved personnel form a chain of custody over the evidence.

---

5. See J.A. Davis, *A Guide To Coordinating and Executing Searches and Arrests*, (Springfield, IL: Charles C. Thomas, 1982).

Another issue in the documentation phase is the sample size of the evidence. In other words, just how much of the evidence is necessary to collect to fully document its authenticity. One must remember that samples of evidence are also pieces of private property belonging to the victim or some other person connected to the crime scene. The over destruction of property—something ultimately the local government will have to pay for—is a question influencing the documentation of the investigation. Then there is the crime lab. Criminalistics will be discussed later at greater length, but it is necessary to consider it at this time in a different context. All evidence needs to be properly documented as it goes from the investigator to the crime lab. This is of particular importance if the material is fragile or has any potential for danger. Contaminated blood samples, volatile explosive devices, eccentric firearms, for example, might be hazardous for lab personnel.

Third Steps

In the third and final phase of the preliminary investigation there are three issues to be considered: completeness, conceptualization and correspondence. Each needs to be addressed separately.

1. *Completeness* simply addresses the desire to have done every thing possible at this time for the future of the investigation by others. For example, there is the matter of "trace evidence." Generally, the larger or obvious evidence has been found. The fingerprint has been collected, the slugs have been sent to ballistics, the blood has gone for typing and DNA analysis, casts of footprints and tire marks have been made. But what of the minute stuff? Trace evidence are those data that are small or invisible to the naked eye. They may be very important. Remember that Wayne Williams—the killer of several young boys in Atlanta, Georgia—was initially arrested and convicted based upon thread evidence. Commonly an investigator will have a small power vacuum cleaner with a supply of clean filters with which to sweep the scene and retrieve otherwise undetected materials. A murder victim's hands might be bagged to examine later for possible evidence under the fingernails.

"Elimination evidence" may become an issue at this time as well. Clearly, investigators seek to find evidence with which to connect or associate a person to the scene of the crime. This process might be made easier if one can eliminate people who had a legitimate right to be at the scene. For example, a house has been burgled. Five people—a husband, wife, and three children—live in that home. Also, the day of the burglary Aunt Matilda paid a visit. Therefore, six different sets of fingerprints might be expected to be on the scene. To better tease out the seventh set of prints—those of the invader—the investigators might want the prints of the entire family so as to eliminate them as suspects.

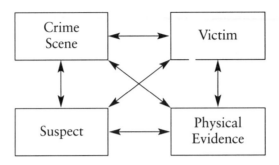

2. *Conceptualization* of a crime means two things. First, it means simply reconstruction of the crime scene itself. One concept is linkage theory. As the illustration above suggests attempts need to be made to link the scene, the victim, the evidence, and the suspect together. This is empirical—that is, the investigator allows the accumulated evidence to lead to an inductive conclusion. Second, and perhaps a little more controversial, is the creating of a hypothesis as to who committed the crime. This is deductive in nature with the investigator having a theory which allows for an "educated guess" as to the perpetrator. Researchers know that the value of a hypothesis is in proving it correct or wrong. Such a hypothesis is not etched in stone, it is a device to focus and test data. An example of a conceptual contrivance might be the following way to think of a range of suspects, it is the DOPE principle.

D	=	Desire	Are there any people who had stronger desires than others to commit the crime under investigation?
O	=	Opportunity	Are there any of those who had a greater opportunity than others to commit the crime?
P	=	Personality	Are there suspects whose personality and past behavior suggest their greater capability to commit such a crime?
E	=	Evidence	Does the preponderance of evidence gathered thus far point to one particular person?

If your major suspect spells out being a dope you may begin focusing the investigation in a manner to prove or disprove the hypothesis.

3. *Correspondence* of the investigative findings rounds out the steps of the preliminary investigation. This means two things. First, the investigator, through bureaucratic forms called "field reports," must convey all that has happened thus far in the crime scene investigation to other investigators. Supervision personnel and plain clothes detectives need the sketch-

es, photographs, witness interviews and lab reports to carry on with the "follow up" investigation. In many respects, later courtroom proceedings are a trial-by-file, and detailed and deliberate files will determine the chances of clearance and conviction. Second, correspondence takes place outside the formal structures and confines of the agency. Much information travels informally. Many uniformed officers who dominate the earliest stages of the preliminary investigation feel that "We do all the work and the detectives get all the credit." The temptation to be careless or withhold evidence in order to exploit it later for personal reasons is great. The distance between the detective and the uniformed officer must be minimized by any crime scene investigative supervisor. Channels of communication need to be kept open if the crime scene investigation is to be a success.[6]

Conclusion

Like all research and investigative endeavors the preliminary investigation of a crime is critical; its success or lack of success likely determines the future outcome of the investigation. Ultimate clearance and conviction may be dictated by what is done at these earliest stages. Beginnings of any research project—be it academic, scientific or criminal investigation —are difficult and decisive. Because of the nature of crime scenes—their impermanence and chaos—many investigative activities are going on at the same time. But they have been sequenced here into three stages. A critical element emerging from the crime scene investigation which will have an impact upon the follow up inquiries is the "junk" or "artifacts" of the crime scene, the physical evidence, a topic to which we must now turn.

---

6. See Charles R. Cox and Jerrold G. Brown, *Report Writing for Criminal Justice Professionals* (Cincinnati: Anderson, 1992).

Chapter 4

Physical Evidence and the Investigative Process

Introduction

It is believed and expected that no one encounters another person or place without leaving some evidence of his or her presence. Therefore, the term physical evidence refers to all objects, large and small, left behind when a person comes to a place or encounters another human. Physical evidence becomes the artifacts of a past event, in this case a criminal activity.[1]

For all investigators, be they college students doing a paper, an academic professor conducting a research project, or a detective investigating a crime, physical evidence is critical. It highlights the importance of details and the painstaking attention to facts, seeing significance in the ordinary. These facts are not abstractions, they are objects that can be seen and handled. They allow for the workings of a very powerful force in modern society, the work of science.

Definitions

Physical evidence is not just the "junk" of a crime scene. It must be looked at in two additional ways. First, physical evidence is defined as associative and trace evidence. Associative evidence connects someone directly to the scene. Trace evidence is minute and easily overlooked in terms of its presence or importance.

Second, two other distinctions need to be made, the difference between class and individualized categories. *Class evidence* is any item that can be placed into a larger category. The goal for any investigation is to classify evidence as specifically as possible. For example, blood may or may not be human; those are two rather large classes. If the blood is human, it can be put into further discrete classes or types such as O, A, B, and AB; these are smaller classes that still encompass large numbers of individuals. A fingerprint might be classed as a whorl, arch, or loop; ridge characteris-

---

1. See C.A. Cook, *A Practical Guide to the Basics of Physical Evidence* (Springfield, IL: Charles C. Thomas, 1984).

tics would compact the classes further. *Individualized evidence* would make the artifact particular to one person. For example, DNA analysis would take the blood sample and connect it to one individual rather than a group. Ridge characteristics in a fingerprint would point to one person rather than to many. Therefore, physical evidence is defined as those large or small items on a scene that directly or suggestively point to the fact that a class of persons or a particular person had been present shortly before, during, or after the criminal incident.

Importance

Physical evidence is very important to the criminal investigative process for the following reasons. First, physical evidence gives direction to the research. In the course of a preliminary investigation, there are a multitude of paths that can be taken. These "leads," or ways the investigator may be led, are many. Physical evidence eliminates some of these possible paths.

Second, the "due process revolution" introduced considerable procedural law which has limited many police and investigative techniques. For example, it is no longer permissible to beat a confession from a suspect. Appropriate searches must be made even if it means that some evidence will be lost. As traditional police techniques have been undermined, the value of physical evidence has increased.

Third, physical evidence gives weight to the case in the courtroom. There is considerable indication that juries and judges are positively affected by the quantity and quality of physical evidence brought to court. Witnesses might lie and victims might forget, but the hard objects of a crime scene—that blood smear, the fingerprint, the DNA match makes the decision process easier.

Fourth, an abundance of physical evidence allows admittance of a special class of testimony in the court, that of the expert witness. Few witnesses in the court of law are allowed to give their opinion, as they must state only the facts of what they saw or experienced. The expert witness, however, can give his or her opinion and interpretation of facts and events.

Thesis

At this stage of discussion most textbooks and handbooks would throw a chaos of physical evidence at the student. While the reader must be introduced to such material, I believe that it must be presented in packages of priority. If all of the following material were on a crime scene, it would not have equal weight. Some items are more valuable than others. Of course, if a crime scene has only a few fabric threads, that evidence is important. But, all things being equal, physical evidence is placed into one of three categories: most powerful, powerful, and less powerful. Placement of evidence in these categories is based how much the class category can be compacted and individualized.

Most Powerful Physical Evidence

Blood and Secretions or Serology

Blood is one of the most powerful elements of physical evidence. It comes in a variety of forms. First, blood can be wet or dry. Wet blood has greater value to the forensic scientist because many more tests can be run on wet than dry blood, thus more conclusions might be reached. For example, the alcohol and drug content of the donor can be ascertained only from samples of wet blood. Blood begins to clot after 3 to 5 minutes when exposed to air. As it dries, the clot darkens to reddish-brown to dark brown. Old dried blood may appear black.

Second, blood can be in the form of pools, drops, smears, or crusts. Being more liquid, pools and drops have greater value. Smears and crusts are likely to be dried and have less evidentiary power.

Blood may be found in a variety of locations that help investigators reconstruct the crime scene. Obviously, one can expect to find blood on the scene of a violent crime. Absence of blood may be a major finding in and of itself. Drops of blood can suggest the height from which the blood fell. Remember blood can fall vertically or at an angle. For example, a blood drop that fell perpendicular to the floor from a distance of zero to two feet would be circular with frayed edges. Drops from two to four feet in height would maintain the circular pattern but have more pronounced tendrils. From four feet and higher, the drop would have definite satellites on the spikes of the sunburst pattern. Therefore, a suspect's story about a murder becomes

Common Blood Drop Patterns

zero to two feet   two to four feet   four feet or more

Typical Smear of Blood Showing Direction of Force

direction of force

incredible if he claims that he struck the victim in self-defense, but a blood drop pattern suggests it fell a distance of only two feet.

In addition, a blood smear on the wall or floor can suggest the direction of the force of the blow. Commonly, blood traveling at an angle due to the momentum of a blow will create an exclamation or baseball bat configuration, with the largest area being the place of origin and the force expending itself on laying down the narrower part. Then at the extreme ending of the blood drop there will be a "wave cast-off" droplet.

Also, there might be "cast-off" splatter, a thin line of blood resulting from the raising of the arm and knife weapon in successive attacks. After the first blow as the knife is pulled out and back a line of blood goes on and over the attacker's shoulder. The number of lines plus one equals the number of blows. The higher and more vigorous the force will give smaller spray back. The lower the force equals larger lines of blood.

Several interesting investigative questions can be raised by blood evidence and addressed by scientific inquiry. First, is there a blood smear? Sometimes blood samples might be so minute or old that they are invisible to the naked eye. Science has progressed with a variety of tests, such as benzidine or luminal tests that can illuminate traces of blood, which allow detection of otherwise undetectable blood.

Second, is it human or animal blood? A suspect covered with blood may claim it comes from an animal he just killed. Scientific tests can not only distinguish between animal and human blood but can in general terms determine the kind of animal.

Third, if it is human blood, what type is it? In the late nineteenth century, it was discovered that human blood could be placed into one of four large typologies based on the presence or absence of an antigen, a protein in the blood system. For example, type "A" has only the A antigen, type "B" has only the B antigen, type "AB" has both A and B antigens, while "O" lacks both antigens. The blood groupings and the percentages of the population that carries them are described as:

O type blood	45 percent of the population
A type blood	40 percent of the population

B type blood   10 percent of the population
AB type blood   5 percent of the population

["A" type blood is most common among Caucasians. "B" type blood is most common among Asians and African-Americans.]

A procedure developed in the early 1940s allowed further compacting of these types by factoring in the Rh component of plus or minus. Approximately 85 percent of the population have Rh+ and 15 percent have Rh-; thus, the presence of the ABO and Rh blood type is:

O   =   39 percent is Rh+ and 6 percent is Rh-
A   =   35 percent is Rh+ and 5 percent is Rh-
B   =   8 percent is Rh+ and 2 percent is Rh-
AB =   4 percent is Rh+ and 1 is percent Rh-

The following chart adds another perspective:

O+:   1 in 3 persons has this typing
O-:   1 in 15 persons has this typing
A+:   1 in 3 persons has this typing
A-:   1 in 16 persons has this typing
B+:   1 in 12 persons has this typing
B-:   1 in 67 persons has this typing
AB+:   1 in 29 persons has this typing
AB-:   1 in 167 persons has this typing

There are 23 blood group systems based on the association of more than 256 antigens. For example, further scientific developments in the 1950s and 1960s allowed for greater compacting of blood types. The MNS enzymes can be used as indicators. Twenty-two percent of the population have an "N" marker enzyme in their blood, 30 percent have a "M," and 48 percent have "S." A person with AB-MN would be a rarity and this information would contribute greatly to individualization of the sample.

Within certain limits the sex of a person can be determined by a blood sample. Seventy-five percent of males have a "Y" chromosome in their red blood cells. The absence of the "Y" chromosome in the red blood cells means that the blood belongs to a female or to the 25 percent of males that do not carry it.

Fourth, blood has become extremely powerful evidence because of the discovery of DNA, deoxyribonucleic acid, in 1984. Since 1984, genetic fingerprinting has been used to type an individual. In theory, the genetic material that determines every aspect of a living thing—in humans from height to hair color to susceptibility to disease—is in every cell. These tell-tale cells can be found in blood, sperm, bone marrow, tooth pulp, and even hair roots. Consequently, on the smallest amount of evidence a person may be "DNA typed" and matched. It is estimated that the chance of having two persons with identical DNA patterns, with the exception of identical twins, is between 30 and 100 billion to one.

How DNA Testing is Done

1. Blood samples are collected from the victim, the defendant, and the crime scene. The type of test, described below, determines the amount of sample needed.
2. White blood cells are separated from red blood cells.
3. DNA is extracted from the nuclei of white blood cells.
4. A restrictive enzyme, which looks for specific chemical sequences in the DNA strand, cuts the DNA wherever it finds those sites. The amount of material between cut sites varies, so the fragments vary widely in length.
5. DNA fragments are put into a bed of gel that has electrodes at either end.
6. An electrical current draws the negatively charged fragments toward the positive end of the gel. The shorter fragments of DNA move more quickly through the gel than longer fragments. Within hours, the fragments are sorted by length.
7. A nylon membrane, placed over absorbent paper, soaks up the DNA and secures the imprint of the sorted fragments. It is radioactively treated and then developed. The Xray is called an autoradiograph.[2]

There are two basic types of DNA analysis. The more conclusive of the two tests, used to determine whether two tissue samples came from the same person, is known as RFLP (restriction fragment length polymorphism). It examines regions of the genetic material—from blood, saliva, tissue, or a hair follicle—where particular small segments of DNA are repeated over and over. Different people have different numbers of repeated segments. If one person has a segment repeated 300 times, that would distinguish him or her from someone whose segment is repeated 100 times. But the RFLP test requires a relatively large sample, about 5,000 cells or one-twentieth of a drop of blood, and the sample must be in good condition. This type of testing can take six to eight weeks.

The second DNA test, a newer method known as the PCR test (polymerase chain reaction), can use as few as 50 cells, which can be found in

---

2. Todd W. Burke, "DNA analysis: The Challenge For the Police," *The Police Chief* (October 1989), pp. 92–95.

a minute speck of blood, and the cells can be somewhat degraded. The PCR test can determine with certainty if a defendant's blood is not in the sample, but it is less definitive than the RFLP test in identifying whose blood is in the sample. Consequently, PCR is more helpful in proving innocence than in establishing guilt, and the test takes only a few days.

DNA analysis allows a variety of other secretions to become powerful evidence. Secretions are other bodily discharges such as spittle, semen, urine, feces, and vomit. Before the discovery of DNA such items were of limited value, as 60 percent of the population were secreters whose blood type could be determined from these secretions. Of course, that meant 40 percent of the population could not be determined. The revolution in DNA typing has impacted here as well, and a match could be made from these secretions.

DNA research and the subsequent "genetic fingerprinting" have revolutionized criminal investigation and made blood and secretions a most powerful form of physical evidence.[3]

Fingerprints or Dactyloscopy

Since the early twentieth century, fingerprints have become one of the most powerful pieces of physical evidence. For discussion purposes, there are two large categories of fingerprints: direct or inked fingerprints and latent fingerprints.

Direct or Inked prints are those prints on file with the police or another governmental agency. They are obtained in a controlled environment using ink as the primary medium, which maximizes their size and clarity. Three large "patterns" emerge from the direct print: arches, whorls, and loops. However, before these patterns are described, some understanding of vocabulary is necessary.

1. *Core* is the approximate center of the print and is used for classification purposes when analyzing prints that have loops.
2. *Pattern area* is the general area of the print that is made up of ridges.
3. *Ridges* are the fine lines that collectively create a pattern.
4. *Type lines* are the two innermost ridges that start as parallel lines, diverge, and surround the pattern area.
5. *Delta* is the area nearest the divergence of the type lines; it is used for classification purposes exclusively in loop and whorl patterns.

---

3. See William G. Eckert and Stuart H. James, *Interpretation of Bloodstain Evidence at Crime Scenes* (New York: Elsevier, 1989).

Examples of Arch Patterns

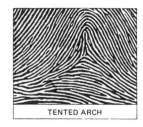

PLAIN ARCH

TENTED ARCH

Patterns

Arches are a general pattern found in fingerprints. Only about five percent of the population have this pattern. The general pattern of arches can be subdivided into plain and tented arches as well.

Whorls are a more common fingerprint pattern with an estimated 35 percent of the population having this design. They are characterized as a spiral in appearance and are classified as clockwise or counterclockwise; in either case whorls can be found in the literature as plain whorls, central pocket, double loop, and accidental.

Loops are the most common fingerprint pattern with an estimated 60 percent of the population having some form of loops. Generally, there are

Examples of Whorl Patterns

PLAIN LOOP

WHORL

CENTRAL POCKET LOOP

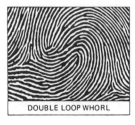

DOUBLE LOOP WHORL

ACCIDENTAL

Examples of Loop Patterns

 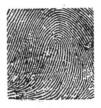

ULNAR LOOP   RADIAL LOOP

two types of loops depending on the general direction of the loop. If it leans toward the thumb it is called a radial loop. If it leans toward the little finger it is an ulnar loop; these are most common. Of course, determining the lean is easy from a card done by the police under controlled circumstances. An individual print at a crime scene is a little more difficult to analyze.

Ridge Characteristics

Pattern characteristics are important indicators of class evidence analysis, but the categories remain too large to make a positive identification. In order to do this, one needs to find unique ridge characteristics in the fingerprint. Ridges are the thin lines that collectively form the pattern. Their characteristics are the distinctive shapes they take, and the most common are: bifurcations, dots, islands, and ridge endings.

In terms of analysis and scientific method, fingerprints are then categorized in one of two classifications, a primary and a secondary. The primary classification is determined by the presence, number, and location of whorls. To start with, all of the fingers are numbered from the right thumb to the left thumb and beyond. On the right hand the thumb is equal to 1, the index = 2, middle = 3, ring = 4, and the little = 5; then the left hand thumb is 6, index = 7, middle = 8, ring = 9, and left little = 10. Then each finger is given a value if a whorl is present. For example, if a whorl is present on the right hand thumb it gets a value of 16, index = 16, middle = 8, ring = 8, little = 4; on the left hand thumb if a whorls is present it receives a 4, index = 2, middle = 2, ring = 1, left little = 1. Arches, loops, or accidentals on any finger have a classification value of 0.

The secondary classification system uses symbols "A" = arch, "T" = tented arch, "R" = radial loop, "U" = ulnar loop, "W" = whorl. The letter for each index finger is capitalized, others will have lower case. If the thumb has a whorl or ulnar loop and the following finger on the right is an arch, tented arch, or radial loop, then the letter is replaced with a dash.

Ridge Characteristics

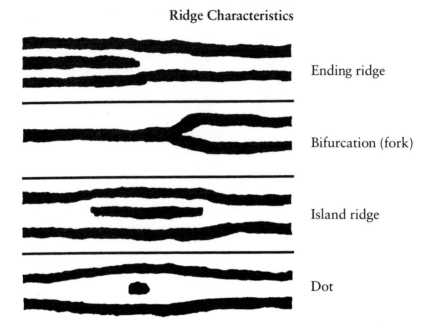

Ending ridge

Bifurcation (fork)

Island ridge

Dot

If two or more fingers past the index finger have the same pattern, the letter is replaced with a "2." For example:

Right Hand

Thumb	=	arch or "a"
Index	=	tented arch or "T"
Middle	=	whorl or "w"
Ring	=	radial loop or "r"
Little	=	radial loop or "r"

Left Hand

Thumb	=	ulnar loop or "u"
Index	=	whorl or "W"
Middle	=	radial loop or "r"
Ring	=	radial loop or "r"
Little	=	whorl or "w"

Therefore the analysis equation would look like:

$$\frac{aTwrr}{uWrrw} \quad \text{or} \quad \frac{aT\text{-}2r}{w2rw}$$

Latent prints or "partials" are those prints found on the crime scene. They are not inked and full. Instead, latent prints are conveyed by natural oils and secretions and are left when a human touches an item. In this case, they may be largely invisible until they are treated or "worked" with a variety of techniques, like dusting, that makes them visible. On occasion prints may be left or conveyed by grease, blood, or dust.

There are several problems with the latent print. First is the issue of having something with which to compare it. Many countries have a universal fingerprinting requirement. Everyone must have a set of prints on file. Of course, this is a boon to criminal investigation. Unfortunately, most countries that have such extensive files are police states. The United States has long avoided such a policy as being contrary to notions of civil liberty. But the absence of a direct print on file limits the utility of the latent print. One cannot compare an unknown with nothing and achieve a known.

On the other hand, there may be too many prints on file with which to humanly examine and make a match. This is like searching for a needle in a haystack. It can take several weeks, if not months, of arduous work to find a match. This has been alleviated considerably since the 1980s with the advent of AFIS (automated fingerprint identification systems.) This system uses computer technology to sort out the more obvious prints and narrow down likely candidates for expert human examination. AFIS technology converts the unique patterns of a fingerprint's ridges, bifurcations, and endings, called minutiae, into a mathematical formula. The fingerprint is scanned into the computer and digitalized. Each minutia, or place at which ridge lines end or split into two, is noted and categorized by its type, location, and ridge direction. Then four neighboring minutiae are also examined. The ridges between the minutiae are counted on a 512 pixel-per-inch scale from landmarks like the core. Pixels are the dots that make up computer images. The computer scores how closely a potential match comes to the search print and ranks the top contenders in descending order. With one good quality print, the system is accurate more than 97 percent of the time. Of course, the computer only gives a number of highly probable matches. The final determination is left to the human eye.

Second, the "point system," or the number of comparisons necessary for a declaration of a positive match, creates some difficulties. After determining the general pattern—doing the simplest thing first—the ridge characteristics are examined. A number of ridge characteristics on the latent print must be found on the direct print on file. Once a certain number has been reached, the prints may be declared a match. Of course, the issue is how many characteristics are enough? For example, France requires 17 points of comparison, and Great Britain settles for 16. Traditionally, the United States has declared 12 points of comparison necessary for a match to be declared. However, professionals in the field, particularly members of the International Association for Identification, have challenged this judicial requirement. They feel the imposition of such evidentiary restrictions is more political than scientific and that the restrictions have no solid basis. But due process, an American means for safeguarding the citizens from an overbearing criminal justice system, requires some sort of evidentiary standard. As the worldwide variation and professional resistance suggests, there is no final answer as of yet to the appropriate number of points needed for a match.

Third, the nature of surfaces complicates fingerprints as evidence. Hard, nonabsorbent surfaces provide the best retrieval prospects of a fingerprint, and soft absorbent materials are much more difficult. So while a student's desktop would be easy to get a print from, the paper on which the student is writing notes would be challenging. The grain and absorption of the surface will distort the ridge characteristics of the print. Surfaces such as skin and clothing can be worked with laser technology but fingerprints will be more challenging to obtain.

Fourth, the nature of humans also complicates matters. The importance of fingerprints has permeated popular culture, and even the most ignorant criminal understands the need to prevent leaving prints on the crime scene. Furthermore, humans have a tendency to grab, handle, and release items so as to minimize the quality of prints. In fact, a topic rarely discussed in such matters, the study of palm prints, may be even more relevant. Some objects, such as the grainy grip of most firearms, are even more difficult from which to obtain useable prints.

Fifth, the effects of nature can limit the possibility of prints. On a hard surface, in cold dry weather, the print may be gone almost instantly. On the same surface, in warm and humid weather, the undisturbed print might last for weeks. Rain, wind, and humidity can distort and destroy prints. Even under the best of climatic situations, prints do not last forever.[4]

Certainly, in the world of physical evidence the greatest power for individualization lies with blood and fingerprints, but other powerful evidence might be available to shape the investigation.

Powerful Physical Evidence

If all possible types of evidence were on the scene, then those discussed above have particular power for individualization and investigative utility. Those that follow have some importance, to be sure, but they are rel-

---

4. See Federal Bureau of Investigation, *The Science of Fingerprints* (Washington, DC: Government Printing Office, 1979).

atively weaker. Of course, if the following types are all that is available, then they must not be discounted and should be treated as major findings.

Dental Evidence or Forensic Odontology

Dental evidence has become important to investigations in two ways in the last generation. First, it has achieved remarkable results in the identification of unknown remains. In the death process, as the body begins to putrefy, the teeth remain long after other means of identification — visual and fingerprinting — have passed. Of course, the dental remains of a cadaver, whether it is a victim of a plain crash, a soldier whose remains are returned from battle, or a badly decomposed victim of a serial killer, are only useful if they match a sample from a known person. This may happen in one of two ways. In the last several years, with greater public attention to dental hygiene and professional dentistry record keeping, the number of dental Xrays have increased. However, unless it is a full mouth Xray, the picture might be too small for useful comparisons. In addition, most dentists create a dental chart or record, updating work done on regular patients and creating a pictorial record of new patients, which shows the history of dental work. All missing teeth, replacements, fillings, and surgery are recorded and provide a picture , and can be as conclusive of evidence as a fingerprint. The reason dental records are not as powerful as fingerprinting, however, is that they are not as extensive or centralized and are a relatively recent development.

Second, dental evidence can be used in bite mark investigation. The earliest use of this type of information was to examine bites left by a suspect on food and pencils. In the more grisly crimes, such as sexual homicides, the victim likely will sustain bites, and beginning in the 1970s, bite mark investigation turned toward that area. An important piece of evidence against Theodore Bundy, the infamous serial killer, was bite marks. And there may be defensive bites that the victim left on the attacker. There are two general bite mark patterns, donut and double horse shoe, as well as slight variations due to missing teeth, overbites, and other aberrations.[5]

Hair

Hair evidence is an important source of information, particularly for those crimes and contacts in which struggle and violence occurred. Homicide, assaults, rapes, and hit-and-runs are criminal events in which hair evidence is likely to be found. As the examples above suggest, hair may

---

5. See G. Gustafson, *Forensic Odontology* (New York: American Elsevier, 1966).

be left on the victim by the assailant or the victim may leave hair on the suspect's person or property.

Hair evidence can tell the investigator several things and expedite research of the crime. For example, is it human or animal hair? There are ample historical examples of a killer declaring that hair evidence belongs to a cat, dog, or horse. Forensic science can easily distinguish between human and other animal hair.

If the hair belongs to a human, several other pieces of information can be obtained. For example, it is important to remember that everyone sheds hair from the head, pubic areas, chest, armpits, beards, eye brows, and lashes, nose and ears, and buttocks areas. Hair will appear distinctive even if it comes from the same person. The origin of hair can be isolated and identified.

Although it can be changed regularly, hair color may help in identification. Types of hair color in the United States are listed below:

> 7 in 10 persons have brown hair
> 1 in 7 persons has blond hair
> 1 in 10 persons has black hair
> 1 in 16 persons has red hair.

In addition, within broad generalizations, hair can be placed into racial groupings of Negroid, Mongoloid, and Caucasoid. Of course, no respectable anthropologist would religate the world to just three broad racial groupings. But they do allow for some preliminary observations. Four variables can emerge in racial hair analysis:

1. Cross section—or when cut what shape will the cross section show.
2. Pigment, or coloring substance.
3. Cuticle, or shape of the hair at its base.
4. Curly, or the amount of natural curl.

Using these variables, racial characteristics are shown:

Race	Cross Section	Pigment	Cuticle	Curly
Negroid	flat	dense	thin	very
Caucasoid	oval	even	medium	rare
Mongoloid	round	auburn	thick	never

Other information about the hair, such as its forcible removal, which can allow for bloody root endings and DNA typing, alcohol and drug use, and dying or bleaching, may be available to help the investigation.[6]

---

6. See B.D. Gaudette, "Some Further Thoughts on Probalities and Human Hair Comparisons," *Journal of Forensic Sciences* vol. 23 (1978), pp. 758–763.

Firearms or Ballistics Evidence

Ballistics is the scientific investigation of firearms, their mechanics, and missiles. For closer examination we can divide them into the firearm and its ammunition.

Firearms may be divided into several categories, such as small arms or assault weapons. For our purposes they will be known as handguns and shoulder weapons such as rifles and shotguns.

Caliber is the diameter of the barrel expressed in hundredths of an inch. Consequently, a .38 caliber gun is one with a barrel that is 38 one hundredths of an inch in diameter. Likewise, .32 and .45 calibers represent the sizes of the barrel diameter of those guns. Caliber is the historical reference measurement for guns made in America. In Europe this measurement is expressed in millimeters. Therefore, a 9 mm gun indicates that the diameter of the barrel is nine millimeters. Increasingly, these guns have been found in the United States, even with many police departments changing from a .38 caliber to a 9 mm pistol. Indeed, many American companies, such as Smith & Wesson and Colt, have added 9 mm semiautomatics to their product line. However, in terms of a measurement device, there is very little difference between a .38 caliber and a 9 mm. Equivalencies in barrel diameters are given in the table below. The top numbers are in millimeters while the bottom are caliber.

Barrel Diameters

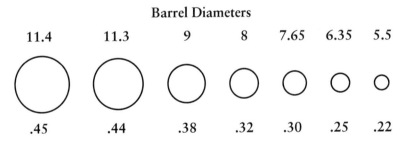

11.4	11.3	9	8	7.65	6.35	5.5
.45	.44	.38	.32	.30	.25	.22

Sometimes the name of the gun expresses the caliber and the year the gun was first introduced to the market. For example, a 30.30 rifle is a thirty caliber gun introduced in 1930. A 30.06 is a thirty caliber gun introduced in 1906.

Gauge is reserved for shotguns. It is the weight, in fractions of a pound, of what a shotgun would fire if it were firing a solid ball instead of pellets. Consequently, a 12 gauge indicates that the imaginary solid ball would have been one-twelfth of a pound.

Bore is the interior of the barrel and it is important because, in the name of having a faster and more accurate missile, the bore is generally rifled. It has a series of ridges that force the slug, after the explosion, to take on a spin, improving the slug's aerodynamics. This results in the slug taking on striations which can have some investigative utility.

Ammunition

Ammunition is also important in ballistic investigation. In terms of structure, bullets and shotgun loads are similar. There is a casing that encloses the materials, primer to ignite the explosion, propellent or explosive material, and the missiles. Sometimes the power of the ammunition allows for a designation to seep into the popular mind. For example, "Magnum" is not the size of the caliber but the power of the propellent. This factor, plus the size of the cartridge explains the difference between a .22 short and .22 long, which most young boys used as their first experience with guns. Variations of the slug may also give rise to different designations. For example, most slugs are lead or lead jacketed. However, some have emerged with Teflon coats which allow them to penetrate bullet proof jackets, and they have become known as "cop killers." Others have hollow points that allow them to break up at the target causing serious wounds even in nonfatal places; these have become known as "dum-dums." A "devastator" is designed to explode upon impact, thus assuring deadly wounds. A "devastator+" has a poisonous substance, lead oxide, that can make a minor wound lethal.

Residues can have investigative importance as well. There are two basic residues: the wading from a shotgun cartridge and the powder from all guns. Powder is particularly useful and may be better understood if thought of in its impact upon the victim and the perpetrator. On the victim two types of powder residue might be found that aid the investigator reconstructing the distance of the firearm from the victim. First, there is the tattooing or burning of the skin around the wound, particularly in a close encounter. This "abrasion collar" is due to the flame and heat expended by the firearm and the heat of the missile as it enters the victim. Of course, the greater the tattoo or abrasion collar, the closer the weapon was to the victim. Second, there is the smudging or grainy, dusty matter around the abrasion collar. This smudge will consist of some dirt but will be mostly grains of unexploded powder and some powder smoke. The tighter the circle of the smudge around the abrasion collar the closer the weapon was to the victim. Of course, if the weapon is too close to the victim, the flame will destroy much of the smudge. The smudge will increase in diameter and decrease in density as the weapon is further away from the victim. Of course, if the gun were fired at a great distance, the pronouncement of tattooing or smudging would decline. Further discussion of this topic occurs later in the death investigation chapter in regards to wounds to the body.

Cross Sections and Side Views of Slugs and Striations

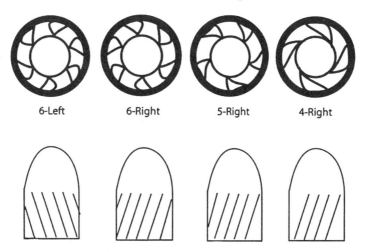

| 6-Left | 6-Right | 5-Right | 4-Right |

Powder residue might be deposited on the hands, wrists and arms of the user of the gun in a "back spray" effect. With lots of firing this might be obvious to the user and a vigorous hand wash might destroy much of this evidence. However, trace amounts might be present and a variety of tests—paraffin and dernol nitrate, for example—might be used to detect its presence.

Slugs or bullets are the missiles hitting the target. Rifling of the bore to insure a spin for accuracy and velocity forces a signature upon the slug that might make for powerful evidence. When a manufacture tools a gun they do not individualize the product. But class evidence—besides the trade name and caliber or millimeter—emerges. For example, a series of striations will be imprinted upon the slug as it explodes from the barrel. Taking a cross section of a slug—as reproduced above—one might see slightly elevated striations; these are called "grooves." The indents are referred as "lands." Any number of grooves and lands might be on the slug but four to six are most common. Furthermore, these striations of grooves and lands might—seen from another angle, also reproduced above—have a slight left or right twist. So a .38 caliber slug might fall into a class of left twist with six grooves or a right twist with four grooves. But these are class evidence designations; large numbers of firearms might produce such features. Class evidence needs to be known first—remember the Law of Parsimony—before the more difficult individualization occurs.

Firearm manufactures, due to the economics of scale, do not individualize their products; it would be too costly. However, the tools that create these grooves and lands wear over time and slowly product variations do occur. Then, also, explosions within the gun as it is repeatedly fired over time begin to individualize the striations on the slugs. Little nicks and scars begin to occur, and once begun they increase dramatically. But how many shots must occur before a firearm begins to individualize? There are two answers. First, a lot depends on the care and cleaning of the firearm; less care equals faster individualization. Second, by one hundred shots the firearm is on the road to individualization. The manufacturer performs numerous test shots, so by the time the product reaches the market it is well on the way toward having its particular signature.[7]

One final point is the "noise signature." Guns of various power have different noises. One reason why professional hit-men favor .22 caliber guns is that their noise signature is low.

Questionable Documents

The authenticity of documents such as in forgeries, ransom notes, extortion threats, and suicide statements are critical investigative problems. They may appear in typewriter, computer word processing, or cut-and-paste formats, or they may be handwritten. For purposes of discussion here, however, the focus will be on handwritten notes and "graphology" or handwriting analysis.

Of course, over time the handwriting of an individual changes. Not only will it do so from adolescence to maturity, but it will also change in the course of adulthood. In addition, it may change somewhat under three direct influences. Shock or fear can force a person to alter his or her writing considerably. Unfamiliar writing materials also can cause temporary changes. And adverse writing conditions like lying on ones back or at a particularly uncomfortable angle can explain a change in style. Nonetheless, according to the experts, if enough indicators are isolated a person can be identified by writing style.

Questionable documents are forgeries. There are three possible forgery styles. First is the freehand forgery where there is no attempt at disguise. Second is the traced forgery in which pressure is applied over and upon an authentic document leaving an indented trace on papers below which are then filled in. Third is the simulated forgery where the bogus author tries to duplicate another person's writing.

Any handwriting analysis and identification of a questionable document must start with a standard of comparison. These standards of comparisons can be obtained in one of two ways—by collected or requested samples.

---

7. V. Krema, *The Identification and Registration of Firearms* (Springfield, IL: Charles C. Thomas, 1971).

A collected document is a found sample that the author never thought would be looked at for comparative purposes. The document might be a letter or note or diary that was written long ago or before the incident under investigation. This type of document can be expected to be as pure as possible.

A requested sample is one in which the author is asked to provide an example of his or her writing. Such a request alerts the person that he or she is under investigation and the potential for deception is great. To minimize the danger of receiving a false sample, the investigator may do several things. First, the material of the requested sample should duplicate as much as possible that of the questionable document. If the ransom note is in pencil on lined paper, the requested sample should be as well. Second, the message the investigator wants duplicated should be dictated. This should catch any peculiarities of grammar and spelling that the subject might have. Third, the message should be comprehensive. It should contain all of the letters of the questionable document, including numbers, lower case and capitals, without duplication of the exact blurb of the questionable writing.

Once the sample is obtained, handwriting analysis may proceed, keeping in mind the following principles. First, generally it is most helpful to initially isolate reoccurring words and letters and to follow them through both the questionable document and the standard of comparison. This is in keeping with the Law of Parsimony discussed earlier. There are three categories of letters based on their frequency in day-to-day writing. These include:

1. Most often used letters presented in order of frequency, E (most often used), T, A, O, N, I
2. Least often used, J, K, X, Q, Z (the least often used letter)
3. Average usage make up the remaining letters.

Second, there are twelve basic characteristics examiners look for:

1. *Line quality.* The skill of the writing, flowing letters and words as opposed to laborious movements, spelling characteristics are also important here.
2. *Spacing of words and letters.* The average amount of space placed between words and the formations of the letters.
3. *Ratio of relative height, width and size of letters.* Consistencies in the formations of letters as to height, width, and size.
4. *Pen lifts and separations.* The manner in which one stops writing to form new letters and words; the study of hesitation dots, those places where the pen starts and pauses, are useful.

5. *Connecting strokes.* Connecting capital letters to lower case letters, connecting strokes within letters and words.

6. *Beginning and ending strokes.* When one begins a letter formation or number and where the stroke ends.

7. *Unusual letter formations.* The formation of unusual letters such as backwards n's, and capital strokes.

8. *Shading.* Also known as pen pressure; how much pressure and ink width is placed on upward and downward strokes.

9. *Slant.* Does the writing slant to the right, left, straight up and down, or a combination? What degree of slant exists (protractor measurements can be useful)?

10. *Baseline habits.* Does the writer write along a straight line, write with a downward slope, upward slope, bent in the middle?

11. *Flourishes or Embellishments.* Fancy writing habits, curls, loops, etc. Also the characteristic manner of letter formations, such as double loops, triple loops, and straight lines.

12. *Placement of diacritics.* Crossing of t's, dotting of i's, and other punctuation marks.[8]

In recent years, application of a field of study called psycholinguistics has been applied to evidence. Students of this science examine the spoken and written word for clues as to background and psychology of the author. They have a computerized "threat dictionary" of over 250,000 words to help study the demographic and psychological profiles of the author, and can calculate a "seriousness probability rate," or the likelihood that threats will be carried out.

Less Powerful Physical Evidence

Glass

Glass evidence has many interesting possibilities. It can be connected to a variety of criminal activities such as hit-and-runs, shootings, and arson. For example, "fracture matching" may help establish an automobile as

---

8. Ordway Hilton, *Scientific Examination of Questionable Documents* (New York: Elsevier, 1982).

Gunshot Sequencing

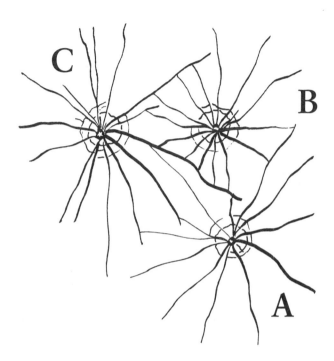

the killing weapon in a hit-and-run. Headlights are made of strong glass that breaks in large jigsaw type pieces. Finding such a fracture on the scene allows one to match it with a broken headlight on a suspects car. The sequencing of gunshots can be determined by the way "radials" intersect in a pain of glass. In the example above the sequence of shots is most likely in this order: "C," then "A," and then "B."

The direction of "rib marks" in a piece of glass might suggest the direction of force as well. In addition, the basic trajectory of the bullet might be determined by the "cone" created at the entry point in a pain of glass.

Of course, such evidence is not shattering, but it does help to reconstruct and interpret the crime scene.[9]

---

9. D.P. Slater and W. Fong, "Density, Refractive Index, and Dispersion in Examination of Glass: Third Relative Worth as Proof," *Journal of Forensic Science* vol. 27, no. 3 (1982), pp. 474–483.

Gunshot and Point of Entry on Glass

Production of Radial and Concentric Fractures in Glass

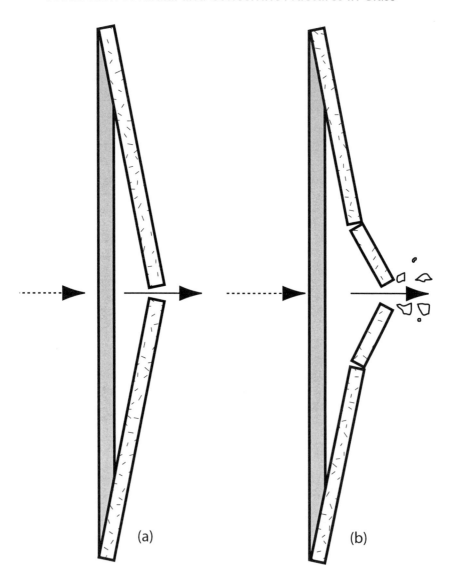

(a)   (b)

Athletic shoe print

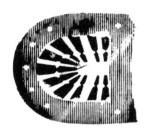
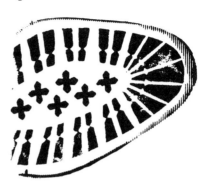

Soil

Soil, dirt, and dust evidence can be useful in two possible ways. First, there is *soiled evidence* or leaving dirt either on the victim—as in a hit-and-run in which the dirt from the automobile may be deposited on or near the victim—or on the perpetrator in pant cuffs or shoes. Of course, the utility here is dependant upon the dramatic variations of soils, such as the red dirt of Arizona found on the scene in Illinois. But local geologists and geographers can be of use in determining the nuance of differences in regional soils. In soil analysis, the first determinations are arrived at by looking at color and density. The color of soil is usually the first examination conducted in a crime laboratory. If two soils are different in color, there is little likelihood they will be similar in other tests. The density of soil samples is one of the most common forensic methods used. Tests can determine with great accuracy differences in soils, due to mineral and chemical makeup, by their density or thickness of consistency. Furthermore, microscopic examination can reveal unique animal or plant matter in the soil that may help in individualization.

Second, there are *soil impressions* or the marks left in dirt and mud by shoe and automobile tires. Of course, shoe and tire imprints have class value. The unique way people wear and wear out their shoes can individualize the evidence. This is called "anatomical wear." The tread markings on athletic shoes have increased and diversified dramatically over the years but may still be put into large product categories. This is true of tire tread marks as well.[10]

---

10. Raymond C. Murray and John C.F. Tedrow, *Forensic Geology* (New Brunswick, NJ: Rutgers University Press, 1975). William J. Bodziak, *Footwear Impression Evidence*, 2nd ed. (New York: Elsevier, 1990).

Fibers

Threads and patches of cloth can become valuable evidence in the investigation of any crime where a struggle has occurred. A hit-and-run victim might leave patches of clothing on the undercarriage of an automobile. A victim of a rape-homicide might have fibers from the clothing of the perpetrator. Fiber evidence was critical in the conviction of Wayne Williams, the serial murderer of young boys in Atlanta, Georgia. Twenty-eight fiber matches were made linking blankets in his car to victims.

Fiber evidence can be separated in large classes according to type of cloth, color, and weave. There are two large categories of fibers from which clothing is made. *Natural* fibers, such as silk, wool, and cotton, and *man-made fibers,* such as acrylic, nylon, and polyester. Another way to look at it is to distinguish four types of cloth materials in the following way: vegetable based materials (such as cotton), animal (such as wool), synthetic (polyester), and mineral (glass). Individualization is difficult, but it can prove useful in directing the investigation toward more solid data.[11]

Tool Marks

Various marks left on home and automobile doors, windows, and locks by makeshift burglary tools can be of some investigative use. Evidence left by tools come in two general categories such as *compressions,* due to hammering and punching, and *striations*, due to scraping. Such marks reveal the point of entry on a crime scene, allow the general determination of the nature of the tool, suggest the general skill level of the user of the tool (clean break-ins indicate a higher skill level than sloppy ones, for example), and the general method of operation that may lead to a positive identification. Such marks are generally found at doors, window frames, safe and vault doors, locks, and chains. Investigators need to obtain actual tool marks from the surfaces by removing them entirely from the scene by cutting or dismantling or making a cast/mold of them.

Other Examples

Finally there are a variety of data that may appear on the scene such as a vile message written in lipsticks or paint, flecks of paint, and strands of rope and string. Duct tape is used so often and in so many ways that it is often called "crime tape." These items have intrinsic worth, but they are limited considerably because of their inability or difficulty to individual-

11. E.P. Martin, "Wool Fibers as Evidence: Their Probative Value in Criminal Procedure," *International Criminal Police Review* vol. 30, no. 288 (1975), pp. 126-137.

ize. The reason they are mentioned here is to introduce the student to another investigative aid, the reference file. Reference files may be found in a variety of agencies, but the most developed are in the FBI crime laboratory. There are two basic types of reference files.

First, there are standard reference files that contain samples of general manufactured items. For example, there is a Cigarette Identification File with samples of 185 American cigarettes. A Firearms Reference Collection has nearly 3,000 handgun and 1,600 shoulder weapon samples. There are Standard Ammunition Files, a Typewriter Standard File, a Shoe Print File, a Watermark Standards File, an Automobile Paint File, a Hair and Fiber File, a Safe Insulation File, and the Explosive Reference File, to name just a few.

Second, there are files of evidence from actual cases that help to identify other pieces of physical evidence or establish the M.O. (modus operandi or the habitual ways a criminal might perform the criminal act) of a suspect. The Anonymous Letter File, the Bank Robbery Note File, and the National Fraudulent Check File are examples of this category of reference files.

Of course, there are reference files for lipsticks, paints, string, and rope, as well, to allow this evidence to have some power but not as much as those forms of evidence discussed earlier.

Conclusion

Frequently criminal investigation is the process of dealing with the artifacts of a past event. Criminal investigators are the archaeologists of crime. These artifacts, the physical evidence, help the investigator reconstruct events and characters in this historical event called a crime. Some of the physical evidence will be unique and particular, such as blood or fingerprints. Most often it will be ordinary, mundane stuff. Its utility will depend on its discovery at the crime scene, determination of class significance, and individualization. Of course, when little evidence is present on the crime scene, then what is found, even if it is a strand of rope, is significant. But if on our hypothetical crime scene all things are found, though they will be treated with respect and professionalism, they do not have equal weight. By realizing the importance of the evidence, the investigator will be more informed and the investigation will proceed more effectively. Of course, most investigators are limited in their knowledge of most physical evidence, and that is why we must turn our attention to a very important aid to the discovery and development of physical evidence, forensic science.

Chapter 5

Forensic Science

Introduction

The importance of physical evidence is connected to the rise and sophistication of science. For university and college students of criminal investigation this area is important for two reasons. Unlike many practitioners, the college student probably has taken some courses in science to satisfy general graduation requirements. And, although much of the information discussed in this chapter is somewhat exotic, the general principles of biological and physical sciences will be familiar. Furthermore, the scientific aspects of criminal investigations opens up career opportunities that may have been overlooked by most students. Students with a facility for science can major in such disciplines as chemistry or biology and find a career in the criminal justice system.

Definitions

Forensic science is defined in two ways. First, the most general definition applies the "three T's" of science to criminal investigative problems and puzzles. The "three T's" are scientific theory, technology, and technicians. Forensic science, therefore, is the application of scientific theory, technology, and technicians to crime and criminal investigation. Second, and more specifically, forensic science is divided into two areas that are discussed at length in this chapter: pathology and criminalistics. Pathology deals specifically with death and has an institutional manifestation in the coroner or medical examiner's office. Criminalistics deals with physical evidence and has an institutional presence in the police crime laboratory.

Role and Importance

Forensic science plays three roles in the criminal justice system in general and criminal investigation in particular. First, forensic scientists collect and preserve evidence. Of course, as discussed in previous chapters, the uniformed police officer and plainclothes detective will find, safeguard,

and collect evidence as well. That is a very important part of the preliminary investigation. But in the larger police departments, specially trained
"technicians" or "investigators" will participate in that activity. Physical
evidence is so important to the success of the investigation, it is believed
that experts should be in charge of it. In that regard, the investigative
process must be shared with others; like any large scientific project a division of labor is established based on specialty.

Second, forensic scientists take the evidence, be it a body of a murder
victim or a crime scene fingerprint, and analyze it using scientific theory,
technology, and trained technicians. All kinds of interdisciplinary sciences
can be used, such as agronomy, anthropology, archaeology, biology, botany,
chemistry, computer science, geology, microbiology, psychology, and
physics, to name just a few.

Third, the forensic scientist may become an expert witness in the courtroom during the trial. Most witnesses during a trial are not allowed to
give their opinion; they must state only the facts of what they saw. Expert
witnesses, however, are given license to give their opinion and interpretation of the evidence. They will be allowed to explain the evidence—some
of it very obscure and difficult for the lay person—and give it special
meaning. Being an expert witness is important because of the weight physical evidence and the testimony of scientists have in a trial. Studies indicate
that judges and juries are predisposed toward science. The more physical
evidence presented, and the more testimony by scientists about that evidence,
the greater the likelihood of a conviction.

All of this is important for two additional reasons. First, in the last half
century science has made some breakthroughs—the discovery of DNA
and computers are two of the more obvious examples—in theory and
technology. Tests and instruments have been developed to take the most
minute evidence and move it from class categories to a greater probability of individualization. Second, the "due process revolution" has placed
a greater emphasis on physical evidence, and its scientific analysis as judicial obstacles has been placed in the way of older police procedures. That
is not to say that forensic science is not challenged by the courts. As early
as 1923, in the court case of *Frye v. United States*, a "general acceptance
rule" was established for forensic science to be admitted into the court.
In that specific instance, the scientific validity of the polygraph was rejected. More broadly, however, was the establishment of the "general acceptance rule," which said that in order for forensic tests and procedures to
be valid, there must be a general agreement by the scientific community
in their validity. The Frye rule existed for seventy years unchallenged. In
1993 the *Daubert v. Merrill Dow Pharmaceuticals Inc.* case overruled
the Frye doctrine and set forth a four-fold guideline on the admissibility of
scientific evidence:

1. Has the theory or technique been tested?
2. Has there been peer review of the theory or technique?
3. Is the rate of potential error known and can it be controlled?
4. Is there general acceptance of the theory or technique in the relevant scientific field?

Forensic Pathology[1]

History

One of the oldest criminal justice agencies in Anglo-American history is that of the coroner. Along with the sheriff, the coroner was created in the twelfth century (1194 A.D.) to extend the king's power into local life and to solidify the notion of a centralized nation-state. Upon the discovery of a violent death, such as homicide, suicide, or accidental, coroners were to come in to a village and conduct a public investigation, or inquest, to determine the cause and specific location of death. Since death and dying was so public, with public executions and plagues commonplace, the general knowledge of the look and processes of death was widespread and lay people often served as coroners. Of course, the level of sophisticated scientific knowledge was limited. As the king's representatives, these medieval coroners were generally disliked and distrusted. Consequently, they were slow to action and a long history of bribery taking and general corruption arose.

As a colonial institution, the coroner system quickly found its way into America. But in the American system of things these coroners were more local in orientation. Their general jurisdiction was the county, but the ultimate responsibility was not to the central government but to the local one. Unfortunately, their history of corruption and ineptitude continued.

For much of the eighteenth and nineteenth centuries two levels of forensic pathology developed. On one level, the ancient coroner system continued. Much of its history and development coincided with the rise of mortuary science and practice. Most coroners, therefore, were untrained in the emerging new schools of medicine growing up affiliated with universities in America, and instead they attended specialized mortuary schools. Furthermore, most coroners were elected and so they often had greater political skills than scientific ones. On the other hand, as the medical

---

1. For an overview see D.J. DiMaio and V.J.M. Dimaio, *Forensic Pathology* (New York: Elsevier, 1989). Also see Werner U. Spitz and Russell Fisher, eds., *MedicoLegal Investigation of Death: Guidelines for the Application of Pathology to Criminal Investigation*, 2nd ed. (Springfield, IL: Charles C. Thomas, 1980).

school and university became fixed in higher education in the late nine-teenth century, a new profession, forensic pathology, began to emerge and was more specialized and scientific. As explained in a previous chapter, some remarkable scientific discoveries were being made during this time and these added to the credibility of forensic pathology. In 1877, Massachusetts abolished the coroner system and established the medical examiner. New York followed in 1915. It was in the New York City medical examiner's office where the discipline of toxicology, the study of poisons, was created. In subsequent decades other states created the medical examiner's office. Many states, such as Illinois, have a medical examiner's office in the larger cities (Chicago established its ME office in 1975), but the rest of the rural parts of the states maintain a coroner system. Ninety-nine of the one hundred counties in Illinois still have a coroner system. In the name of professionalism, however, some coroners administer their offices while a pathologist is hired to conduct more scientific aspects of autopsy.

Structure and Science

America, today, has two systems for forensic pathology. It is important to highlight the distinction because the kind of services an investigator can expect is predicated upon the kind of system existing in the officer's jurisdiction. First, a word of caution. Often an investigator will find very competent forensic services from a coroner, and, in some places, a medical examiner might do poor work. That aside, however, some generalizations might be made.

Coroners continue to be elected officials. The largest single career path for these coroners is mortuary science, as they come up from the undertaker occupation. Indeed, they can maintain a lucrative funeral business as they act as a coroner. They may be trained and talented in handling dead bodies, preparing them for viewing by loved ones, and disposing them by burial or cremation, but their grounding in forensic science is limited. Furthermore, since they are politicians looking to favorable publicity and the next election, they may conflict with the police on crime scenes. In some cases a coroner may hire a forensic pathologist to scientifically carry out autopsy procedures, but the scientist remains subordinate to the politician in such a situation.

The medical examiner is generally appointed for life, and, therefore, formal politics is not an important concern. In addition, medical examiners are trained medical doctors with further specialization in the science of *pathology*. Pathology is the study of reasons why people get sick or injured and the kinds of dysfunctions that result from such illnesses and injuries. Certainly, a large part of this science is death and dying. At this point it would be useful to introduce basic themes and terminologies of forensic pathology.

First, some general definitions are in order. "Dead" means the cessation of life, when a person is lifeless. But a dead person may be revived and brought back to life. "Death" is a more permanent state in which cerebral functions cease or brain death has occurred. No one returns from such a condition. In terms of a medicolegal definition, therefore, death occurs when there is (1) a dilation and fixation of eye pupils, (2) an absence of all reflexes, (3) no breathing without assistance, (4) no heart beat, and (5) a flat brain wave tracing. The term "time of death" refers to the legal time of death and is the moment that a professionally trained person declares a body to be dead. A cadaver may have been dead for several hours, but it is not legally dead until pronouncement. In another way, death is a long process in which the body undergoes numerous changes as it returns to its more basic elemental state. In that context, the death process continues for hours and days after the appearance of life is gone and as the body breaks down.

Bodies take on certain characteristics at the onset of the dying process. For discussion purposes this description is divided into two areas: "fresh" and "ripe" bodies.

Fresh Bodies

Fresh bodies are those within the two-hour range of the event that caused the death. This is not a random notion. Certain dramatic things begin to happen at the two-hour mark that warrant this designation as described below in order of occurrence:

- All vital signs, such as breathing (there may be one last deep gurgling breath called the "death rattle"), heart beat, and reaction to stimuli, will cease.
- Second, the body temperature will rise slightly. This is due to the fact that during life heat is given off from the body by respiration and perspiration. With death this heat loss is lessened.
- The color of the body will become pale, waxy, and almost translucent in appearance. Of course, certain types of death may give a body a particular look. For example, carbon monoxide poisoning gives a cherry red tone to the complexion. Choking and asphyxiation gives a blue tint and lips and nails become pale.
- After five minutes the eyes will dilate and will not react to light. Then the eyes will begin to flatten as loss of fluid and/or eye pressure occurs.
- From five to ten minutes after the event any wounds will begin to clot, and by thirty minutes mucous membranes will be dried.
- From ten minutes onward insects, particularly flies, will nest and lay eggs in the mouth, nose, and eyes.

The Crossley Checklist Death Time Determination System

IF YOU FIND:	MINUTES SINCE DEATH	
	Least	Most
Absense of vital signs (pulse, respiration, etc.)	0	0
Dilation of pupils	0	5
Clotted blood (cases of wounds)	4	10
Pallor (pale, white skin)	0	20
Mucous membrane dryness	0	30
Incontinence (bowel and/or bladder evacuation)	5	35
	HOURS SINCE DEATH	
Tendon reflexes present	0	2
Clouding of cornea (pupil or eye) – eyes open	½	2
Cadaveric spasm (death grip – electrocution, head injuries)	0	3
Dried blood (wounds) – estimate by drying of pool from periphery, inward	½	4
Livor mortis – mild (pink coloration of lower portions of body)	½	4
Tympanic abdomen (resonant)	½	5
Rigor mortis – onset (stiffening of muscles). Subtract one hour for each 10°F average temperature above or below 70°:		
Jaw muscles	2	6
Neck and fingers	3	7
Wrists	4	8
Elbows	5	9
Shoulders and knees	6	10
Hips	7	11
Abdomen (complete rigor mortis)	8	12
Livor mortis – livid (do not confuse with lividity of asphyxiation)	8	12
Blanching of livor (finger pressor on livor areas)	8	12
Indicative acts and indicative factors*	12	24
Disappearance of cutis anserina (gooseflesh, exposure cases)		24
Clouding of cornea – eyes closed	12	24
Loss of optic turgor (softening of eyeballs)	20	30
Rigor mortis resolution (disappearance). Subtract one hour for each 10°F above 70°. Accumulate one hour for each 10° below 70° (1 + 2 + 3, etc.):		
Jaw	26	30
Neck and fingers	27	31
Wrists	28	32
Elbows	29	33
Shoulders and knees	30	34
Hips	31	35
Abdomen (complete resolution)	31	36

The Crossley Checklist (cont.)

IF YOU FIND:	HOURS SINCE DEATH	
	Least	Most
Putrefication: Grade body 0 to + + + + obesity. Subtract four hours for each + of obesity. Subtract four hours for each 10°F above 70°. Add eight hours for each 10° below 70°. Note well head condition factors:		
Veneral discoloration (genitals)........40	40	56
Dependent portions of body........48	48	72
"Skin slip" (separation of outer layer of skin)........60	60	84
Blisters........72	72	96
	DAYS SINCE DEATH	
Immersion cases:		
Fingertips swelling........½	½	1
Hand swelling........3	3	5
Separation of epidermis........4	4	6
Flotation (running of warm water — less; cold water — more)......6	6	18
Adipocere (saponification of fat)........14	14	21

* There are few corporeal findings of value in the attempt to determine the time of death occuring between 12 and 24 hours previous. Indicative acts (meals prepared, newspapers read, etc.) and indicative factors (snow above but not below a body, run-down timepeaces, spoiled food, etc.) may be very accurate and valuable.

- Between five and thirty-five minutes after death the sphincter, the ring-shaped muscle at a body orifice, loses tone as muscles relax and bladder and bowel contents are discharged. This is called incontinence.

Ripe Bodies

Ripe bodies are those experiencing numerous changes beginning at the second hour after death and continues until complete decomposition has occurred. For ease of analysis, we can consider this process as early versus advanced ripeness.

Signs occurring during the *early stages* of ripeness, that period from two to twelve hours, are:

- First, lividity begins to be noticeable. Actually, lividity, known as the settling of the blood down through the tissues due to gravity, began in the earlier phases but it will not be noticeable until about the third hour. A definite purplish bruise-like appearance will occur. At first, the skin will blanch, or a white finger mark will appear upon touch. As time passes, to the sixth and eighth hour, lividity will become fixed and no blanching will occur upon touch. Lividity might be useful to determine if the body has been moved. Also, lividity must be kept in mind so these bruise marks are not misinterpreted as beating and abuse.

- Second, the body, which had remained relatively warm to the touch, begins to cool at a rate dependant on a variety of conditions such as climate, obesity, and location. The formula for calculating the rate of decline in temperature is:

$$\frac{99.6 - T}{1.5} = N$$

[99.6 = average living temperature, T = temperature of cadaver, 1.5 = average drop of temperature after death, N = hours since death]

- Third, rigor mortis sets in by the third and fourth hours. It begins in smaller muscle groups, such as the fingers and jaw, and progresses through the larger ones. By the twelfth hour, rigor mortis will be dispersed throughout the body and the cadaver will appear stiff. Rigor mortis is due to the disappearance of the source of energy required for muscle contraction, ATP (adenosine triphosphate). If violent exertion occurred shortly before death, the process of rigor mortis is expedited because the ATP energy source was already depleted.
- Fourth, insect activity becomes more pronounced. At the twelfth hour insect eggs hatch and maggots feed on the tissue.

Advanced stages of ripeness might be marked from the twelfth hour onward and are characterized by some of the more dramatic changes:

- First, cooling of the body continues based on the formula given above until the twenty-fourth hour when decomposition has progressed enough to keep the cadaver at the temperature of the surrounding environment.
- Second, rigor mortis begins to let go of the cadaver. Again, starting at the smaller muscle masses like the neck and jaw, rigor slowly leaves so that at thirty hours the body is softened and flaccid.
- Third, facial features are largely unrecognizable by the twenty-fourth hour.
- Fourth, beetles arrive to feast on the dry skin. Spiders and mites follow shortly to eat the earlier bugs. By forty-eight hours the cadaver will be covered by a variety of abundant insect life.
- Fifth, discoloration begins to spread. At first there is a greenish discoloration, particularly around the genitals and abdomen. As

time passes this darkening spreads and deepens to a black and brown appearance. In people of color, African-Americans and Latinos, this will give a marbling look that will appear as streaks of darker color.

- Sixth, putrification (Latin for "to stink") accelerates from the thirtieth hour onward. Besides the smell, which is particularly pungent, gases begin to be produced as tissue decays. Fluids begin to leak from the orifices. If there is no outlet for these gases because wounds and orifices are sealed or obstructed due to the crusting of the fluids, the gases will build up and bloat the cadaver. If not relieved this bloating may lead to the bursting of the cadaver.

Any of these levels of decay if occurring in watery environments will occur four times as fast. In addition, in such immersion cases some other elements are present. For example, finger tips and hands will begin to swell. By the fourth day of immersion, there will be a separation of the epidermis. Flotation will occur from six to eighteen days. Finally, adipocere, the saponification of fat, will be pronounced from the fourteenth to the twenty-first day. This will appear as a greasy soap-like substance which develops on the surface of any body lying in a wet or moist environment due to a chemical action of decomposing body fats.

System and Procedure

There are several procedural steps for forensic investigation that occur in most large jurisdictions. These steps can be classified by the work done by medical examiner investigators, morgue processing technicians, autopsy, pathology laboratory work, and presentation of findings to the police detectives and the prosecutor.

Forensics Investigator. Generally, when the police have been called to a death scene they must quickly notify the coroner or medical examiner's office. The body should not be touched until an investigator, frequently referred to as a "body bagger" in police slang, arrives from the morgue. This investigator takes pictures and notes about the scene and then releases the body to be taken for official pronouncement. Official pronouncement may occur at the local hospital.

Morgue Processing Technicians. After pronouncement the police officers who discovered the body transport it to the coroner's or medical examiner's office. At that time all possessions of the deceased are inventoried and signed for by the police and morgue technician. After the body is weighed it is toe-tagged for identification purposes and placed in a waiting room. If the body is particularly advanced in decomposition or had a traumatic and violent death, it might be placed, in a closed refrigerated compartment. Otherwise, especially in large morgues where there is considerable volume, cadavers might be placed in a large chilled area and stacked in racks similar to a library book storage. There are two types of bodies at the morgue: those awaiting an autopsy, a process that will occur in a short time, or those already autopsied and waiting to be picked up by a relative, those purchased by a medical school for class dissection, or those awaiting public burial in a potter's grave. In Cook County, Chicago, for example, approximately 300 bodies a year are buried in mass graves at the county's expense.

Autopsy, Greek for "to see with one's own eyes," is a common surgical process used to determine and document cause of death. In the 1940s and 1950s autopsies were done quite often. In reaction to such apparent undignified treatment of the dead, a federal law was passed in 1954, the Model Post-Mortum Examination Act, which most states have followed, that limits and defines the circumstances under which an autopsy would occur. All suspicious deaths justify an autopsy. These include homicides, suicides, accidents, all inmates who die while in custody, and those in which the person seemed healthy at time of death. In the latter case, all jurisdictions have a time line for when a person had to see a physician last to avoid an autopsy. The press of business might even require changing the criterion. For example, in Chicago's Cook County Medical Examiner's Office the old rule was that if a person had not seen a doctor within three months and died, an autopsy was performed. Because of the volume of bodies needing autopsies, the new rule — not seeing a doctor in six months — was implemented. Those who will be cremated or buried at sea are autopsied. Exceptions are made, if possible, to honor religious desires, but criminal justice should take precedence over personal desires. Generally, in any given population, one percent will die each year. Of that one percent, about 25 percent will be autopsied. For example, in a city of 100,000 people 1,000 will die each year. Of that number about 250 will be autopsied. Given such a simple formula, one can imagine the volume in places such as New York City and Los Angeles. For example, in Chicago in 1990, 8,000 bodies were brought into the medical examiner's office for investigation. Five thousand of these were autopsied.

The procedure of an autopsy is fairly consistent nationwide. There are three types or levels of autopsy. First, there is the complete autopsy in which the entire body and head are surgically examined. Second, there is the limited autopsy in which the body but not the head is examined. Third, a selective autopsy studies only a few organs.

It appears that the common training and career path for most of these autopsy technicians is mortuary school. First, a general external examination, similar to one that you might receive in a physician's office, is done to the body. An accurate detailed description of all wounds and marks is

"Y" incision

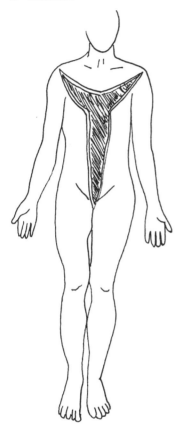

recorded. The entire procedure is recorded for documentation purposes. Second, a dissection and internal examination occurs with a "Y" incision, a cut across the chest from shoulder to shoulder dipping down over the breasts. Then another incision extends down the length of the abdomen to the pubis. Then the ribs and cartilage are cut to expose the lungs and heart. These are dissected, as are other organs in the abdomen area, and are weighed. Samples of these organs are taken for laboratory work. Samples of fluids are taken as well. Third, the head and brain are examined. This may be done to get a brain temperature to help establish time of death or to see if any other illnesses or injuries are present. Most often head and brain examinations are done in the name of scientific completeness. The examination begins with an incision through the scalp behind one ear and across the top of the head to the back of the opposite ear. The scalp is then peeled forward and away to expose the skull. Then the front section of the skull is cut through by a saw and removed, exposing the brain. The

Scalp cut

Incision

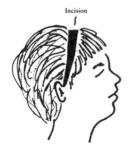
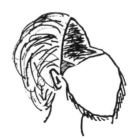

brain is removed, examined, weighed, and sectioned for microscopic analysis. At the end of this procedure the remaining organs are put in a sack and placed back in the body cavities and the wounds are synched up. More cosmetic procedures are left for the mortuary.

Laboratory analysis shortly follows autopsy. The tissue samples are taken to the coroner's or medical examiner's laboratory for a variety of tests. The tests may be toxicological to determine the presence of substances such as poison, alcohol, and drugs. One important test has to do with AIDS. This disease has made the work of autopsy technicians very hazardous. The body and blood they worked on in the morning might be shown to be HIV-positive in the afternoon. If maintained in cold storage, at 40 to 45 degrees Fahrenheit, the AIDS virus will survive 23.5 hours in a dead host. For safety's sake, many medical examiners run such screening tests before an autopsy is initiated.

A *Presentation of Findings* goes to the investigators and becomes part of the case file. In addition, the medical examiner might provide special advice and clarifications to the prosecutor at more advanced stages of the case. Finally, the coroner or medical examiner may be called upon to act as an expert witness in court. This activity will be discussed in a later chapter relating to the courts.

Criminalistics[2]

History

Criminalistics, or the application of the physical sciences such as chemistry and physics to criminal investigative problems, is a fairly recent development. It is connected to the rise and development of the sciences in the nineteenth century. Mathieu Orfila (1787–1853) published the first scientific work on the detection of poisons in 1814. Alphonse Bertillon (1853–1914), in 1879, began developing anthropometry, a system of taking systematic body measurements as a means of distinguishing one person from another. Frances Galton (1822–1911) began a study of fingerprints

---

2. For an overview see Peter R. DeForest, R.E. Gaensslen and Henry C. Lee, *Forensic Science: An Introduction to Criminalistics* (New York: McGraw-Hill, 1983) and Richard Safferstein, *Criminalistics: An Introduction to Forensic Science*, 4th ed. (Englewood Cliffs, NJ: Prentice Hall, 1990).

and their classification, leading to the first book on the subject in 1892. Leone Lattes (1887–1954) discovered in 1901 that blood could be placed into groupings of A, B, O, and AB. Calvin Goddard (1891–1955) began using comparison microscopes to examine bullets found at the crime scene and those from a known gun. He became famous in Chicago in 1929 when he studied the ballistic evidence connected to the infamous St. Valentine Day massacre. In that incident, several gangsters dressed as Chicago police officers shot and killed members of a rival gang. In a sense, Goddard was able to clear the Chicago police from any wrongdoing. In 1910 Albert Osborn (1859–1946) published the classic *Questioned Documents* and led the way for such items as forged notes to be accepted in the court as evidence. The oldest forensic laboratory in the United States is at the Los Angeles Police Department; it was established by August Vollmer the police chief of Berkeley, California, who was a visiting chief at Los Angeles. Vollmer went on to establish the School of Criminology at the University of California at Berkeley and his colleague, Paul Kirk, taught generations of forensic scientists and coined the word "criminalistics." In the meantime, J. Edgar Hoover, while reforming the Bureau of Investigation, created a crime lab in 1932.

Hierarchy of Criminalistic Laboratories

Criminalistic services in any given jurisdiction are dependent on the proximity and sophistication of the crime laboratory. Such facilities may be classified accordingly:

1. *Closets and cooperation.* Many police departments are small operations and cannot afford some of the instruments and personnel to have anything more than an evidence closet. These departments establish relationships with larger departments, sheriffs offices, or state police facilities and send much of their evidence to other places for analysis. They have photographic capabilities, of course, but they might be of a Polaroid variety which do not call for darkroom skills. They may have a ballistics retrieval system, such as a water tank, into which a gun can be fired so that a spent slug can be retrieved.

2. *Simple laboratory.* This is a lab with some microscopes (especially the comparison variety), more photographic capability than an evidence closet, and certainly a water tank or other means to retrieve ballistic data.

3. *Basic full-service laboratory.* For those cities, counties, and states with full-service labs the officer can expect the following units:

- *Physical science unit.* This unit is filled with people trained in the principles and procedures of chemistry, physics, and geology, and various instruments are used. For example, there may be spectrographic analysis instruments to identify organic substances by the spectrum of the gas they emit while burning. These instruments are most often used to analyze metals, oils, ashes, glass, cloth, and paint. Emission spectrographs work on basic elements while mass spectrographs are used for low-level trace elements. Spectrophotometry, however, is limited because the material being examined needs to be in a pure state, a rarity for physical evidence of a criminal investigation. Consequently, more important for the analysis of physical evidence is chromatography. Chromatography is the process of separating and identifying the components of a mixture. Obviously, this has become most important in the examination of drugs. Both spectrographic and chromatographic processes identify an element's signature, usually in a graph-like illustration, of chemical elements that allows for identification. In addition, laser technology is used to discover otherwise invisible fingerprints.

- *Biology unit.* These personnel study dried blood and other body fluids, hairs and fibers, and botanical materials such as wood and plants.
- *Firearms unit.* These scientists examine bullets found on the scene and compare them to known guns. Also, they might study garments of a gunshot victim to determine the closeness of the firearm when fired.
- *Document unit.* This unit studies questionable documents in terms of handwriting and type-written papers.
- *Photography unit.* These personnel record physical evidence the laboratory receives, prepare photographic exhibits for court, and use sophisticated photographic techniques, such as infrared, ultraviolet and X-ray photography, to help investigators with their cases.

4. *Sophisticated full-service crime laboratories.* These laboratories have the instruments described above in addition to the following:

- *Toxicology unit.* These personnel would concentrate on body fluids and organs to ascertain their presence or absence of drugs and poisons.
- *Latent fingerprint unit.* This unit processes, compares and identifies fingerprints found on the crime scene. As the collections of inked fingerprints increased, finding a match became a herculean task. Beginning in the 1970s the classification and retrieval of fingerprints by computers, generally referred to as AFIS or automated fingerprint identification system, has expedited the process considerably. The heart of the AFIS technology is the ability of

The Basic Gas Chromatograph

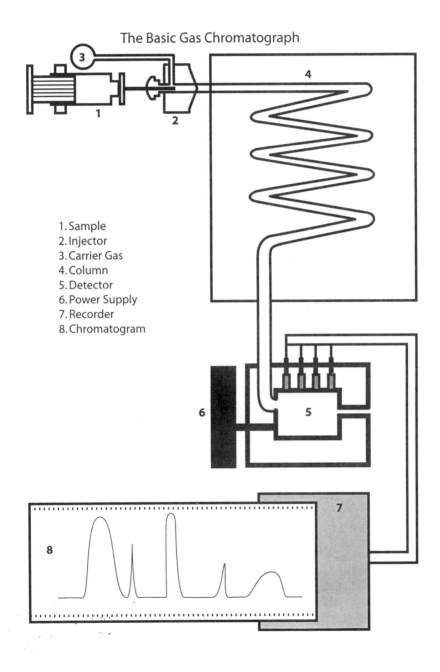

1. Sample
2. Injector
3. Carrier Gas
4. Column
5. Detector
6. Power Supply
7. Recorder
8. Chromatogram

a computer to scan and digitally encode fingerprints so they can be subject to high-speed computer processing. A set of ten fingerprints can be searched against a file of 500,000 sets of ten fingerprints in about eight-tenths of a second. When the Los Angeles Police Department implemented AFIS the city was being terrorized by a killer of 15 persons. This "Night Stalker" was identified as Richard Ramirez. Police estimate that it would have taken a single technician, manually searching the city's 1.7 million print cards, 67 years to match the perpetrator's prints. The AFIS search took 20 minutes. Furthermore, the national "hit rate," or making a match, is only five percent. AFIS approaches a 20 percent success rate. Actually AFIS does not make a match; it narrows down the number of close possibilities and then a trained expert makes the final match.

- *Polygraph unit.* Although this lie detector technology is not part of forensic science, it was one of the earliest "scientific" devices used by the police and found its way into the early crime laboratories where it remains. Most likely it will be used by criminal investigators and interrogators, at least by those trained in its use, rather than a forensic scientist.

- *Voiceprint analysis.* In those investigations where a voice is recorded, such as a telephone threat or tape recorded message, and the detectives want an identification, a voiceprint can be obtained. A sound spectrograph takes the voice sample and transforms it into a visual graphic display. This technology and investigative tool is based on the premise that the sound patterns produced by speech are unique to the individual and the voiceprint displays that uniqueness.

- *Evidence collection unit.* This unit is made up of specially trained police officers (or sometimes nonpolice personnel) who go to the crime scene to discover, collect, preserve, and transport physical evidence to the crime laboratory.

- *Exotic tools.* Depending on the lab, there might be additional exotic capabilities. For example, some labs have "age progression" computer functions. If a child disappeared at the age of five years, and ten years have passed, how might he look at the age of fifteen? This computer program allows for such a rendition as age progression. Perhaps, one of the more exotic and expensive tools would be neutron activation analysis instruments. This form of analysis makes very small samples of evidence radioactive, down to the neutron level, and makes an identification. It can analyze samples 100 times smaller than those needed for spectrographic analysis.

Compound microscope

1 eyepiece and body tube
2 objectives
3 stage with stage clips
4 mirror
5 fine adjustment
6 coarse adjustment

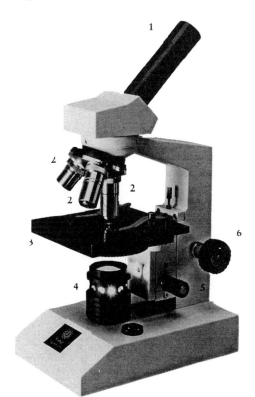

5. Specialty laboratories. Although many crime laboratories on the state and federal levels have the facilities similar to the more sophisticated full-service laboratory, there are some unique qualities that deserve mention.

- State police systems have crime laboratory facilities that are frequently used by rural and small towns of the state. These laboratories are unique in terms of their geographic coverage. The state of Illinois is illustrative. The state police crime laboratory system is divided into nine districts. The desire is to put a crime laboratory facility not more than a two hour drive from any local police department. Each of those district crime laboratories becomes a self-constituted, full-service facility.

- Federal law enforcement crime laboratories are famous. The FBI.'s lab is recognized worldwide. It has all of the operations listed above. Money and resources allow this lab to have even more sophisticated tools and personnel than most. In addition, the FBI crime laboratory has a "reference file" system. Reference files are samples of commonly manufactured items that may be found on a crime scene. Reference files become for some physical evidence what an inked print is to a latent print; they provide items of known origin with which a comparison can be made with objects found on the crime scene. Reference files may include:

  1) *Cigarette Identification File.* There are nearly two hundred different types of cigarettes made in the United States and other key countries on file. Therefore, a cigarette remnant found on a crime scene can be identified according to manufacture and product date.

  2) *Standard Ammunition File.* Over 13,000 specimens of commonly manufactured ammunition in the United States and key countries are included in this file. Therefore, a shell casing found on the scene can be identified by manufacturer and production date.

  3) *Firearms Reference Collection.* About 3,000 types of handguns are referenced in this file. In addition, 1,600 shoulder weapons are included in the sample.

  4) *Shoe Print File.* Photographs of all the major shoe soles and heels manufactured in the United States are in this file.

  5) *Tire Tread File.* All the tire treads made in America are in this file.

  6) *Watermark Standards File.* This provides an index to all the watermarks used by manufacturers of paper.

  7) *The National Fraudulent Check File.* This file contains over 100,000 samples of bogus checks.

  8) *Bank Robbery Note File.* This file contains photocopies of hold-up notes written by known bank robbers.

  9) Other files are the Explosive Reference File, Automotive Paint File, Hair and Fiber File, and Blood Serum File, to name a few.

Other Federal Agencies—such as the Drug Enforcement Administration; Alcohol, Tobacco and Firearms; and Pure Food And Drugs—would have even more specialized reference files. The Bureau of Alcohol, Tobacco, and Firearms, for example, has three laboratories that specialize in the bureau's work dealing with explosives and arson.

Conclusions

Forensic science has had a remarkable impact on criminal investigations. Increasingly, more information can be found with smaller and smaller pieces of evidence. Early resistance by detectives to turn over their occupational standing to outsiders, such as scientists, has been overcome to the point of detectives becoming too dependent upon forensics. The truth of the matter is that forensic science has limitations. First, science has its shortcomings. The famous murder cases in Narborough, England, can be taken as a case in point. In 1983, and again three years later, young girls were abducted, raped and murdered. The investigation was carried out systematically but to no avail. In the meantime, a scientific breakthrough occurred at a nearby university as the principles of DNA were discovered. This led to the "Blooding," the taking of blood samples, of over 4,000 men. Even at that, however, the killer slipped through, having a friend to substitute for him. It was only when the friend was overheard talking about the giving of blood that a tipster called the police to alert them to Colin Pitchfork. Forensic sciences confirmed Pitchfork's guilt, but good old investigative techniques actually led to his arrest.

Second, staffing of scientific personnel has problems as well. People completing rigorous college training to become scientists find all kinds of lucrative careers in universities and private industry. As of 1996 the average starting pay of a laboratory technician ranged from $25,000 to $30,000. The relative poor pay of police work does not always attract the best of technicians. Furthermore, recent revelations of shoddy and corrupt work by lab technicians both at the local and federal level have aroused public concerns. One cover story of *Time* magazine put the FBI crime lab "under the microscope."[3]

Third, the workload and backlog of cases have become a national problem. The average crime lab examiner works on 700 to 1,000 cases a year. Reliance on crime labs has increased, but funding and resources have not. While awaiting conclusive evidence examination, many suspects are allowed to go free and commit new crimes. This problem has become so grave that many criminalistics labs have resorted to various strategies such as:

1. Prioritizing, in which the most serious cases and cases with set court dates are worked first. Some states, California, Indiana, New Mexico, and Delaware, do minimal work on cases without a suspect.
2. Charging fees of up to $150 per hour for services. Those police departments with modest budgets may find a county or state lab too expensive, thus the case goes unsolved or is not adjudicated because of a lack of expert interpretation of evidence.

---

3. *Time*, April 28, 1997.

3. Random sampling of large quantities of evidence. This is done most often for drug crimes. For example, if the police seize hundreds of bags of cocaine, the lab will test random samples from a given percentage of the bags. This is done in the name of economy, but it flies in the face of basic science that preaches "completeness" and "comprehensiveness." Police and prosecutors would feel more comfortable with a more thorough examination process as well.

4. Training the police to do fundamental "field testing" of evidence is another option. For example, in New York City the police have been trained to field test suspected drugs. That way they can hold defendants for a grand jury indictment. Otherwise, the suspects would have to be released in five days. In some jurisdictions officers are given kits to test for gun residues on the hands of suspects.

5. Automation of evidence analysis can be more efficient. In the short run such machines can be expensive but in the long run it would be more efficient to put a large quantity of material in an automated analysis device and let the analysis go on during the night.

6. Making analyzing systems compatible. In recent history police departments have had a choice between two data bank systems to analyze ballistics. They are the Drugfire System of the FBI and the Integrated Ballistics Imaging System (IBIS) of the ATF. Therefore, those local departments having the money to purchase the necessary equipment have two systems to choose from, but the systems do not communicate or link with each other. Agency pride and rivalry has gotten in the way of cooperation.

7. Accreditation by the American Society of Crime Lab Directors (ASCLD) is advocated. This would include having a series of rigorous standards set up by a professional association with a means to check and certify a lab's compliance. As of 1996 only 40 percent of the crime labs of America were accredited.

In spite of the widely publicized setbacks to forensic sciences during the O.J. Simpson trial and acquittal, the rapid and exciting advances in science in the last century have made forensic science a critical helpmate in the criminal investigative process.

Chapter 6

Witnesses and Interviewing

Introduction

People are a major source of information in most research endeavors, and criminal investigations are no exception. Many scientists, particularly social scientists, use interviewing as a research technique. This "qualitative research," whether through structured sampling or snowball techniques, is a vital and respected part of information gathering in sociology and marketing research. Of course, the overall project and questions must be designed to maximize information gathering and minimize problems of bias.

Like the chapters on physical evidence and forensic science, this information is offered because both the crime scene investigator and the follow-up researcher will participate in this activity. Uniformed officers on the scene must interview witnesses at points of high tension and excitement, and plainclothes officers will later re-interview them as conditions become more stabilized.

Due to the dramatic, even traumatic, nature of criminal events and the awesome repercussions of a successful investigation, soliciting information from human beings, rather than collecting physical evidence, presents a series of challenges. In fact, obtaining and documenting such information presents issues that transcend criminal investigation.

Witness testimony and interviewing techniques highlight the importance of *observation*. In general, even under the best and most benign circumstances, people go through everyday life largely oblivious to the human and natural environment around them. College students wearing headphones sauntering across campus completely oblivious to anything but the latest top forty tunes coming through the ear phones is a glaring example of this total lack of awareness. Many people—especially the young and the adolescent, are so self-absorbed that they are largely ignorant of their immediate environment.

Not only are people unaware, but their memories are often weak and fragile. The ability to recount clear, detailed, and distinguishing information is nearly impossible for most. The number of proven cases of people going to prison for a long time based upon erroneous identification has increased over the years.

Interviewing becomes another issue in this process. It highlights the importance of creating an appropriate environment for the interview and then asking and framing questions in such a way as to trick the witness's memory but not contaminate the information with leading and suggestive queries. Interpersonal and social skills are very important here, and the public relations aspects of interviewing may be as important as the information obtained.

Definitions

Actually there are two types of witnesses that must be kept in mind at this stage of the criminal investigation. First, there are the "direct" witnesses, victims or nonvictims who saw the criminal activity. The role of the interview, in this context, is twofold: to obtain information for the police that moves the investigation along and to give information to the direct witnesses that gives them positive impressions of the investigation. Second, there are the "indirect" witnesses, those people who may not even be aware of the crime, but due to their lifestyles and job they are near the crime scene. Indirect witnesses will be discussed later in the context of the follow-up investigation and the neighborhood canvas.

One other distinction must be kept in mind; the interview is an information gathering and giving process. It occurs early in the investigation, and it is generally benign in nature. Another process, the interrogation, resembles the interview. While information is desirable in the interrogation, more prized is the confession and admission of guilt. Interrogation occurs later in the investigation and is certainly more accusatory. Distinctions are presented below:

Interview	Interrogation
1. Involves a witness and/or victim	1. Involves a suspect
2. No custody	2. Involves custody
3. No Miranda rights	3. Requires Miranda rights
4. General information	4. Specific information
5. Less demanding	5. More demanding
6. Casual	6. Structured
7. In the field	7. In the office
8. Information not known	8. Information to be confirmed[1]

Problems

This process also highlights several problems. First is the problem of the unreliability of witnesses and their memory. Studies indicate that there is a

---

1. Don Rabon, *Interviewing and Interrogation* (Durham, NC: Carolina Academic Press, 1992), p. 5.

curve of forgetting. This means that people forget at a more rapid rate short-ly after an event but as time goes by that rate of forgetting tapers off more slowly. Of course, such a curve is important in structuring interviews and reinterviews. The slope of forgetting is steeper with recent occurrence of the event and special techniques that are discussed below need to be applied.

Criminal events happen quickly and are intimidating, thus it would be easy to misperceive and misinterpret the scenario. Even under the best of situations a person might forget—indeed the trauma of the event might demand some sort of self-protective forgetfulness. However, the concept of *flashbulb memory* can be helpful in a criminal investigation. Flashbulb memories are snapshots of events so personally important that the witness can remember everything with clarity. The assassination of President John F. Kennedy or the destruction of the Challenger space shuttle are likely examples of this. Years later, many people remember exactly where they were and what they were doing at the time of those events. Witnessing a criminal event can have the same effect. However, *Yerkes-Dodson's Law* may counterbalance this advantage. According to this law a little stress is beneficial; learning and performance is enhanced with a little stress. But there is a level beyond which learning and performance decrease. Consequently, tremendous stress can degenerate the abilities of the victim/witness to remember.

Not only might people not remember but they may *confabulate*, a process of filling in forgotten or unknown information. Incidents of false memory have marked the criminal justice process. For example, Steve Titus was arrested and identified by the victim as a rapist in Seattle, Washington, in October 1980. After Titus spent eight months in jail, the real culprit was found and identified. In another case, Frank McCann, an undercover Treasury agent, was identified and convicted of 32 counts of rape. After six years of imprisonment all convictions were reversed due to mistaken identity. In 1990, George Franklin was convicted of first-degree murder due to "recovered memory." Apparently, his daughter in 1989 suddenly remembered that he had killed her girlfriend twenty years earlier. In 1995 his conviction was overturned and the prosecution declined to retry him.

Daniel Schacter's study *Searching for Memory* shows that a person's mind can be tricked into false memory. For example, volunteers heard lists of semantically related words such as:

1.	Thread	8.	Point
2.	Pin	9.	Hurt
3.	Eye	10.	Knitting
4.	Injection	11.	Prick
5.	Syringe	12.	Thimble
6.	Sewing	13.	Haystack
7.	Sharp	14.	Pain

When asked to identify words on the original list, many incorrectly picked decoy words like "needle." Fifty-eight percent of the words remembered were not on the list.[2] Subjects of this research simply misremembered.

Second is a problem of public relations. Studies indicate that the chief complaint of victims and witnesses in any criminal investigation is that the detectives do not keep them informed of the case. Victims and witnesses feel very close to a case, it is an intensely personal event, and they disapprove of being neglected or treated in cavalier ways. Interviews, therefore, are not just ways of receiving information to lead the investigation progress to a successful conclusion, but they are a public relations tool to shape societal impressions of the system of criminal justice.

Witnesses

To be prepared for the encounter with a victim/witness, the officer should realize the variety of possible witnesses likely to be encountered and what motivates them to be cooperative or uncooperative.[3] For this purpose victims/witnesses are divided into two large categories, uncooperative witnesses and cooperative witnesses.

Uncooperative Witnesses

First are the uncooperative or silent witnesses or those people on or near the scene whom you know have valuable information but refuse to cooperate. There may be one of three reasons that these witnesses are silent.

Uncooperative witnesses may be *timid* and intimidated by the police. A child who is a victim of parental abuse or incest or pedophilia may feel uncomfortable discussing such issues with a stranger like a police officer. A rape victim may not want to discuss such a personal sexual matter with a male officer. Recent arrivals to America from a country with a long tradition of an oppressive police system may want to avoid involvement. Strategies, both personal and institutional, need to be made so as to waylay this timidity. For example, female officers may interview rape victims and children. Public relations campaigns need to be in place to inspire immigrants with confidence. Acquiring officers who speak foreign languages might facilitate interviewing victims/witnesses in their native language.

---

2. Daniel L. Schacter, *Searching For Memory* (Basic Books, 1996).

3. For an overview see Frank J. Cannavale Jr. and William Falcone, *Witness Cooperation* (Lexington, MA: Lexington Books, 1976).

Some witnesses may chose to be silent out of *fear*. They may fear the police, or more likely, fear the people they are being called upon to witness against. For example, victim and witness intimidation is epidemic in neighborhoods infested with gang activity. There are four factors that increase the chance that a victim/witness will be intimidated:

1. The violent nature of the crime.
2. A previous personal connection to the defendant.
3. Geographic proximity to the defendant.
4. Cultural vulnerability—being a member of a group easily victimized, such as the elderly, children, or recent or illegal immigrants.[4]

Police are the strangers but the suspected ones are neighbors. Such problems need to be addressed in broader terms than the individual interviewer by public relation policies that waylay any negative images the victim/witness may have regarding the police. Some individual solutions, however, can be done. For example, promises of confidentiality can be made to the prospective witness. Painting pictures of future crimes by the perpetrator and harm to the neighborhood if he goes undetected can be helpful as well.

Some uncooperative witnesses may just be *hostile*. These people—based upon racial, ethnic, class, or gender orientations—may simply view all police as the enemy. Radical college students in the 1960s chanted and taunted the police, calling them "pigs," and they tried to obstruct and hinder rather than help law enforcement. There is not much one can do to cultivate these witnesses except, perhaps, build an individual reputation of friendliness, fairness, and professionalism.

Cooperative Witnesses

Second are the *cooperative* or *talkative* witnesses. There are several subcategories here as well. There may be *hostile* persons who pose as being helpful to mislead the investigation. The hostile witness may be a criminal or may be a member of a group that dislikes the police and desires to misdirect the investigation. They may say that a six-foot-four-inch black man ran north on the street and turned west at the corner, when, in reality, it was a five-foot-six-inch white man who drove east on the street and turned south. The investigator, from past experience in the area and using carefully crafted questions on the scene may detect such deception.

---

4. Kerry Murphy Healey, "Victim and Witness Intimidation: New Developments and Emerging Responses," National Institute of Justice Research in Action (October 1995).

Then there are those witnesses who are ready to give information, but it is clouded because they were *under the influence* of alcohol or some other drug during the crime event. Their inhibitions may be down, but so are their perceptivity and clarity. Furthermore, what they so boldly state now may be recanted later as the power of the alcohol wears off. Such information can have some slight investigative utility, but it is likely to be worthless in the courtroom.

Then there are always some individuals who are ready to give as much information as possible to receive recognition and gratuities from the police. These *groupies* probably always wanted to be police officers and they participate vicariously through the media. Their information can be quite reliable but it needs to be seen against the backdrop of exaggerated ingratiation.

Finally, there is the *good* and cooperative individual who courageously steps forward, in spite of the inconvenience, embarrassment, and possible danger, to do an appropriate civic duty. Good witnesses are so important that their witnessing must now be seen and tested against two additional principles. Information from even the most cooperative good witness may be flawed based on the issues of competence and credibility.

Competence has to do with the personal qualifications of the witness/victim. There are several indicators of competence.

Age may determine a witness's competence level. The younger the witness/victim the more the investigator needs to take care over his or her competence. The younger a person the greater the dangers of being led or fed suggestive ideas by the interviewer. In addition, the level of perceptive and interpretive power is lower for younger people. Adolescent people are so self-absorbed, caring less about what environment they are in and more about how they look and fit into their society, that they are not good observers. On the other hand, the older segment of society may be more alert to their environment, but the likelihood of various impediments, such as short term memory or bad eyesight or bad hearing, will diminish their competency.

Intelligence levels may determine a person's general competence as well. Of course, an idiotic and ignorant person would be a difficult witness/victim to question for meaningful information. But even children and educationally deficient adults might have difficulty sorting out and understanding the complexity of events in a criminal scenario. On the other hand, those with superior intelligence might be troublesome as well because their minds might be elsewhere; they might be dealing with levels of higher abstraction that give them an air of preoccupation.

The *mental state* of the witness/victim will obliviously be disturbed after the crime event; a personal and traumatic event has just occurred in the encounter with a criminal. An individual's ability to cope with such a highly charged emotional state might shape their competency.

Finally, the *relationship* of the person being interviewed to the victim or the suspect can complicate the interview. For example, a victim's close friend or loved one—say, a father to a rape victim—might be so emotionally charged as to distort the information. Or a witness might be close to the suspect—a mother of a rape suspect, for example—and cannot believe or support the accusations. In short, factors of age, intelligence, mental state and relationship need to be weighed against a witness's competency.

Credibility is an additional but independent issue as well. A witness can be competent, having the right age, intelligence, mental state and relationships, but may still be incredible due to the following factors that may cloud their perceptions and memory.

The *surprising nature of the event* will determine the witness's credibility. As discussed in an earlier chapter, the criminal will alleviate his own anxiety by transferring it to the victim. Of course, this will be done by threat and intimidation. Also, it will be done by quickness. The witness/victim will not have the ability nor the inclination to look for and remember details, as he or she is caught off guard.

The *length of time of observation* will also have an impact. The shorter the time of observation, the less likely information will be observed and remembered. Conversely, the longer the period of contact, the greater the likelihood of seeing and remembering details of the crime.

Conditions of the event will determine what is seen and remembered as well. The distance from the event and the nature of the lighting, for example, will have an impact on seeing details.

Psychological factors such as previous encounters with criminals as a victim, stereotypes currently in vogue and one's own prejudices will have an impact. For example, let's suppose that a street robbery has been witnessed in which a young white person robs a woman in a parking lot. But the witness had been robbed last year by a young African-American. Furthermore, street crime has been stereotyped as a young black man's occupation. The witness, given the problems of distance and the darkness of the scene, "sees"—due to a psychological process called expectancy—a black person robbing a white person. In short, even the best witness can have credibility problems, which is an assessment that needs to be made as the interview begins.

The Interview

The interview process is a very important part of the criminal investigation where information is obtained and messages of assurance are directed to victims and witnesses to crimes. The information that follows has utility beyond criminal investigation. Other careers, such as journalism, marketing, or personnel services and activities like seeking employment, use these techniques.[5]

Basics

Before beginning a more detailed discussion of the interview process, some basic considerations are in order. Perhaps the fundamentals in the preparation of any interview scheme come from the journalism profession. As any student who worked on a school newspaper can remember there are the essential guides of who, what, when, where, why and how. While they may not be of equal value in a particular criminal investigation they certainly are an essential starting place in the construction of any interviewing format.

A second basic consideration is the creation of an appropriate interview environment. The beginnings of this process may be summarized in the "three C's" of good interviewing; the interviewer should "connect," "converse," and "communicate." Connecting with the person being interviewed is critical in order to maximize the information gathering process. It may help if two principles are kept in mind. One principle is the "Eye" concept. The best communications begin with eye contact. Looking a person in the eye suggests your attentiveness and interest in what is being said. Of course, there can be some exceptions. For example, a rape or incest victim might feel embarrassed and humiliated recounting their story to a male officer. The diverting of the eyes might be considered a more friendly gesture in such cases. Or perhaps maintaining eye contact but emphasizing a sympathetic and empathetic look in that posture. Another principle is the "I" concept. A certain way of connecting and conveying a message that you are listening and caring about what is being said is to paraphrase back such statements as "I understand..." or "I see how you feel...." By taking in information then giving it back in a personal way you firmly establish paths of communication. Conversing is more than just asking a set of previously established questions, that is too bureaucratic and unfeeling. To be conversant is to be well read. As mentioned in earlier chapters, in the name of professionalism the police have learned to speak two languages: "bureaucratese" (a stilted clinical approach) and street lingo (a vulgar slang talk). Neither may be appropriate for the interviewing of a victim/witness of a crime. A good conversant interviewer is one that knows a little about a lot, one who reads newspapers and books, and who can adjust and set up friendly and informed beginnings and transitions in the

---

5. See Raymond L. Gordon, *Interviewing: Strategy, Techniques, and Tactics,* 4th ed. (Florence, KY: Wadsworth, 1987). Also helpful are R.L. Kahn, *The Dynamics of Interviewing: Theory, Techniques and Cases* (Melbourne, FL: Krieger, 1983).

interview process. By doing so one inspires confidence in a process—and the actors in that process—for someone whose confidence in the power of the police and criminal justice systems ability to serve and protect has been severely undermined.

Communication is a two way street. At first glance one would think that the purpose of the interview is for the investigator to receive information and the witness to give it. This is wrong headed. Of course, the detective must get information to expedite the investigation. And, indeed, in the name of the investigation some prized information must be kept secret. For example, in one college town a young female student was found murdered. Everyone assumed it was her boyfriend, the result of a lovers quarrel. Until the case was further advanced the victims parents, the press and public had to be kept uninformed. But in many circumstances, either during the early or ending stages of the investigation, the victim and witness should be kept informed of the progress of the investigation. In fact, a convenient ploy for subsequent re-interviews might be the desire to bring witnesses/victims up-to- date on the investigation.

The Process

Like any teacher of freshman English would say at the start of an essay assignment, the interview process has a beginning, a middle and a ending.

Beginnings

In the formal beginning of an interview four considerations must be kept in mind: they are the elements of purity, privacy, control and courteousness. The P.P.C.C. of all interviewing.

Maintaining the *purity* of the witness is essential. Witnesses and victims are indeed in a fragile condition, they have seen and heard things of monumental importance but most likely there will be gaps in their information, and the natural impulse—in a self protective way—is to forget unpleasantness. Therefore, witnesses need to be separated from others as quickly as possible so as to prevent contamination and tainting of their information. There is always the danger that the witness will hear whispers and rumors about things one is ignorant or unsure of and then unconsciously incorporate that second hand information into their own testimony. This is confabulation.

Privacy becomes a critical issue to maintain this purity. Everything seems so public to the witness/victim—they have been violated in some way by another individual, crowds of curious have assembled and several police are busy at work at a place in which the witness is a central character—and it now becomes essential to establish private space in which to discuss the incident. However, too much privacy may be inappropriate for some witnesses/victims. For example, a victim of child molestation—having been attacked by an adult stranger, perhaps—now has to confront an adult stranger who is a police officer. Certainly, that witness needs the support of significant adult figures such as parents. Of course, then, those people—with their overwrought and emotional concerns and attitudes—become a consideration of the interviewer.

Control is another important part of the beginning phases of the interview. In any interview situation someone will always be in control. Either it will be the interviewer or the subject. The interviewer must establish and maintain control or the chaotic impressions and perceptions of the witness will confuse the process and compound the work. The witness/victim is like a drowning person struggling against the rescue attempts of the lifeguard. For the greater good of rescuing the swimmer the lifeguard must vigorously keep in control. Decisions must be made as to where the interview must take place to maintain this control. But this is not as simple as it first appears. For example, the maximum control would occur by taking the witness to police headquarters. But that is such a busy and intimidating place the process of communication might be damaged. On the other hand, the interview might take place in the victim's home. Certainly subsequent follow up interviews will most likely take place there. But in this crime scene interview the interviewer would most likely relinquish too much control. Consequently, in the name of privacy and control, most likely the crime scene interview would take place quickly in the police car or some other reasonably private place in an otherwise very public environment.

Lastly, all of the above must be done in a *courteous* manner. There should be no physical, emotional or verbal abuse. Interviewers and investigators must remember that it is the perception of abuse by citizens that is more important than the reality. An officer may conduct an interview and investigation in absolutely appropriate ways but if the citizenry interprets it as inappropriate then an investigative and public relations crisis has occurred. Choices of the interview place, care for the creature comforts of the witness/victim, determination of the questioning style and language, the use of the interviewers body language, and the timeliness and convenience of later interviews all send messages to the witness about the police in particular and the criminal justice system in general.

Main body

The main body of the interview is based upon the premise that the witness/victim does have useful information to impart but that they need to be brought along to cooperate fully and to remember the details of the criminal and the criminal event. Before we turn to some specific helps in that process some general things might be kept in mind.

Rapport

What is rapport? It is a relationship based upon trust and harmony. The investigator and the subject are strangers brought together by a horrendous event. To expedite the interview and achieve a maximum of cooperation and communication a bridge needs to be built by the interviewer; this bridge is rapport. This may be accomplished in two ways: reading and responding to the subject's body language, and conveying messages by the investigator's body language.

Communication from the subject may be read in numerous ways but the more accurately indicators come through their eyes. Three channels of information may be utilized. They are eye movements based upon the memory of things visual, auditory, and sensory. *Visual eye movements*, when remembering past events that were seen, will be upward and to the subjects left or directly forward. If the events are constructed, responding to a hypothetical story offered by the interviewer or fabricating events that were construed as visual, the eyes will look upward and to the right of the subject. *Auditory eye movements*, when remembering past events that were heard or said, will be left ward. Down and to the left means remembering of things heard. Horizontally left would connote remembering sounds or things said by the subject in the past. When constructing auditory images the eyes will be down to the right of the subject. *Sensory eye movements*—when remembering sensations such as sorrow, anger, fear—will be downward, downward and to the left, eye closing and eye fluttering. There does not seem to be any patterns for sensory construction. It is not the purpose of such readings to call into question the veracity of the subject; this information is to be used to better establish rapport. By understanding the recall and reconstruction process of the subject the interviewer can better tailor make the questions and show empathy more honestly.[6] Nonetheless such analysis tells the investigator the type of witness being interviewed: if the person is more visual then they will be good at physical descriptions of facial features, clothes and cars; if the person is more auditory they will be best at the sounds of voices and other noises; while the sensory person was too scared to see or hear much of value.[7]

The investigator might ease the process with intelligent use of body language as well. *Mirror reflection* techniques might be used to advantage. The interviewer can give the subject a mirror reflection of themselves and thus build rapport. For example, if the subject is sitting with their right leg

---

6. Don Rabon, *Interviewing and Interrogation*, pp. 25–37.
7. Ibid., p. 21.

crossed, the interviewer would subliminally send a message by sitting with the left leg across, the mirror image of the subject. If the interviewee is fidgeting with their left hand, the investigator would mirror that action discretely with her right. Enough of these subtle signs would build a bridge between the two people. To test the success of such a strategy, to see if rapport has been achieved, the interviewer could introduce some new signs to see if unconsciously the subject returns the mimicry.[8] If there is no imitation then rapport has not yet been achieved. If there is a repeating of the gestures then rapport likely has been completed and the rest of the interview should proceed accordingly.

Questions

Questioning sequences need to be considered and employed at the outset. There are two possible sequencing strategies. First, is the *inductive sequencing* which starts with the quest for details and then moves to generalizations. Second, there is the *deductive sequencing* which starts with general questions and then moves to particulars.[9] The choice of each strategy may be determined by the *mental state* of the subject. For example, since inductive questions seem cold and hard edged they would be reserved for the relaxed subject. A tense subject would be approached with a deductive questioning strategy at first. The *memory state* of the subject might be a variable as well. For example, a person who has trouble remembering might be given confidence by a series of short and easily answered questions, the inductive strategy. On the other hand, a person with apparently good recall might be given greater room to maneuver the memory with a deductive approach. Finally there is the *control state*. Since an interview is a tug-a- war between two people for control the interviewer would not want to give too much power to some one who constantly tries to take control, something they could best do with the deductive approach. On the other hand, if issues of control have been worked out then greater freedom might be given to the subject.

Language is an important aspect of the interview process. The way a subject uses the language might help direct the questioning process. For example, there are *false sounds* or *hesitation patterns*. These are words and insertions—such as "uh," "um," "ya know"—that do not add meaning to the sentence. Of course, a person who speaks constantly with such patterns may have an idiosyncrasy. But an individual whose story is initially fluent and then falls into false sounds is sending a message. In a sense, the subject is really saying "I want to communicate but just not now." Rec-

---

8. Ibid., p. 38.
9. Ibid., pp. 93–94.

ognizing this the interviewer can mark off and return to develop this material later. There are *qualifiers* and *hedges* as well. These are attempts to limit or hide the real meaning. For example, if you ask a person "What did you do on the evening in question?" and you receive an answer: "Mostly, I watched TV" you are a victim of a qualifier or hedge. "Mostly" is an ambiguous term and hides a considerable amount of meaning.

Interviewers need to be careful in the language they use as well. They need to direct the flow of the discussion without providing leading questions. Those being interviewed are in a highly suggestive state and the information that comes from them should be theirs and not something unintentionally planted by the interviewer. Care over the use of language is critical at this point. For example, notice the difference in a question just with the use of an article. "Did you see the broken window ?" As against "Did you see a broken window?" The first example implies that there was a broken window.

The most logical means of questioning to inspire memory is chronological. Just as historians discuss the Civil War before World War I the interviewer should initially sequence the questions in a chronological format, However, problems of recall still might persist.

Restoring Memory

One of the more powerful aids for interviewers to use in maximizing remembrance is *Cognitive Interviewing Techniques*.[10] Cognitive interviewing is based upon two theoretical assumptions. First, a memory is composed of a collection of several elements. The more elements a memory retrieval aid has in common with the memory of the event, the more effective that aid will be. Second, a memory has several access routes and a memory that is not accessible with one memory cue may be accessible with another one.

There are four general methods for jogging the memory. First, the witness would be asked to reconstruct the circumstances surrounding the incident. A description of the area of the crime scene—be it a room, store, or street—the kind of weather, or nearby people would enhance memory of the specific criminal event. Second, the witness would be asked to report everything they can remember about the event. Many people edit their memories, leaving out things they think are unimportant. By recalling everything associations are established that help trigger the memory of something otherwise forgotten. Third, recall things in a different order. Earlier the witness was asked to remember in chronological order because

---

10. Margo Bennett and John E. Hess, "Cognitive Interviewing," *FBI Law Enforcement Bulletin* vol. 6, no. 3 (March 1991), pp. 8–12.

such sequencing had a logical order. But such a process had the danger of people reconstructing the past event based upon hindsight, shaping differently what had happened earlier based upon what they know what eventually happened. Now the witness would be asked to become an archaeologist of the mind, discovering facts from the most recent to the most ancient. Fourth, the witness would be asked to change perspectives, to adopt the perspective of someone watching from a distance or role playing that they were the victim.

Besides these four basic techniques there are some additional memory-tricking aids. For example, when it comes to physical appearance, it might be useful to ask the witness if the assailant reminded them of someone and why. Did the voice and speech patterns remind the witness of someone they know? If names were used but forgotten it would be helpful to concentrate on the first letter of the word and go through the alphabet until it was remembered. If numbers were evolved how high or low did they seem to be? Were there any in sequence?

Studies comparing cognitive interviewing with the other two major processes—hypnosis and standard police interviewing—indicate it to be superior in soliciting more correct and less incorrect information from witnesses/victims. When eighty nine students from UCLA were tested they remembered correctly at a rate of 41 facts for cognitive interviews, 38 for hypnosis and 30 for standard police techniques. Furthermore, cognitive interviewing takes less training than hypnosis and is less controversial.[11]

Checklists of various kinds might help the witness to remember otherwise unfamiliar items. For example, realizing that most people are not familiar with guns, the FBI has published *Firearms Identification: A Visual Aid* a small document containing pictures of common types of handguns, rifles, shotguns and submachine guns.

Some items are so familiar that people have trouble separating them out and find their distinctiveness. In terms of personal identification there is a checklist of physical identifiers. For example:

Anatomical

1. Ethnic/race
2. Sex—male, female, transsexual, bisexual
3. Height
   a. Less than five feet
   b. 5 feet to 5 feet six inches
   c. 5 feet six inches to 5 feet 10 inches

11. R.E. Geiselman, F.R.P. Fisher, I. Firstenberg, L.A. Hutton, S. Sullivan, I. Avetissian and A. Prosk, "Enhancing of Eyewitness Memory: An Empirical Evaluation of the Cognitive Interview," *Journal of Police Science and Administration* 12 (1984), pp. 74–80.

    d. 5 feet 10 inches +
4. Weight
    a. Less than 100 pounds
    b. 100 to 140 pounds
    c. 141 to 180 pounds
    d. over 180 pounds
5. Build—heavy, medium, light
6. Head shape—flat top, straight back, round, sloping forehead, long
7. Face shape—round, square, oblong, triangle, inverted triangle, oval
8. Complexion—light, dark, brown, black, ruddy, swarthy, sallow
9. Hair—color, texture, style, hair line
10. Facial hair
11. Eyes—color, type, defects, eyelids, eye brows
12. Noses—frontal and profile
13. Mouth—lips, teeth
14. Chin—frontal and profile
15. Ears—frontal and profile

Behavioral

1. Speech—soft, gruff, accents, defects
2. Habits—nail biting, gum chewing, body and head scratching
3. Walking patterns
4. Nervous disorders
5. Substance use—alcohol, drugs, tobacco

Such a checklist informs the interviewer and might inspire the memory of the witness.

Hypnosis is another way to refresh the memory of a victim/witness.[12] It is particularly valuable in crimes with high degrees of trauma: witnessing a murder, being a victim of rape or child molestation are examples.

As when considering other scientific contributions to criminal investigation the "Three T's" should be kept in mind: theory, technology and technicians.

Hypnosis is based upon the theory that humans take in and store vaster amounts of information then they are actually aware. This storage, in an area that might be called the subconscious, remains there for years waiting to be accessed. As any one who has ever had a flash of memory can

12. Harry Arons, *Hypnosis in Criminal Investigation* (Springfield, IL: Charles C. Thomas, 1967) and Martin Reiser, *Handbook of Investigative Hypnosis* (Los Angeles: Lehi Publishing, 1980).

testify such hidden memories might come to the surface on there own at any time. Or—too painful to remember—they may remain hidden for decades. But by putting aside the conscious levels, with all of its preoccupations and diversions, the subconscious levels might more easily be brought to the conscious level.

In theory hypnosis is a valid tool but their are a few problems for the criminal investigator. Obviously, suspects may not be hypnotized. In the name of efficiency it would be an advantage to hypnotize suspects into a confession. Of course, in the United States, dedicated to the adversarial system of justice and due process, this would be impossible; it would be against the fifth amendment guarantees against testifying against ones self. Unless, of course, the hypnosis of the defendant would likely call for an acquittal.

This leaves witnesses/victims as likely candidates but there are a few problems here, as well. First, there is the problem of "garbage in-garbage out." Hypnosis will only bring to the surface what the witness perceived but that might have been a misperception. For example, on a dark night a witness thought they saw a six foot black man rob a person on the street. Actually the robber was five foot 10 inches and Puerto Rican. The subject of hypnosis will remember the original misperception. Indeed, there is the danger that the subject of hypnosis will confabulate, that is actually fill in details from the imagination in order to make an answer more coherent and complete.

Second, there is always the problem of being misled while undergoing hypnosis. Most people can be hypnotized but the easiest and the best are those people who are more susceptible to suggestion. In other words, those most likely to be hypnotized are the same who are most vulnerable to suggestion while undergoing the hypnotic interview. Consequently, it is the hypnotist and their types of questions that might be the main problem. This problem is confounded when the hypnotist is a police officer. In one study done at Illinois State University, it was found that 26 percent of forensic hypnotism was done by a police officer, someone who had a direct interest in manipulating the remembrance. If one takes and factors in other police connected hypnotists that percentage comes closer 40 percent.[13]

Third, many attorneys dislike the "memory hardening" aspects of hypnosis. That is, subjects of hypnotism become very difficult for cross-examination. The process makes them intractable, they become convinced of their testimony and their confidence and self-assurance makes them very powerful witnesses on the stand.

This presents a moral dilemma. Of course, a distinction might be made between investigative information—those leads that help the investiga-

---

13. Robert Bradley, "Hypnotism in the Courtroom: Science or Suggestion," paper given at the Southern Political Association meeting, November 1991.

tion along—and evidence that the prosecutor hopes to use in a trial. However, the judicial doctrine of the "fruit of the poisoned tree" implies that evidence obtained inappropriately will itself become tainted. On one hand, this means that hypnotically induced witness testimony should be avoided. On the other hand, many investigators would use such information but stretch the chain of connection so far as to remove it from consideration.

The history of forensic hypnotism is interesting and revealing. Originally, in the late nineteenth century, hypnotism was controversial because it was felt someone might be led to commit a crime under the suggestion of some evil hypnotist. Such a fear lasted well into the modern times, consider the argument made be several that Sirhan Sirhan—the murderer of Senator and Presidential candidate Robert F. Kennedy—had been induced to commit the crime while under hypnosis. From 1900 to 1960 hypnosis disappeared as an instrument and issue in criminal justice. There had been a general loss of interest of it in the scientific community and consequently its use declined. From 1960 to 1990, however, there began an awakened interest and acceptance of the practice. The medical profession recognized it. The American Psychological Association accepted it as a legitimate tool in psychotherapy in 1958. Popular culture was aroused with the "age regression" techniques in such people as Bridy Murphy. In that instance a woman was taken back in time to a previous life, causing quite a stir in society. "How-to-do-it" books began to appear and the number of parlor-room hypnotists increased. The Los Angeles police department even set up a training institute in the 1970s to train officers to use hypnosis in investigations.

However, there were some legal concerns as this practice continued to grow. For example, the Minnesota State Supreme Court, in its famous 1980 Mack Decision, declared hypnosis to be unscientific and inadmissible. The Washington State Supreme Court in 1985 reversed the conviction of a person previously imprisoned as the "South Hill rapist" based upon the hypnotized enhanced testimony of four victims.[14] "The unreliability of hypnosis as a means of restoring memory makes the use of hypnotically aided testimony unacceptable in a criminal trial," declared the court. The California State Supreme Court had reached the same conclusion three years earlier. The Illinois State Supreme Court, in 1989, concluded that testimony aided by hypnosis should not be allowed, except by a defendant, because its reliability was suspect. In that particular case a police officer was hypnotized to remember an automobile license plate of suspected gangland assassin. By 1990, 25 states and one federal circuit

---

14. *Newsweek* (February 4, 1985), p. 27.

excluded hypnotically enhanced testimony because of its unreliability. They note—and in keeping with the "general acceptance doctrine" forged in Frye v. U.S. in 1923—that the relevant scientific community did not give "general acceptance" to forensic hypnosis as a dependable method of refreshing recollection. Such decisions now were going to have to be gauged against thinking going on in Washington D.C.

In 1983, Vickie Loren Rock was convicted of manslaughter in the death of her husband. Mrs. Rock's lawyer had her hypnotized so as to better remember the event which she had blotted out of her mind. According to Arkansas case law—and in keeping with the growing direction of State Supreme Court decisions—the hypnotically enhanced testimony was not admitted and she was convicted. The case eventually made it to the United States Supreme Court in Rock v. Arkansas (1987). The issue in Rock was the blanket conclusions made by the various State Supreme courts disallowing hypnotically enhanced testimony because it was not "scientific." That might be an appropriate standard for witnesses for the prosecution, declared Rock, but it must not be so for the defendant. In short, the new rule was that hypnosis might not be good enough for the prosecution but it was alright for the defense. Opening a door for a future decision, the Court declared in Rock that Arkansas "had not shown that hypnotically enhanced testimony is always so untrustworthy and so immune to the traditional means of evaluating credibility that it should disable a defendant from presenting her version of the events for which she is on trial."

As public patience over growing crime rates wore thin another case provided an open door for hypnotism as an investigative tool. In 1992, Dawbert v. Merrill-Dow challenged the ancient "general acceptance" rule of Frye v. U.S. In that decision it was declared that it no longer was necessary for the scientific community to accept or reject a scientific piece of evidence or test. It was up to the judge to make that decision. The implications were profound. Now a judge can accept or reject DNA, for example, or hypnosis based upon their own notion of its scientific validity.

One of the possible ways the police might maintain hypnosis as an investigative tool is to establish strict guidelines as to how it is to be carried out. Clearly, one of the major issues is the possibility of intentionally or unintentionally leading the witness to remember and reconstruct things that did not occur. One way to safeguard against that possibility is the audio and video taping of the session. As of 1993 only about one sixth of the nations police departments video interrogations where standards of propriety are most important. That is to say, that most likely police departments notoriously do not video witness/victim interviews even to the degree they do interrogations. While this may be a particular point for hypnosis, it leads to a final important point of documenting the interview.

Documentation is another important part of the middle stages of the interview process. It fits into the general thesis of this chapter; human memory is bad. If that is true of witness/victims it is also true for detectives. Therefore, to guard against forgetting and to be able to pass on to subsequent investigators it is necessary for the interview process to be fully documented. There are several ways this documentation process might take place. Obviously, some sort of note taking strategy must be decided upon. The interviewer might choose to take full notes, writing down everything the witness has to say. Of course, this gives an air of preoccupation and eye contact is broken. Another approach would be to take done sketchy notes and flesh them out later. There is always the danger that the interviewer will forget some important information in this process. The presence of another person, a partner or recording secretary, to take down extensive notes while the interviewer devotes undivided attention to the witness. Finally, there would be the video taping of the interview session but as mentioned earlier the police as yet have not adopted this tactic.

Endings

The third major section of an interview is the ending. It is at this time that the witness must be prepared for the likelihood of a re-interview. There are several reasons for the re-interview. First, a new set of investigators might come on to the investigation and they need to establish contact with the witness/victim. Second, as the investigation proceeds and new information and perspectives come to light there is a need for clarification of past statements. Third, there is the notion of "twice told tales" or that stories told over again away from the immediate time and place of the crime might inspire remembrance. And, finally, officers should find ways to convey messages to witnesses that real work is being done on the case.

Conclusion

Often overlooked, the understanding of witnesses, their unique problems and prospects, will help the investigation in two ways: it will maximize the amount of information that can be obtained in any investigation, and it will be a positive force in the creation of public relations. Both in the preliminary investigation and in subsequent "latent" inquiries contact and communication with victims and witnesses is essential in the methodical search and analysis for information. It is so important that such interviews might need to be duplicated in the latent investigation, a topic to which we now turn.

Chapter 7

Latent Investigation I

Introduction

The latent investigation, sometimes known as the follow-up investigation, marks a distinct change from the preliminary activities discussed in chapter three. First, it is different in terms of the types of police personnel who dominate. In the preliminary investigation a variety of police were involved. There were the uniformed officers, some expert technicians such as evidence collectors and medical examiner investigators, and the earlier arrivals of plainclothes detectives. In the latent investigation these plainclothes detectives clearly dominate. Second, the focus of the geography shifts. During the preliminary investigation most activity was tied to the crime scene. In the latent investigation much of the work is far a field from the original scene. Third, the time factor is different as well. The preliminary investigation is abbreviated when it comes to time; the scene is still alive with activity and it must soon return to public use. The latent investigation, however, can take considerable time, even months to years. Fourth, due process becomes increasingly important. Many things—such as search and interviewing—can be done during the preliminary investigation that might be obstructed by rules of evidence and the dictates of the Supreme Court in the follow-up stages.

But it may be said that the latent investigation is that series of research following the preliminary investigation that is conducted by special police officers called detectives using clearly defined methods that if successful end with a clearance or arrest and presentation to the prosecutor of a case ready for the court trial and conviction.[1]

The Process

Field Reports

In any research activity the transference of information is a critical step. To maintain clarity, correctness and completeness special attention needs

---

1. Very useful here is William B. Sanders, *Detective Work: A Study of Criminal Investigations* (New York: The Free Press, 1977).

118 Foundations of Criminal Investigation

to be paid so that information goes from one party to another expeditiously. This most likely will be done in a criminal investigation with the field report. The field report is simply the documentation coming forward from the preliminary investigation—including searches, sketches, photographs, and witness statements—crime labs and forensic pathology. It is the total history of the case to the point of the follow-up stages. It is necessary so that detectives can proceed with some important decisions and procedures.[2]

Case Disposition

One of the first decisions to be made is whether or not to even accept the case, a process known popularly as "making a case." If the case is not made—that is the detectives determine that not enough information is present, that witnesses have disappeared or recanted, that the preliminary investigation was poorly done—the case might be declared "unestablished" or "unfounded." The statistical standard for success for the police in general but the detective in particular is "clearance" or the ability to close a case with an arrest. Clearance rates in the United States are not particularly good. Homicide has higher clearance (around 70 percent) because of its sensation and the fact that so many victims were acquainted with the killer. Robbery has much lower clearance (about 14 percent) and the national average or clearance rate for all crimes is 20 percent. Consequently, detectives have a vested interest—in terms of economical use of their resources and occupational status—to select those crimes likely to be solved and neglect those were chances of success are slim. Other reasons for the unestablished character of a case might be: it is really a civil and not a criminal matter, the victim is suspect and this might be a phony complaint, and this case is of such low visibility and importance that it can be safely set aside.

A "righteous" case is one that has been made, it is one that will demand the efforts of the detectives. Several factors go into the righteousness of a case.

First, is the sensational nature of the crime and/or its victims. The press and the public might demand that something be done and they follow the case closely. The public not only wants something done but in a ravenous way they want to follow the case development. In a democratic society they have a right to know these things. This gives rise to the problem of secrecy and the lie. Much publicity may not be beneficial to the investi-

---

2. Clarice R. Cox and Jerrold G. Brown, *Report Writing for Criminal Justice Professionals* (Cincinnati: Anderson, 1992).

gation. In spite of the procedural steps of the investigative method so much of the criminal investigation is achieved serendipitously and monotonously, and revelations might be embarrassing and trying to the public patience. Therefore, many detectives practice the lie of commission, giving wrong information to the press, or more commonly the lie of omission, neglecting to tell the full truth. A classic example was the coverup by the Alcohol, Tobacco and Firearms agency in the Waco debacle in 1992. A corollary here is the relativity of importance depending upon the nature of the specialized detective bureau. For example, a case that is not important to homicide may be very important to juvenile squad.

Second, a righteous case is determined by its solvability. Many cases solve themselves. An incident with a woman holding a smoking gun standing over a dead husband pretty much is a case with high solvability. At the opposite end of the spectrum an incident of a street holdup of a prostitute by a masked man late at night with no witnesses present has low solvability. Of course, many cases fall between these extremes. Studies suggest that there is a thirty three percent chance of an arrest if the crime is detected in progress. But if it is one minute old the changes fall to a 10 percent probability of an arrest. If it is 15 minutes old or older the chances slip to 5 percent. Some may have a potential for solution but need to be nibbled at over time when time and resources are not pressing. These might be placed in an "inactive" or "cold case" file. There might be a special cold case squad created to work on old cases.

Another element of solvability infrequently examined is not the nature of the case but the nature of the detective personnel. One study by the Institute for Law and Social Research found that commonly detective departments can be made up of two types of detectives. Twelve percent of detectives (High-conviction rate or HRC officers) made 50 percent of arrests. That means that the other fifty percent was done by the 88 percent low conviction rate (LCR) officers. A supervisor of detectives, therefore, must make solvability decisions based upon availability and skills of detectives, as well.

Third, a process of *selectivity* or *screening* must occur. In the past the selection of cases (or case disposition) was haphazard and informal. According to the Rand Corporation's Study of Detectives, most cases received attention of one day or less. The Stanford Research Institute and the Police Executive Research Forum (PERF) developed one model for screening burglaries. Factors associated with the crime would be assigned a number. A description or name of a suspect might receive nine points. An eyewitness account of the incident might earn seven points. A useable fingerprint might warrant seven points. Cases that have earned ten points have a higher degree of solvability and would be selected for follow-up investigation. Those with less than ten points would be screened out or assigned a low priority.

Once issues of sensation, solvability and selectivity have been resolved and the righteous nature of the case has been determined, the follow-up investigation begins in earnest.[3]

Re-interview

One of the earliest phases of the follow-up investigation is the re-interviewing of witnesses/victims. There is undoubtedly some aggravation over this policy and witnesses are apt to cry out that "I already told the police this stuff before!" "Why do I have do go through this again?" There are at least three good reasons for the necessity of the re-interview.

First, is the "forest and the trees" principle. Initial interviews were conducted by uniformed officers and/or detectives on the crime scene. That procedure—and its problems and prospects— were discussed earlier. The information gathered at that time must be seen against the backdrop of the clutter and chaos of the crime scene. All of the preliminary investigation had not been done but was in the process of being done. All of the physical evidence had not been gathered and analyzed. All of the witnesses had not been interviewed. By definition everything was still incomplete and unconnected. Information was scattered and incoherent. Investigators were in a maze of trees, too close and involved to see connections and coherence. Now in the follow-up stages everything previously done has been studied and perspectives developed. Perhaps the initial facts are not needed but clarifications of older information might be critical. New questions emerge as the investigators have been able to step back away from the trees and see the totality of the forest.

Second, is the "twice-told-tales" phenomenon. Witnesses who were interviewed during the preliminary investigation were too close to the events themselves. In all likelihood they were on or very near the crime scene, a place still charged with the emotion and excitement of the event. People were very active all around them adding to the very nature of complexity. In the follow-up investigation, however, the witness has established some geographic and chronological distance from the scene. Having the witness/victim now go over the same story a second or third time— after time, security and comfort have been allowed for—would allow for greater opportunity for remembrance of things previously forgotten or overlooked.

3. J. Petersilia, A. Abrahamse, and James Q. Wilson, "A Summary of RAND's Research on Police Performance," *Journal of Police Science and Administration* vol. 17, no. 3 (1990), pp. 219–227.

Third, there is the principle that "it is better to give than receive." Clearly, the obvious reason for interviewing is to obtain information. But there is a larger aspect, more public relations reason, for the interview. Studies show that the chief complaint that witnesses/victims have with the criminal investigative process is the feeling of being neglected and uninformed over the progress of the case. Consequently, the follow-up interview might have as a hidden agenda the clarification of information and the re-doing of questions to stimulate memory but it might be publicly cast as the giving rather than the receiving of information.

Neighborhood Canvass

Another form of interviewing would be questioning indirect witnesses. These are people who did not see the criminal incident but by the nature of their living and working patterns they would be near the crime site and might have heard or saw something that could be useful. This type of canvassing, then, would be extending the questioning to people who lived and worked around the area of the crime. In that context it is geographical, perhaps extending the interviews in a concentric circular pattern with the crime scene being at the center. But two additional things must be remembered in such canvassing. First, the timeliness of the interviews must be kept in mind. For example, a break-in into a home at 3:30 p.m. would require the interviewing of people who would be at their homes or in the area at that time. Other day street people, such as postal workers and bus drivers, might be useful. But people who were at work and far away from their homes and neighborhoods, of course, would not be useful. Strange sounds, smells and sights—anything out of the ordinary—might be recalled by people who otherwise had no idea that a crime had occurred. Second, is the problem of secrecy. On one hand, the canvass alerts many others who might have information. Successful criminal investigation is very often predicated upon the contributions of ordinary citizens. Witness the rise and popularity of television programming such as "America's Most Wanted." On the other hand, the more confidential and secret the investigation the less likely that suspects will be alerted into defensive strategies. Many robbers and burglars live within short distances of their victims and canvassing might inform them of the progress of the case. Nonetheless, very early in the latent investigation the interviewing of people will expand into a neighborhood canvass.

Crimes Analysis

While many of the previous steps are being carried out another process might be coming into play. Simply defined, crimes analysis is the identify-

Locating Murders in 1993

Although murders in New York City declined in 1993 for the third year in a row, figures show they were becoming more clustered in certain neighborhoods.

Total in New York City: 1,960

	Total killings	Highest number	
The Bronx	517	44th precinct	71 killings
Manhattan	418	34th precinct	75 killings
Queens	279	113th precinct	39 killings
Brooklyn	721	75th precinct	126 killings
Staten Island	25	120th precinct	21 killings

Source: The New York Times.

ing of criminal patterns, trends and styles where they exist. It is based upon the assumption that the more experienced criminals will have niches or established activities and that they repeat or do things in similar ways providing a signature of their presence. This system has far reaching utility. For example, it might be used to identify hot stops in a given city and inform decision-making as to the deployment of patrol personnel. For investigations it helps establish lists of suspects especially in the area of professional or repeat criminality. Crimes analysis might take two forms in any given detective bureau: informal or formal.

Informal crimes analysis has existed for years; it is probably as old as the occupation of police detection itself. This is based upon the experience of the criminal investigator. Years of practical experience and acquaintance with the criminal world and the individuals in it inform the investigator as to styles and modes of operation of hundreds of criminals. A given investigator might come upon a crime scene and recognize immediately certain signature qualities that point to a known operator in the criminal world. In the early history of police investigation many detectives learned the trade by going to the underworld hangouts and just observing. This was called "getting a spot on the underworld." Informal crimes analysis is based upon the sacred notion that "experience is the best teacher." The problem of this non-institutionalized system is that it takes along time for an officer to become proficient as a walking encyclopedia of criminals in the area; the start up cost are too great. Furthermore, personal reasons of glory and indispensability might make the investigator reluctant to share personal expertise. The very volume and variety of crime might make it increasingly difficult to take in and process and use the information effectively. Finally, when this investigator retires much of the special information that had been accumulated over the years disappears, as well.

Formal crimes analysis would be an attempt to institutionalized and control the process along more scientific lines. Some sort of crimes analysis unit—operated by one or more personnel—within the police structure would characterize the formal approach. Rather than going out and watching and interacting with criminals these officers use social science techniques and geographic mathematics to study the problem. But it too can go from a simple to a sophisticated means of analysis. For discussion purposes formal crimes analysis might be seen in two areas: pictorial displays and categories of analysis.

Pictorial displays center around the academic discipline of geography and the mapping of crime hot spots. It can range from simple to sophisticated approaches. For example, on the simplest level would be providing pin maps of the city with different colored indicators where certain crimes occur. It may be a mixed map showing a variety of crimes or it might be specialized as to one particular activity. The next stage of development would be to give a spacial sense to the map by drawing circles, ellipses and isopleths of criminal activity. The final stage of sophistication here is the use of computer programs to map current hot spots and predict future developments.

Analytic categories are another attribute of crimes analysis. The rule of thumb here is that the ever narrowing of category, or the greater specificity, marks a more powerful crimes analysis tool and professional unit. For example, there might be some broad or universal factors of categorization: crime type, location of crime, time of day, day of week, and nature of victim, that act as broad units of analysis. The next level of sophistication would compact the categories even further. For example, instead of the simple category of burglary it would be

1. Residential burglary
   a. Type of premise
      1. House
         a. occupied or unoccupied
         b. point of entry
            i. window—front or back
            ii. door—front or back
         c. method of entry
            i. tools
            ii. smashing
      2. Apartment—and same analysis as above
   b. Time

      1. season of year
      2. day of week
      3. time of day
  2. Commercial burglary (and continue same as above)[4]

Internal informational sources[5]

There are research sources more easily accessed by police officers than ordinary citizens. For convenience these materials may be discussed by placing them in geographic categories of international, national, state and local.

International sources might begin with the International Criminal Police Organization—commonly referred to by its acronym Interpol. Interpol is headquartered in Lyon, France and has around 150 members. Each member nation has a national central bureau through which it accesses information from the headquarters. The purpose of Interpol is to record, analyze and disseminate information contributed by member nations on criminals who operate in more than one country, criminals who flee from one country to another, and criminals whose crimes in one country impact upon other countries. In its personnel files are listed over 150,000 persons. Its property files have lists and descriptions of items stolen. Interpol has considerable information about international drug dealers, as well.

National sources on crime and criminals are as varied as the nations of the world are different. In the United States the National Crime Information Center (N.C.I.C.) is particularly useful. It is a computerized data resource operated by the F.B.I. Over 350,000 wanted persons would be on file here. In addition, over 70,000 missing persons have their identities on file. One million stolen vehicles are on record with the NCIC as well. Three million stolen guns are on file. Even the presidential protective service of the Secret Service has on file all those suspected to be a possible threat to the President of the United States. The National Law Enforcement Telecommunications System has a computerized network of information on criminal histories, drivers licenses, and vehicle registrations. The El Paso Intelligence Center or E.P.I.C. has extensive information of

---

4. Thomas F. Rich, "The Use of Computerized Mapping in Crime Control and Prevention Programs," *National Institute of Justice: Research in Action* (July 1995).

5. John M. Carroll, *Confidential Information Sources: Public and Private*, 2nd ed. (Boston: Butterworth-Heinemann, 1991) and Harry J. Murphy, *Where's What: Sources of Information for Federal Investigators* (New York: Quadrangle/New York Times, 1976).

drug traffickers, gun smugglers and aliens. The C.P.I.C. or Canadian Police Information Center is also very useful and illustrates the availability of information from neighbor countries.

On the state level there are numerous sources of information. A System for Electronic Analysis and Retrieval of Criminal Histories or S.E.A.R.C.H. has been in operation since 1969 and exists in all states and can be accessed from one state to another. Most states have something comparable to New York's N.Y.S.I.I.S. (New York State Information and Intelligence System) which has fingerprints, names, rap sheets, wanted persons and missing persons files of the particular state.

On the local level police officers have, in addition to those sources discussed above, other information opportunities. First, like most non police personnel they have local materials such as city directories, real estate records, tax documents and other public government documents housed at city hall. City directories are particularly interesting and even the ordinary citizen has access to them. Knowing only the address on a house one can determine the name of the resident, ownership or renting of the place, and even occupations. Various documents in the local city hall would allow the investigator to trace the history of a houses ownership. Divorce records, on file where the divorce took place, are rich in information. The number of information sources for non-police personnel is surprising.

Second, there are those materials of an in-house nature that only the police may use. Obviously, the field reports and crimes analysis unit reports discussed earlier fall into this category. In addition, there are the Daily Crime News Recap, a listing of crimes reported during the previous 24 hour period. This daily document gives the type, time, location and evidence of a crime that might have been committed while the investigator had time off from work. Another example might be the Known-Offender file containing information on all known offenders in the area. They might be divided into "active" or "inactive" categories. The former is for those known to be still practicing their criminal life while the latter has to do with those who apparently have gone legitimate. Modus Operandi files and Mug Shot files would be important research tools as well.

Other items might be suggestive. For example, federal social security numbers are coded in such away that geographical regions of the country might be ascertained.

First three numbers of issuance	State
001-003	New Hampshire
004-007	Maine
008-009	Vermont

010-034	Massachusetts
035-039	Rhode Island
040-049	Connecticut
050-134	New York
135-158	New Jersey
159-211	Pennsylvania
212-220	Maryland
221-222	Delaware
223-231	Virginia
232-236	West Virginia
237-246	North Carolina
247-251	South Carolina
252-260	Georgia
261-267	Florida
268-302	Ohio
303-317	Indiana
318-361	Illinois
362-386	Michigan
387-399	Wisconsin
400-407	Kentucky
408-415	Tennessee
416-424	Alabama
425-428	Mississippi
429-432	Arkansas
433-439	Louisiana
440-448	Oklahoma
449-467	Texas
468-477	Minnesota
478-485	Iowa
486-500	Missouri
501-502	North Dakota
503-504	South Dakota
505-508	Nebraska
509-515	Kansas
516-517	Montana
518-519	Idaho
520	Wyoming
521-524	Colorado
525	New Mexico
526-527	Arizona
528-529	Utah
530	Nevada
531-539	Washington
540-544	Oregon
545-573	California
574	Alaska

575-576	Hawaii
577-579	D.C.
580	Virgin Islands
581-585	Puerto Rico
586	Guam, American Samoa, Philippines

Many states use the social security number as a basis for the driver's license number, as well. However, some states (Florida, Illinois, Michigan, Missouri, Maryland, Minnesota and Wisconsin, for example) use the soundex system and it might be revealing. At its simplest level take this driver's license number:

M650 2783 7271

M	=	the first initial of the last name
650	=	code for remainder of last name
278	=	code for first name and middle initial
37	=	year of birth
271	=	day of birth for male

1–365 for males

366 + (or in Illinois starts with 600) for females

Another area of possible evidence would be the vehicle identification numbers or VIN. For example, a typical VIN might look like this:

IGIAZ3735BR123456

I	=	location of origin of manufacture (USA)
G	=	Manufacture code (GM)
I	=	Make and type (Chevrolet Passenger)
A	=	Restraint System
Z	=	Car Line/series (Monte Carlo)
3,7	=	Body type (Two Door Coupe)
3	=	Engine type and make (3.8l Buick)
5	=	Check Digit
B	=	Model Year (1981)
R	=	Assembly plant (Arlington)

123456 = Sequential no.

Informants[6]

Generally an informant is any human source of information. This information can come from a known or an anonymous source. The number of cases solved due to an anonymous tip are legion. Frequently, police will offer rewards or anonymity to inspire these tipsters. More specifically, however, informants may be questionable as to veracity and reputation. In fact, an informant who maintains strong ties to the underworld maybe more valuable because they have better access to information. These informants are people who for a variety of reasons give information to the police. They are not traditional direct or indirect witnesses because generally some sort of transactional agreement characterizes the informants motivation. Frequently, these sources are shady themselves. On one hand, this makes their information all the more valuable because they have accesses not generally available to others. On the other hand, their motives and general character might taint the information. Therefore, a good investigator must do three things. First, a string of informants should be developed. Second, one must recognize the possible types of informants to better judge their motivation and quality of information. Third, these informants and their information need to be constantly tested as to worthiness.

The first category of informants might be called *civic minded*. They see it as their duty as a citizen to cooperate and bring forth information to the police. *Mercenary* informants are those willing to give information for money or some other commodity such as drugs. Historically this was more common in foreign countries but it has grown considerably in America in the last generation or so. Many police departments have a "hidden fund" that officers might draw upon for such informants. In addition, individual investigators might keep a private stash of money and drugs to use as negotiations with such informants. *Plea bargain* informants are those who give information in exchange for leniency or reduced severity of treatment by the investigators, they simply want to avoid punishment and use their special commodity, information, as a way to receive favorable treatment. *Sycophants* are those who feel important if they are recognized and treated well by the police. They look out for and give information in hopes of being recognized by the police; vanity is a motivation for their actions. *Rival* criminals might give information to the police in order to get a competitive edge or eliminate a competitor. *Fearful* informants come in a variety of types. There might be those — like the mother whose son claimed he was going out to hurt someone — who fear for possible victims and even

---

6. Michael F. Brown, "Criminal Informants: Some Observations on Use, Abuse and Control," *Journal of Police Science and Administration* vol. 13 (1985), pp. 251–256.

the assailant. Then there are those who fear a particular menace and want him removed from the streets. Some informants are seeking *revenge* for past wrongs. Finally, there is the *false* informant, a person who for a variety of reasons wants to mis-lead and divert the investigator.

Of course, many ethical issues come to mind when discussing informants. Clearly, it does not seem proper "to deal with the enemy," or "dance with the devil." Not only do the police exploit these shady people but they sustain them by providing goods to satisfy their habits, give them money, and provide protection from arrest by other officers. Furthermore, the information can not be readily trusted. A corruption of the fruit of the poisoned tree might be applied. In other words, how can anything trustworthy come from such proven untrustworthy sources? And, indeed, besides creating a string of informants the investigator must test and corroborate the information coming from informants. In that way many informants come and go, the less reliable going earliest, as the officer deals with the ethical issues by subscribing to the doctrine "the end justifies the means."

Social Network Analysis

Many crimes and criminal enterprises are done in collective ways. Gangs and groups of criminals are present everywhere. For example, there are youth gangs, terrorist groups, organized crime "families," racketeering enterprises and vice operations to name just a few. A useful way to study people and their relationships in a group environment is social network analysis. All groups have four levels of commitment, responsibility and power. There would be the core group made up of leadership and true followers. Then there is the general follow-ship, people who belong to the group but do not take leadership positions. Then the marginal group of people who are leaving or just arriving in terms of group affiliation. And then there are the sympathizers, those not belonging to the group but are sympathetic to it and its members. Social network analysis is a device to ascertain the power center of a group, the flow of information within the group, the roles of people within the organization, those who are weak in commitment to the mission of the group, the presence of any rival clusters in the structure and cohesiveness of the gang. At the simplest level this analysis would be the spying on a group and watching the interaction of its members. To do this a couple other investigative techniques might be necessary.

Surveillance[7]

Simply put, surveillance is spying by the police. It has several purposes. First, it seeks to learn the true identity of a person, not just names and addresses but the detailed life style—the comings and going—of an individual. Second, it hopes to develop leads to further the investigation. Third, surveillance may give officers information to establish probable cause and eventual arrest. Fourth, it would be useful in obtaining information to be used in subsequent interrogations. Fifth, it may end in the obtaining of legally admissible information in subsequent trials. Sixth, surveillance might be used to "test" information given by informants. And, finally, it is a necessary practice in order to obtain background information for undercover operations.

There are several things to keep in mind in any decisions relating to a surveillance strategy.

First, should it be a discreet or indiscreet surveillance? A discreet strategy operates under the assumption that the subject does not know they are being followed and that any indication that they have become aware of being followed suggests a failure and the possibility that it should be brought to an end. An indiscreet one assumes that the subject suspects the surveillance but the purpose is not so much to find information but to intimidate and modify behavior. For example, an organized crime figure known to be a hit-man might be a subject for surveillance so as to scare him out of the jurisdiction and prevent him from fulfilling a contract. The Presidential Protection Service of the Secret Service displays this indiscreet surveillance as officers conspicuously look into crowds of people watching for the suspicious and deterring the dangerous.

Second, should it be a fixed or a moving surveillance? Actually any surveillance strategy should account for a mixture of both types. The fixed, or stakeout, of a known place frequented by the subject would be appropriate for the beginning of the surveillance and returning to when the subject was lost in course of the moving phases. The stakeout, then, would be comprised of sitting in a car or some other inconspicuous place waiting for the subject to be up and out. In this context, it might be useful here to obtain something called a "mail cover." If the subject is a suspect in a felony case the postal officials will provide to the police the return addresses of all first class mail delivered to the subject. Another form of stakeout would be the examination of the suspect's garbage. Waste material might contain much useful information. Naturally the moving strategy would be the most common and most challenging. A variety of styles might be present here as well. For example, there might be the "loose tail" and the

---

7. Gary Marx, *Undercover: Police Surveillance in America* (Berkeley: University of California Press, 1988).

"close tail." As the names suggest, the former implies keeping some distance while the latter demands being closer. Factors going into the decision will be discussed shortly. In addition there might be a "rotating" or "progressive tail." To protect the surveillance from being detected the members of the team might come on and drop off the surveillance.

Third, should the surveillance be a foot or automobile type? Actually, the wisest approach—given the factors to be discussed shortly—would be to make account for both. People's lives are a mixture of walking and riding and all surveillance should have a healthy mix of walking and riding members of the team. Indeed, if the subject should take large trips, by train or airline, the team should be prepare to respond.

Fourth, should it be a single or a group effort? Depending upon the nature of the case and the resources available the surveillance should always have teams of people. Danger and inefficiency necessarily follow the single surveillance scheme.

Fifth, should it be a human or electronic effort? Again, it depends upon the nature and extent of the case. Some simply do not lend themselves to anything more than human surveillance. Others might demand a variety of tools of electronic eavesdropping. A further word is necessary about electronic surveillance.

Of course, historically all surveillance was regarded as slightly un-American. This was even more true for governmental intrusion by electronic means. Its use as an investigative tool has been limited over time by two considerations. First, public tolerance for this activity in a democratic society. Of course, the public does shift its attitudes and tolerances. In periods of a more "due process mind set" there might be concerns over this strategy. Such intrusions into the lives of citizens—even if they are criminal—smacks of a police state. Those of a more liberal persuasion might hold to this opinion. In periods of a more "crime control mind set," or when the conservative ideology holds prominence, there is likely to be greater tolerance of such police activity. The Omnibus Crime Control and Safe Streets Act of 1968—coming in the midst of a particularly sensational crime and disorder filled decade—established some procedural guidelines for the police using such surveillance. The least controversial were based upon the doctrine of "consentual third party eavesdropping." Under this notion if anyone who is a party to a conversation consents to the eavesdropping—even if other parties are unaware of it—it is permissible. This gave rise to a procedure of wire and taped participants in a conversation. Of course, more controversial were telephone taps. The number of federal court approved wiretapping has increased throughout the 1980s and early 1990s.

Second, has been the nature of the technology. Earlier electronic surveillance was limited to telephone taps and concealed microphones or "bugs." Modern day technological developments, however, have expanded greatly the tools of electronic surveillance. For example, the further miniaturization of devices for audio surveillance has increased dramatically in the last decade. Light weight video devices with special capacities for better night vision have been developed. One example might illustrate. It is possible to place a microscopic listening device on a telephone—let us say in Los Angeles, California—and trigger it in New York City. The eavesdropper would dial all the digits of the phone number except the last one. Then a special code is dialed before the final regular digit. When that last number has been done the phone will not ring but the listening device will have been triggered and the person on the East Coast can hear everything going on in the house on the West Coast. On the federal level the agents predominating in electronic eavesdropping have been—in order of importance—the Drug Enforcement Administration, the Federal Bureau of Investigation, U.S. Customs and the Air Force Office of Special Investigation. Largely this is a reflection of the United State's growing concern and combat with drug crimes.

There are several factors that might determine the type of surveillance strategy as described above. First, the general importance of the case. Some cases are so important that they require extraordinary efforts. For example, the U.S. Customs has something called "extended search privilege." As long as they keep a surveillance "unbroken" they can go anywhere in their investigation. Consequently, they might keep a person under surveillance from El Paso, Texas to Chicago. Second, the availability of resources such as personnel and automobiles. Smaller departments or detective bureaus simply might not have the resources to expend adequately on a case no matter how important. Of course, if it has a federal dimension maybe the various federal agencies might come in to carry out surveillance. Third, general conditions of the surveillance. For example, daylight v. night time conditions might shape decisions about a loose or close tail. General traffic—pedestrian or automobile—might shape the same decisions. Lastly, the general wariness of the subject might shape strategies. If the subject begins to suspect being followed then calling off of the surveillance or the changing of personnel or styles might be demanded.

Undercover

Undercover work is another device in the latent investigation to obtain information. It is the posing of a police officer as a criminal or non-police person in order to obtain information about criminal activities and make arrests. It might be thought of in several ways. First, it might be "light" v. "deep" undercover. The distinction varies from agency to agency but the F.B.I. believes that the six month mark is an adequate cut-off. Undercover operations lasting less than six months are considered light and the resources are relatively small. Those over six months are deep and get more commitment. Another distinction might be drawn by preliminary undercover — or those before crimes have been committed in which the hope is to discover and stymie future plots — and ensuing — or those after some crime has been committed and the operation is to discover the culprits.

Historical development of police undercover operations in America is revealing. Most probably the first real undercover activities in America were done by the private police, most notably the Pinkerton detectives in the nineteenth century. Indeed, when the Northwest Police Agency was established by Pinkerton in 1855 its main job was to have operatives pose as railroad passengers and watch conductors for dishonest acts. In the 1870s James McPharland posed as an Irish coal miner in the Pennsylvania coal fields and joined the infamous Molly Maguires, an organization believed to be killing several foreman and mine operators. This Pinkerton infiltrator began working in the mines, joined the Mollies and eventually worked his way up to be a high official. After several years he exposed the group sending several to the gallows. The Pinkerton Agency continued to send operatives into undercover in the labor unions exposing any secret plans for strikes. Later, in the early twentieth century, another Pinkerton, Charley Siringo, did the same thing in Colorado and Idaho.

The public police were pretty slow to become involved in undercover work. The posing as victims — one manifestation of light undercover — became important as certain activities were labeled vices and outlawed. Its first manifestation came with the purchasing of illegal goods. The first Supreme Court test of such investigative techniques occurred in 1932 — with Sorrells v. U.S. — when an undercover officer's purchase of liquor was admitted as legitimate evidence. Such activity would continue as officers would pose as men looking for commercial sex or drugs. Indeed, as the drug wars were declared in the 1980s undercover work of this nature became much more important. People like Mark Levine became legendary for their exploits for the Drug Enforcement Administration.

Of course, in the 1930s — as the threat of Communism allowed the expansion of the F.B.I. — greater infiltration of radical groups began and lasted well into the 1960s. Many big city police departments by the late 1960s had a "red squad" made up of young officers posing as students in universities to find radicals. The FBI successfully infiltrated organized crime families ending in several convictions. Agent Joe Pispone, for example, went undercover for six years to infiltrate an organized crime family.

Undercover operations are a controversial and dangerous investigative tool. On a positive note the public seems to condone underwork in the name of "fighting fire with fire." On the other hand, some feel that there is something basically immoral in such police deception; that it requires the police to stoop to the level of criminality in order to catch criminals. In addition, there is the defense that a person was "entrapped" to commit a crime by the encouragement of an officer undercover. To what extent does an officer, in hopes of making an arrest, tempt people with weak moral — rather than strong criminal — tendencies to commit crime? Finally, what is the price paid by the police? Undercover officers, to be effective, are not known to other officers and may be in harms way from their own. Several large departments address this problem with a policy of "colors of the day." An undercover person should wear some items of clothing with colors known by patrol personnel as a mark of an undercover officer. In terms of danger, stress and temptation is the price worth it? Apparently yes because the number of undercover operations have increased considerably in the last twenty years.[8]

Psychics[9]

One of the themes of this work is that there is a slight tension, a love-hate relationship, between the "competent craftsmanship" of the detective officer and science. Faith is placed upon the investigative method and the common sense experience of the investigators. Under ordinary circumstances this procedure should be enough. Of course, as outlined earlier, science has become a significant helpmate but slight tensions remain. This tension is even more pronounced when it comes to psychics. Psychics are those people who claim to possess certain skills and abilities unavailable to ordinary people. This parapsychology — extrasensory perception and clairvoyance — gets considerable media attention and compels even reluctant investigators to consider them when other techniques seem to have led to nowhere. It is estimated that 49 percent of the American population believe in ESP. Psychics might use different styles. For example, they might want to see a piece of personal property of a missing person which will give them feelings about the owner. They might dream in which they see the scene in general terms. Or they may have a feeling of how the victim felt at the time of greatest anxiety and trauma. Psychics have been used in determining the whereabouts of missing persons and helping police artists reconstruct pictures of otherwise unknown villains. For example, during the investigations of the Green River serial killings in the Seattle area a psychic was able to locate one of the bodies of the victims. The Dallas police were able to find the body of a missing person in the Trinity River about two miles from where a psychic said it would be. The St. Louis

8. Ibid.
9. *Chicago Tribune* (October 27, 1992).

police used a psychic to find the remains of a missing housewife. The killer of three young people in California was found when the psychic helped an artist develop his likeness. Our knowledge of this kind of gift or ability is limited. Research designed to test this phenomenon has been flawed. But, ever the pragmatist, the investigator should recognized the possibility of parapsychological people in their areas and use them quietly and un-dramatically when all else has failed. However, their use indicates some other things going on in the investigation. For example, the case is likely to be at a dead end with few if any investigative clues available. The police mood might be one of frustration. Finally, the desires of friends and relatives of victims might demand such extraordinary diversions from the scientific methodology.

Conclusion

The latent investigation is an important follow up in any criminal investigation. It is procedural in nature and the steps above have been placed in a rough order of occurrence. Of course, this has been done for pedagogical purposes and the reader must remember that many of these steps are going on at the same time. One general characteristic of the above steps, however, is that they are information gathering. Sometime during the latent investigation this information gathering aspect—though never completely at close—changes in style. Another area of the latent investigation is of a more accusatory nature. It is to that part of the latent investigation we must now turn.

Chapter 8

Latent Investigation II

Introduction

This is a continuation of the latent or follow up investigation described in the previous chapter. What distinguishes it from the earlier chapter is that the investigation has progressed to such a place that the mood shifts from pure information gathering to a more determined accusatory style. Evidence and testimony has narrowed down the investigation to a small number of suspects. Even though actual guilt has not been determined by the courts, which operate under the due process notion of "presumption of innocence," investigators by this stage are pretty sure of a persons guilt. As "competent craftsmen" (or those people who through long experience feel they know best in spite of opinions to the contrary by outsiders) they know that the person is *factually guilty* but that if previous procedure and especially current activities are not done correctly the *legal guilt* might be in jeopardy. Indeed, it is at this more accusatory stages of the latent investigation that the Supreme Court and principles of due process loom largely.

The Process

Search

Definitions

Certain types of search have been discussed in earlier chapters on the preliminary investigation. The crime scene search must be seen as different from what is to follow. It was more immediate and its purpose was to gather information to further the investigation. This search, however, is more directed and the implication is that it is accusatory. That is, the person being searched at this stage is felt to be a prime suspect. So while the crime scene search is general, this search is specific. Furthermore, the constitutional restrictions and due process procedures are much clearer at this stage.[1]

---

1. George T. Felkenes, *Constitutional Law for Criminal Justice*, 2nd. ed. (Englewood Cliffs, NJ: Prentice-Hall, 1988).

Landmark Cases

The constitutional case law on search and seizure has grown considerably as the Supreme Court has identified this aspect of the criminal investigation as a key difference between a despotic and democratic police. The Fourth Amendment to the Constitution does not protect people from search, but from unreasonable search and seizure. In 1967 the Supreme Court—in Katz v. United States—determined that the Constitution protects people not places. In other words

> What a person knowingly exposes to the public, even in his own home or office, is not subject of Fourth Amendment protection.... But what she seeks to preserve as private, even in an area accessible to the public, may be constitutionally protected.

Katz dictates then that the person searched must have a reasonable expectation of privacy in the place searched. If no such expectation of privacy exists, the Fourth Amendment protections do not come into play.

Types of Search

For purposes of discussion here there are two types of search, warrant and warrantless searches.

Warrant searches are those in which prior approval has been obtained from a judge or magistrate. The advantage of a warrant search is that many procedural and constitutional issues have been resolved and in all likelihood the search will be a good one. Of course, it takes time to get a search warrant and suspects and evidence may disappear. In addition, on occasion a judge may even deny a warrant. Three qualities—the three P's —are necessary for a search warrant.

Probable Cause must be established by the investigator petitioning for a warrant. Actually, there are two sets of probable cause. Probable cause to make an arrest requires that the officer has personal knowledge, a set of facts and circumstances which would lead a reasonably intelligent and prudent person to believe that a particular person had committed a specific crime. It is reasonable grounds by a reasonable person that a crime has been committed by the person under investigation. It is the foundation upon which much of modern-day police arrest is built. Probable cause for a search, however, is slightly different. Here, there must be a substantial belief that certain items are fruits, instrumentalities, or evidence of a crime. Due to informants and tipsters, however, the certainty of the particular knowledge of the investigator is more problematic. In 1983, in Illinois v. Gates, the Supreme Court set forth the doctrine of the "totality of circumstances." This doctrine allowed the courts greater freedom and leeway in accepting information originally supplied by an informant when granting a warrant.

Particularity means that the warrant should specify in clear detailed ways what is being searched for and expected to be found. There must be a description and identification of the person, place and property to be searched and seized. Blanket warrants allowing the investigator to roam and recover things at will smacks too much of a police state and is forbidden. The particularity of the description of the place to be searched is usually enough if it is such "that the officer with a search warrant can, with reasonable effort, ascertain and identify the place intended." If the warrant is sufficiently particular on its face, but results in confusion when it is carried out, it is permissible for the investigator to use common sense to resolve the confusion. However, if the warrant is too broad on its face it will be void. The warrant should be sufficiently detailed so that an officer can recognize the items sought. If the items are contraband, the warrant need not describe them in the same detail as is necessary for other items. A search for narcotics—since they can be hidden so easily—gives the officer greater leeway in the search. One legal doctrine that applies here is the "elephant in the match box" principle. One needs to be particular enough as to size of objects so as to not look for large objects in small places.

Proper procedure in carrying out the warrant is necessary, as well. In order to issue a search warrant an impartial magistrate must make two separate findings. First, the connection between the items sought and any illegal activity must be established. Second, the magistrate must determine that there is a great likelihood that the items sought will be found in the area to be searched. The search must be done in a timely way. Usually the execution of a search warrant must occur within ten days of its issuance. However, the key is that the probable cause still exists at the time of its execution. Consequently, even if the warrant has been executed in four or five days if probable cause has diminished the viability of the warrant is in question. Furthermore, most states provide that all search warrants be executed during day hours, but under certain circumstances special permission might be granted for a nighttime execution. Finally, both search and arrest warrants to be executed appropriately must adhere to the "knock and notice rule." First, the officer must knock and identify police authority. Second, the purpose of the knock and visitation—serving a warrant—must be made. Third, a reasonable period of time needs to be allowed to let people legitimately respond. Exceptions may be made in this waiting period if the police expect that evidence might be destroyed or that they might be placed in greater danger. Fourth, forcible entry then may occur.

Warrantless searches are those searches that are an exception to the principles discussed above. They are those searches in which special conditions are such that prior judicial approval is not necessary. They have the benefit of quickness, without the bureaucratic process of confronting a judge. However, they might have the problem of propriety and can be thrown out later as corrupting due process. There are several likely situations in which a warrant is not necessary.

Consent

There may be searches of a person if they give permission. Two problems may be associated to this type of search. First, the person later may change his story and recant the permission. In that case, it is the officers responsibility to prove that permission had been granted. Second, the consent for the search must be voluntary and not a product of coercion. The courts may look at several indicators in the determination of voluntary consent. For example, the age of a person giving consent will be taken into consideration. Very young and old people might tend to give consent because they feel intimidated. Second, the courts will look at the personal qualities of the person giving consent. Education, intelligence and timidity would be relevant issues when considering voluntary consent. Third, the court might consider if the individual understood they had the right to deny consent. Fourth, different rules apply if the person is in custody. For example, giving consent in the public areas of a street surrounded by non-criminal justice people is quite different than the "voluntary" nature of admissions when one is in the police station. Another consent issue arises when a third party consents to a search of commonly shared space such as an apartment. However, that consent does not extend to areas of "exclusive control" of the other person. For example, one roommate might consent to the search of the general apartment but not the exclusive bedroom of the apartment mate.

Plain View

The plain view exception has to do with that inadvertent discovery the police make when being in a place the officer has a right to be and when the criminality of the evidence is clearly apparent. This plain view exception allows the officer to seize the evidence.

Open Fields

The Supreme Court has held that in certain public places such as open fields and parks there is "no expectation of privacy" and therefore the Constitution does not protect them from police search. Items found in such places can be seized without a warrant because a search — which connotes the expectation of privacy — could not be expected and assumed by a citizen.

Exigent Circumstances

A series of emergency situations in which justice and safety might be jeopardized by seeking a warrant give the police officer an opportunity to search without prior judicial approval. For example, if an officer is in hot pursuit of a person and probable cause is strong enough to make an arrest, and the pursuit goes from public areas to a private ones the officer may follow and search for the suspect without obtaining a warrant. Similarly, if the police is patrolling outside a home and hears cries and screams from inside the officer may enter without a warrant to save life. In either case, once inside anything in plain view may be seized.

Automobile Searches

Motor vehicles are easily moved and can make it very difficult to keep track of and obtain suspects and evidence. Furthermore, the Supreme Court "Katz standard" does not apply as strongly; that is by venturing out on to public roads a person has a reduced expectation of privacy. Of course, if an officer is arresting the person in the car a thorough search of the interior and all closed compartments is permissible as incident to the arrest. In addition, an automobile might be "impounded" and the contents "inventoried" without a warrant. All apparently abandoned cars can be seized and searched, as well. Increasingly, the Court has opened up the automobile and its compartments to search without a warrant.

Incident to an Arrest

Arrest is a seizure covered by the Fourth Amendment. If an officer has probable cause to arrest then a search may logically follow. This search is largely to protect the officer from potential harm from one resisting the arrest and the Court decided in Chimel v. California (1967) that not only the suspect but the area in the suspects immediate control (the arms length or "lunging" radius) could be searched.

Stop and Frisk

In the less obtrusive field stop an officer may pat down the outer garments of a person without probable cause to insure the safety of the officer and surrounding citizens. It is based upon the desire to stop possible crime from occurring rather than arresting some who has already committed a crime. The Court, in Terry v. Ohio (1968), allowed another standard other than probable cause for this procedure and it was called "reasonable suspicion."

The searching power of the police in general and the investigator in particular is an ominous one and the Supreme Court has seen fit to develop an elaborate series of case law to guide the procedures of investigation.

Entry and Arrest

Entry is the dramatic encounter of the police with the suspect. Its purpose is to effect an arrest, prevent flight and destruction of evidence, and safeguard the safety of the officers. Historically, officers had to always announce their presence and purposes. They could not open up or break in a door without first making their announcement. Some "competent craftsmen," however, approached this in a darkly humorous way; they might have a battering-ram device that they called "announcement" or "knock" and simply brake down the door claiming it to be announced. As discussed earlier, as the drug problems and crime rates escalated — and as people and politicians moved to a more crime control mind set — "no knock laws" came into existence allowing greater leeway for officers to break into a persons domicile.[2]

Arrest is one of the most awesome activities of the police; it is the taking away of liberty, the placing of someone into custody with the purpose of prosecution. There are two types of arrest as well: warrant and warrantless.[3]

Warrant arrests are similar to those discussed earlier in terms of search. It is the prior approval by a judge to make the arrest. It relieves the police from the burden of proving the legality of the arrest later. It also allows for an independent evaluation, by a magistrate, of the evidence. There are some drawbacks, however. It does take time and the suspect might flee. And it is possible that the judge might deny the petition. The officer must establish probable cause and execute the warrant in a timely fashion.

Warrantless arrests are quite common in policing and they are based upon personal observation of a crime occurring, citizen complaint in which the complainant in a sense does a citizens arrest through the officer, and probable cause by the officer that a crime has occurred and the person probably committed.

Media

Media relations are critical parts of the criminal investigative process. It must be remembered that the press in reality or in appearance due to the quest for a story will appear to be adversarial. In some instances — since the media tends to be more liberal and also has its own agenda in getting news stories — the press will either appear to be or will really be an enemy to the police. In any given jurisdiction a generalization can be made. The local media will likely to be more friendly to the police than the national news gathering establishment. Local news print and broadcast — though having a higher concentration of crime and criminal justice coverage —

---

2. *New York Times* (May 22, 1995).

3. Wayne R. LaFave, *Arrest: The Decision to Take a Suspect into Custody* (Boston: Little, Brown, 1965).

tends to be more sympathetic and empathetic than those who come in from the outside. Of course, a generalization may not hold up in some jurisdictions where there is a particularly strong crime reporter or syndicated columnist. But there are other problems, as well.

In every investigation that remains in progress there is always the danger that too much information made public will alert and inform the perpetrator. In addition, news revelations put the investigative process public and raises societal expectations and criticism. On one hand, media exposure brings accountability of the process. On the other hand, some bureaucrats resent how it hampers the operations of the investigation.

Furthermore, there are some controversial areas needing to be considered. For example, crimes involving children as victims need special attention when it comes to publicity. So do adult victims of sex crimes. Of course, police-media relations address issues of due process as well. For example, there is the freedom of the press guaranteed in the Bill of Rights. Such a freedom, however, might get in the way of an efficient investigation by revealing too much information. Pre-arrest information might inform and distort the opinions of potential witnesses and jurors as well.

Finally, in America there is a presumption of innocence and any pre-adjudicative information might jeopardize that presumption. The moment when a captured suspect is displayed publicly, a process called "walking the perp," images come forth that might have impact upon subsequent adjudication. The "perp walk" has a long and important history in policing. In effect, it was one way the police created favorable relations with the press. It appears to have three historical stages in its evolution. First, up to the 1940s recently arrested suspects were paraded across a stage in front of reporters who assessed their newsworthiness. Second, from the 1940s through the 1960s reporters were allowed to sit around booking areas of the police department chatting with suspects and getting photo opportunities. Third, from the 1970s onward some guidelines emerged from the New York Fair Trial, Free Press Conference in 1969. The press should be allowed to photograph suspects in public places but any police posing of the perp was forbidden. However, four natural perp poses seem to have emerged. They are:

1) *Beast at Bay*, or the crimes are of horrendous nature and the suspect is treated as a captured animal. They seem totally subdued. Charles Manson might be an example of this public display at the time of arrest.

2) *Grinning Punk* pose is that of defiance. This person is unrepentant and plays this moment as a triumph. Lee Harvey Oswald did this.

3) *Old Pro* pose is one of arrogance and confidence. Organized crime figures serve as a stylish example of this.

4) *Shamed* pose is one in which the suspect hides the face and ignores the press cameras.

There are several possible general approaches that might be taken. First, there is the centralizing of the police news information. Most large police departments create a public information office in charge of press releases. On the crime scene, however, before the press officers are alerted, the supervising officer should be the only one to speak to the media. Second, another approach might be that police simply not talk to the media. This is not advisable because existing adversarial stances by the press might be exacerbated. Third, the police might lie to the media but such action might return to embarrass. Fourth, an "off the record" approach might be taken in which some information is leaked on condition of anonymity. Fifth, and more likely, relations will be developed with all or "favored and friendly" press.

In the name of professionalism there should be no posing or posturing. If no one has been arrested as yet it is advisable to withhold certain details of the crime which only the offender and the police know. Witnesses and victims should be cautioned not to talk to the press as well. In some cases, such as child molestation and rape, the names of the victims would be withheld. It might be appropriate to make appeals to the public for support and information at this time.

If someone has been taken into custody a series of new concerns emerge. First, no prejudicial comments about the suspect should be made. Second, the "perp" should not be posed. As discussed above the perp will intentionally or unintentionally pose themselves for the press. However, picture taking by the press cannot be stopped. Like it or not these immediate public appearances have an impact upon general feelings toward the suspect and the police who are processing him.[4]

Lineups

Lineups may be defined as public displays of the suspect among decoys so as to allow witnesses to make identifications. They are important because they allow for the release of innocent people and the placing into custody of suspected guilty persons. Furthermore, they are important to bolster the confidence of witnesses and victims and prepare them for courtroom identifications later in the process.

---

4. Arthur H. Nehrbass, "Promoting Effective Media Relations," *The Police Chief* (January 1988). Rod Bernsen, "Meeting the Police," *American Journal of Police* vol. 7 (1988).

There are some problems with this process. A 1987 study concluded that in America nearly 80,000 trials a year rely mainly on eyewitness testimony. In 1993 a study of 1,000 convictions of people who were later found to be not guilty revealed that eyewitness error accounted for half the cases. One psychologist, Gary L. Wells, conducted a study in which 100 people watched a staged robbery. They were asked to view a lineup in which the real culprit was absent. Twenty one percent still identified someone as the thief. Another problem is that of "false confidence." Witness grow confident if their decision has been bolstered by the knowledge that other witness made similar identifications. Furthermore, police officers after an identification strengthen it by acknowledging they have more evidence. Bolstered, the witness appears in court as confident. And juries are more impressed by confident than hesitant testimony. In addition, there is a problem in the process of recall. For example, if a person really knows the face it comes forth quickly and effortlessly; such identifications are accurate around 70 percent of the time. However, those who do not really remember go through a laborious process of elimination and are inaccurate 70 percent of the time. Frequently, they simply give the next best selection. Consequently, investigators must access the witness accordingly. If they scan the array of images and quickly make a decision they are using the process of recognition and are more reliable. If they take longer to come up with the identification they are using an entirely different thought process and are likely to be wrong. Recommendations given by these researchers suggest then that witnesses should be presented the image (in the lineup or a picture) one at a time and asked "Is this the person or not?" before moving on. In lineups the witness should be informed that one of the possible answers is that the real culprit is not present.

The procedure of a lineup should be such as to not bias the witness. Many investigators, as competent craftspersons, want a "positive id." so bad that they "bull's-eye" the suspect. That is they arrange things in such a way as to predispose the witness to make the "right" identification. This is wrong. Indeed, the suspect should be free to pick out their spot in the array of people. There should be ample decoys, or persons not suspected or connected to the case, with at least a ratio of two decoys for every suspect in the lineup. Everyone in the lineup should have general racial and physical characteristics. They should display a uniformity of appearance and decorum. If the identification cannot be made the suspect in all likelihood should be released. If the identification can be made, however, this provides ample reason and ammunition to move to the interrogation.[5]

---

5. *New York Times* (January 17, 1995).

Interrogation

Definitions

Next to search, the interrogative process has become one of the more controversial aspects of the latent investigation.[6] Interrogation is another interview-like process but its mood and methods are different. For example, it seeks confessions and admissions; it is more accusatory in nature. Two assumptions are at play by this time. First, the person being interrogated is guilty; the presumption of innocence may be appropriate for the court but "competent craftsmen" at this point have a presumption of guilt. Second, everyone lies and the detection and depletion of deception is critical.

Landmark Cases

The Supreme Court has been very active in this area of the investigative process, as well.

Coercion and confessions. For much of the history of criminal investigations and interrogations brutal treatment was commonplace. In fact, a phrase was coined for the beating of a person for confession and it was the "Third Degree." In one of the earliest cases addressing the interrogative process, Brown v. Mississippi (1936), this practice was struck down.

Custody and confession. Another popular approach was to put a person into jail and leave them there until out of despair a confession was forthcoming. This smacked of a police state, as well, and the "prompt arraignment rule" was put into place with the McNabb v. U.S. decision in 1943. In short, it was not permissible to have long delays in the criminal justice process to coerce a confession.

Counsel and confessions. The next area addressed by the Court was the role of legal counsel and the interrogative process. The first landmark case, Escobido v. Illinois (1964), declared that whenever the process shifted from general investigation to an accusatory style the defense counsel could be present. This, of course, pushed the interrogation concept out of the police station and on to the streets. If the person were ignorant and did not know that they might have the counsel then they should be informed of that right (Miranda v. Arizona, 1966).

---

6. Richard O. Arthur and Rudolph R. Caputo, *Interrogation for Investigators* (New York: William C. Copp and Associates, 1959). Clifford H. Van Meter, *Principles of Police Interrogation* (Springfield, IL: Charles C. Thomas, 1973).

The case law has grown considerably over the last two decades and does not need to be gone over here. But the above cases illustrate the point that interrogation certainly is one of the more important and controversial aspects of the latent investigation.[7]

Interrogative Procedure

The procedure of an interrogation may be broken down into three parts: the interrogator, the setting in which it occurs and the actual interrogation.

The Interrogator

First, the interrogator and the "magic moment." Every interrogator must make several assumptions. The person to be interrogated is guilty and will lie to you. Furthermore, there is a "magic moment" in which the person will confess. The interrogator must look for signs of the suspect coming to that turning point and help them achieve the confession.[8]

There are several "plays and ploys" the interrogator might use to get to the magic moment. First, generally the interrogator should read the subject. What is the level of experience of the subject? Veterans of crime will be different than rookies. Is there a weak spot? Some one concerned over their reputation, family or friends might be exploited to confess.

Second, rapport should be established. Previously rapport was sought with victims/witnesses so as to build bridges of communication. However, now rapport is sought for a different reason. It is harder—but not impossible—to lie to someone with whom you are connected. Rapport allows the interrogator to more clearly see when deception is practiced. Signs of deception are more dramatic when done against the backdrop of rapport.

Third, there are several styles of interrogation that might be utilized. One such ploy is to come across as a mean, rough and harsh person. This "tough cop" approach is to intimidate the suspect into a confession. This style is frequently used because the suspect puts on macho airs. Another ploy might be more sympathetic and caring. This good-guy approach is meant to make it appear that the interrogator understands and is a friend in an otherwise harsh frightening environment. This type may be manifested in

---

7. F.E. Inbau, *Criminal Investigation and Confessions*, 3rd. ed. (Baltimore, MD: Williams & Wilkins, 1985).

8. Hugh C. MacDonald, *The Practical Psychology of Police Interrogation*, (Santa Anna, CA: Townsend, 1963).

a variety of ways such as: "father confessor," "concerned listener," "protector." Of course, the best approach might be a combination of the good-guy/bad guy strategies, frequently called the "Mutt and Jeff" approach. One member of the team poses as unsympathetic and intimidating while the other plays the role of restraining the pent up angers and energies of the other. Slowly the body language of the suspect can be seen shifting to the good guy even as the bad guy has the floor.

The Setting

Second, the setting—just as the main interrogators are playing roles—should be staged as in a play. We might even call it the "prop room." Unlike the interview situation, in which all the creature comforts are given special attention, the interrogation room should maximize the discomfort levels. It is likely to be deep within the interior of the police station. This is to maximize police safety but also to symbolically give a message out to the suspects of the hopeless irretrievable condition in which they find themselves. They are layer upon layer removed from supportive environments. It is likely to be sparse with few furnishings. The Gulag approach may apply here. That is, when there is so little creature comfort available any gain or loss, no matter how little, assumes tremendous proportions. It presents an atmosphere of alienation, distance and dashed hope. Some interrogation rooms might even have reminders of the crime, gruesome pictures and artifacts. In the old days many interrogations took place in the morgue standing over the cadaver.

The Interrogation

The actual interrogation needs to be seen in terms of theme development, detecting deception and helping along a confession and documentation.

Territorial zones need to accessed and exploited. As humans we have four zones. The intimate zone is from 6 to 18 inches. A personal zone goes from 18 to 58 inches. A social zone, 4 to 10 feet, and a public zone, 10 feet and beyond, extend outward. At first, the interrogator might assume the outer limits of the social zone. But eventually the personal zone needs to be invaded. The area of operations should eventually be less than 24 inches.

Theme development is the stylized procedure that most interrogations follow. For example, a common practice of the interrogator is to initially confront the suspect with a statement of the police knowledge of his guilt. Of course, such a presumption of guilt flies in the face of due process but at this level it is quite common and even appropriate. The purpose here is to crumble any defenses the suspect might have in hopes of an early admission. Failing in that this strategy hopes to test the suspect and see the degree of denial ready to be used. Next, even though the guilty and innocent will exercise their right to deny, it is always harder for the guilty person to reach the magic moment if they have a long string of denials. Consequently, the interrogator needs to block—by interjection statements and looks of impatience and incredibility, perhaps—and hold down the number of denials. This denial of denials is necessary to keep the interrogator in command and push the subject closer to the magic moment. But there is a major problem here that many interrogators overlook, and that has to do with the slight differences in denials. For example, there is the denial that is a lie told by the liar: "I didn't do it!" Such denials will likely be nipped in the bud to show that the interrogator is in control and is incredulous. On the other hand there are "technical denials," these are truths spoken by the liar. For example, to say "I didn't steal!" may be a denial that is a lie, but to say "I don't have the money!" would be a technical denial that might be true. The interrogator needs to recognize the difference and exploit them more fully. Another opening gambit is the "moral justification" statements. Most people redeem or rationalize themselves by placing blame on others. Therefore, the interrogator might help along the suspect by allowing them to place part blame on others. For example, a person who has been stealing from their employer might find it comforting to hear the interrogator say that "everyone seems to be doing it." Finally, the interrogator might introduce "alternative questions." That is posing the question in a framework of premeditated v. spur of the moment situations. For example, the interrogator might ask: "Did you plan this thing or did it just happen?" The implication, of course, is that there was no real question of the culpability of the suspect but that it was degree of involvement and intent that was at issue.

Approaches to the question need to be considered. There are two general approaches plus some side shows that might be instructive. First, there is the "direct" approach. This is characterized by close-ended questions. The interrogator is in complete and tight control. Questions and atmosphere are highly structured. This approach is best for those close to the magic moment. They are first offenders who have committed crimes of passion, anger and jealousy. Second, there is the "nondirect" approach which is a more opened questioning style. Interrogators would appeal less to the emotions and more to the logic of the offender's mindset. This would be better for the career criminal who feels little remorse. By pointing out the over whelming nature of the evidence and the futility of denial appeals to the logic thinking powers of the subject. No matter the approach taken any one of several side shows might be utilized. They are:

1. *Complete File Technique.* In this case a very thick file is visible illustrating the nature of the investigators knowledge of the subject. It sends a message that we know a lot so rethink your lie strategy.

2. *Incentive Technique*. In this case, after reading and accessing the subject, a determination is made over what is important or a weakness of the subject. Using this information the interrogator gives the subject reason or incentive to confess.
3. *Quick Question Technique*. In this case the rapid firing of repetitive questions are given in hopes to inspire inconsistencies in the subject's story.
4. *Silent Technique*. Most people in discourse dislike silence, they feel self conscious. As long as there is noise they feel attention is deflected from them. Long periods of silence focuses attention to them and in trying to end it they might stumble into incriminating admissions.[9]

Stress response states need to be assessed. There are five of these that emerge as questioning progresses. They are anger, depression, denial, bargaining and acknowledgment.

Detecting of Deception

Detecting of deception is another major problem in the interrogation. Of course, a major assumption at this point is that the suspect is going to lie. Consequently, the detection of deception is important to use against the individual so as to finally get to the truth. There are several ways of detecting the lie. Two will be discussed here highlighting their promise and problems. They are body language and the polygraph.

Body language is the set of messages sent by the position and positioning of the body.[10] Sigmund Freud once said "If his lips are silent, he chatters with his fingertips; betrayal oozes out of him at every pore." Reading this language is very useful because it may be sent in more loud and truthful ways than what is actually being said. By recognizing these mixed messages the interrogator might more effectively manipulate the questions and the suspect.

It should also be remembered at this point that all people have a personal privacy halo, an area around their body that they want to keep free and clear except for those people and moments designated for intimacy. By recognizing the boundary of this private space and getting as close to it as possible the interrogator might read better or force a greater expression of the body language.

---

9. Don Rabon, *Interviewing and Interrogation* (Durham, NC: Carolina Academic Press, 1992), pp. 102, 105, 114–117.

10. Merlin S. Kuhlman, "Nonverbal Communications in Interrogation," *FBI Law Enforcement Bulletin* vol. 49, no. 11 (November 1980).

There are some clearly *obvious body messages*. This elementary vocabulary is essential to begin an understanding of the complex language of the body.

Before we start it might be useful to place this all in a broader context. Most police agents do not understand the principles of body language. Perhaps, the one that has arrived at that knowledge inadvertently is the Presidential Protection Service of the Secret Service. Anyone who has attended a public gathering where high governmental officials are to speak would readily recognize the presence of Secret Service agents blatantly staring out at the audience. Clearly, they are looking out for probable assassins. Besides knowing the faces of known suspects, what they are really looking for is the face of some one who is deceptive, that is for some one who seems "out of the ordinary" from the rest of the crowd. They have become quite adept at reading body language, looking for those messages that suggest a dangerous mission. What are some of the more obvious body messages?

One of the more obvious sections of the body that sends out messages is the face, particularly the lips. For example, the pursing of the lips connotes two possible readings, concentration and/or disapproval. The excessive licking of the lips suggest nervousness. Biting of the lips might mean self reproach. But the lips might join with other parts of the face to send a message. For example, the eyes.

It has been said, with considerable truth, that the eyes are the window of the soul. When the lips are genuinely smiling, for example, eye muscles are effected and the eyes will echo the smile. On the other hand, a disingenuous smile will not do so and the eyes will be out of congruence with the smile. Furthermore, the drawing of the eye brows together suggests anger and/or anxiety. The staring with narrowing of the eyes means aggressive attitudes. Eye contact suggests interest, and, conversely the failure to keep it means a lack of interest, timidity and anxiety. The looking at someone sideways might mean there is distrust. The cocking of the head and looking at someone means a genuine interest in what is being said.

One police interrogator and student of this phenomenon basis his interrogations on the fact of that eye movement. To him most right-handed people look up and to the right when they are creating, something they would not do in remembering. Left-handed people would look to the left. "They move differently when you're remembering and when you're creating. And if you're creating when you're talking to me about a crime, you're lying." There are some popular misconceptions that need to be corrected. For example, many believe that dominant people look you in the eye more. Actually, submissive people, in an attempt to overcompensate, do so while dominant types—in disdain or boredom—may actually look away. Finally, there is considerable evidence to suggest that the pupils of the eye dilate when a lie is told. The interrogator might get close to the threshold of the persons' halo boundary and look into the eyes for this indicator.

The rest of the body tells tales, as well. For example, the way a person sits, crossed legged or a more open sprawl, may suggest defiance and distrust or openness and confidence. Leaning back in the seat implies that the person is relaxed and confident. Leaning forward means interest and attentiveness. Legs and arms that are crossed are barriers. A figure four crossing of the legs suggests confidence. When seated a liar leans toward doors and windows. The constant fidgeting of the body might imply impatience and/or nervousness. Excessive tapping of the foot might be interpreted as nervousness, annoyance and impatience. The biting of the fingernails means fear and/or aggression. Hunching the shoulders suggests discouragement and/or fear. The sticking out of the chin tells of belligerence. Finally, auto-contact, or self touching, behavior indicates lying. People who lie touch their nose or other face areas. It displaces some of the anxiety that accompanies the telling of a lie.[11]

Some *less obvious* signs might be called micro-expressions. These are those small and fleeting signs a person subconsciously makes that reveal true communication. Two elements seem to characterize these micro-expressions. First, there are those features that are out of sync or give an asymmetrical expression. For example, prolonged smiles or looks of amazement that linger too long are probably false. Most authentic facial expressions fade after four or five seconds. A person who bangs the table but then waits a split second to produce an angry face is probably faking. Crooked, or asymmetrical, facial expressions are usually deceitful. In 70 percent of people tested, the pitch of the voice rose slightly when they were upset, afraid or angry, a broad clue to the possibility that they were lying. In addition, speech errors, such as slips of the tongue and odd pauses, often reveal lying. Second, there is something called "emblem leakage," or the unconscious misuse of common symbolic gestures. For example, displaying the A-O.K. sign, the thumb to forefinger configuration making a circle — but below the waist rather than commonly above — and the one-shoulder shrug are suggestive of deception.[12]

There are at least two main *problems with body language* as a tool for the criminal investigator. First, there is the issue of "normalcy." Some people have told lies so often that it has become normal for them. In fact, certain occupations — such as diplomacy and acting — actually train and encourage the art of deception. Pathological and trained liars, therefore,

---

11. P. Ekman and M.V. Friesen, "Leakage and Clues to Deception," *Psychiatry* vol. 32 (1969), pp. 88–106.

12. *Time* (April 22, 1985).

might disguise their deception better than others. In terms of crime, the habitual and professional crook—ones with considerable exposure to the criminal justice system—might more effectively cover their lies. There is even a greater problem with this normalcy issue. Many normal people under extraordinary circumstances will give off many of the signs indicating deception. It would be normal to sweat, fidget and contradict oneself under such circumstances. And studies indicate that the population in general and the police in particular are over confident and generally mistaken when it comes to reading body language.

Second, there is the problem of interrogator misinterpretation. This might be illustrated by something called the "cool pose." The cool pose might be defined as the aloof swagger, exaggerated masculinity, fearless styles of walk and talk and the wearing of provocative unconventional clothes by certain segments of the population, particularly the young male.[13] This is the only source or sign of competency and control in the general face of frustration and failure. They are generally young men whose interpretation of maleness comes from female dominated households or from inappropriate male models. The police will view these young men as rebellious, uncompromising, irresponsible people. While that interpretation might be true partially it becomes misbegotten self-fulfilling prophecy as the police treat them as enemies. In short, the body language can be seen as only partially useful and indeed as misleading. In light of these problems of detecting deception with body language many investigators prefer science in the form of the polygraph.

The polygraph, or lie detector machine, arose in the 1920s just as constitutional law was putting restraints on the Third Degree, or brutal obtaining of a confession. A discussion of this procedure will be couched along the notion of the "Three T's": theory, technology and technicians.

Theory. The theory behind the polygraph is sound. Simply put, it posits that there are physiological changes that occur in most people when they tell an untruth. These changes are discernable from respiration rates—the nature of a persons breathing—heart beats and pulse, blood pressure, and skin sweat on the hands and fingers. Of course there are some people who can "trick" the theory but their number is so small as to be statistically insignificant.

Technology. In 1921, J. Larson—under the guidance of the pioneering police chief, August Vollmer—devised an instrument for making continuous readings of both blood pressure and breathing. In 1930, L. Keeler refined

---

13. Richard Majors and Janet Mancici Billson, *Cool Pose: The Dilemmas of the Black Male in America* (New York: Simon & Schuster, 1993).

the Larson apparatus by adding a means for measuring Galvic Skin Response (GSR). With slight variations this Keeler device is the one used today. The modern polygraph is a brief-case size machine that records skin resistance (GSR) by two electrodes attached to the finger tips. A standard medical blood pressure cuff is on the arm. Finally, changes in breathing are recorded by hollow corrugated rubber tubes, one placed around the abdomen and one around the upper thorax, which expand and contract with movements of the chest cavity during inspiration and expiration. All of these readings are recorded on a paper chart by a mechanical pen-and-ink system.

Technicians. One of the possible problems with the polygraph is in the technician and the way they might ask questions and interpret the answers. To safeguard against this possibility the polygrapher needs voluntary clearances showing that the subject permits the questioning, a pre-test that is gone over and evaluated, and then two official tests with the same questions in different order.

Historically there have been two major testing techniques. The oldest is the Relevant/Irrelevant (R/I) test. In this test some relevant questions are interspersed among irrelevant ones. An example would be:

R: "Did you steal the money on September 23rd?"
I: "Are you over 18 years of age?"

In such a questioning it is assumed that truthful persons will not react too differently to relevant and irrelevant questions while liars will. In 1950, John E. Reid developed a new method called the Control Question Technique (CGT) which is the most popular style presently. It is similar to the R/I system except it introduces a control question. An example would be:

R: "Did you steal the money on September 23rd?"
I: "Are you over 18 years of age?"
C: "Did you ever steal?"

In this case it is the response variance between the relevant and the control questions that is important. Consistently and greater physiological responses to relevant questions rather than to control questions indicate lying on the relevant issues. Conversely, greater physiological response to control rather than to relevant questions indicate truthfulness in the case being tested.

Police use the polygraph in two ways. One, to pretest prospective employees for their honesty. In that regard it is an instrument for personnel. Two, it is used as an investigative tool to determine honesty or dishonesty during interrogation. Field practitioners claim a success rate between 90 and 95 percent. Controversy surrounds the polygraph with many believing that its findings are generally inadmissible in the court. The original judicial decision, Frye v. U.S. in 1923, did exclude polygraph evidence but many jurisdictions still use it. By the 1980s more than twenty states-including the District of Columbia — limited the use of the polygraph. In fact, a federal polygraph act of 1988 outlawed the use of lie detectors by employers in the private sector to study and make policy decisions about their current or future employees. This Employee Polygraph Protection law did not apply to federal, state and local government employers, however. More importantly, this law allowed the use of the polygraph as an investigative tool. Perhaps its greatest utility is not in detecting deception but in intimidating a person into confessions and admissions.[14]

Confessions

Confessions are both highly prized and troublesome.[15] Prized because they validate the investigative process and hold out promise for closure. And they are troublesome because they can be recanted later or claims might be made that they were obtained under duress. One safeguard, of course, is to document them, an issue to be examined in a moment. But first the arrival at this "magic moment" must be discussed.

There are two basic types of people who eventually confess to a crime under investigation. These reasons are important because the informed interrogator/investigator might see their elements or better prepare the person under interrogation for the magic moment.

First, there are the guilty. Many of these people confess because they are genuinely sorry and fearful for what they have done and they are slowly rehabilitating and repenting their acts. Interrogators need to watch for such signs, reading the character of the suspect, and encourage them along the way to admissions. The "righteousness" of the action, its moral correctness, might be emphasized. Promises that they would feel better, "confession is good for the soul," might be made. In addition, and more commonly for hardened criminals, confessions come as a result of realizing that the state's case is too big and solid to overcome. Any further resistance would just add years to the punishment. Interrogators need to remind the suspect of that fact and intimidate them into confession. Finally, the stress and strain of the investigation and interrogation simply wear down those people who are guilty.

Second, some innocent people rush to confess, as well. There are always a number of people, messianic in type, willing to take on the sins of everyone else. They get some satisfaction from confessing. Also, these people

---

14. J.K. Murphy, "The Polygraph Technique: Past and Present," *FBI Law Enforcement Bulletin* vol. 49, no.6 (June 1980), pp. 1–5. David T. Lykken, *A Tremor in the Blood: Uses and Abuses of the Lie Detector* (New York: McGraw-Hill, 1981).

15. Yale Kamisar, *Police Interrogations and Confessions* (Ann Arbor, University of Michigan Press, 1980).

might be stressed over the interrogation and confess to shorten that unpleasantness.[16]

There are some confessional signs, body indicates that the magic moment is near. For example, there may be a cleansing breath — an exaggerated inhale or exhale of breath. Hands, legs or arms that had been crossed or clenched before might open up. Shoulders may droop and chin drops and quivers. In a final plea for connection and understanding the suspect may now lean into the interrogator's territorial space.

Documentation

Documentation of the interrogation is important to validate it and the appropriateness of the interrogative process. Of course, it is important to have witnesses in attendance. There are several ways to document the interrogation. First, note taking as discussed under interviewing techniques might be used. Most likely, these notes should be done by a third party. The interrogator or interrogators have too many other roles to play. Second, in this modern day of electronics the use of audio and video recording machines might be most appropriate. These would clearly document the truthfulness of the confession and the integrity of the interrogative process. Furthermore, many people under interrogation, while interrogators are out of the room, harm themselves and later lay charges upon the police. A video documentation would deflect such bogus charges. But as of the early 1990s only one-sixth of the law enforcement agencies of America used them. Third, a statement prepared from the notes or recordings should be made, read and explained to the suspect and signed before witnesses.[17]

Conclusions

The latent investigation may be divided into two phases, the information gathering and the more accusatory phases. The former proceeds relatively value free. The method is more scientific. The latter occurs under the assumption, growing stronger as the process proceeds, of a presumption of guilt. Competent craftsmen, those experienced practitioners of criminal investigation, reach a point that they know the guilt of a suspect. The Supreme Court has recognized this distinction and has created a body of procedural law to curtail the efficiency of these craftsmen in this stage. In

---

16. See Richard Ofshe and Ethan Watters, *Making Monsters: False Memory, Psychotherapy and Sexual Hysteria.*

17. William MacDonald, "The Use of Videotaping in Documenting Confessions," *The Police Chief* (February 1983).

effect, there are two worlds: the one of the investigator craftsman who values efficiency above all else and subscribes to the notion of the "end justifying the means," and another world of the courts and due process which believes that the police must not descend to the level of those they apprehend. There are too many dangers of being burnt when you fight fire with fire. Investigators need to operate in their world but recognize that ultimately they must collide with the other. Clearance, the statistical measure of their success, means little with out conviction. So while they have finished one important task, the latent investigation, they have another one to perform in a world that is questioning of their procedure and motives, a world that not only puts on trial the suspect but also the investigators and their methods. This will be played out in the court and brings into play a new set of strategies and characters.

Chapter 9

The Criminal Investigator and the Courts

Introduction

This chapter is concerned with a very important part of the criminal investigation, that is the connection of the investigator to the courts — its main functionaries and rituals — and the law. It is important to us as students of the investigative process because it is one more type of documenting the process. Like all research methods this allows the public scrutiny of the method and its findings. In a larger sense the craftsman-like qualities of the investigator — constantly under close scrutiny by partners and peers within the police department — now are examined by another more exacting and less sympathetic set of critics in the courtroom environment. Prosecutors, who are busy building their own careers and reputations, make judgements about the skill of the investigators and might even refuse to accept and prosecute a case if it appears to be weak, a process called *nolle prosequi* or "I refuse to prosecute!" In short, the prosecutor at this stage questions the skill of the investigator.

In addition, the legal standards to be discussed shortly inform the process that has been under discussion for the previous several chapters as to the perimeters of appropriate detective conduct; and it validates or invalidates its ethical nature. That is to say, that due process, which is a motivating force here, now collides with the detectives quest for efficiency. In many respects, the investigator and the investigative process are on trial as well. Indeed, for reasons not always clear to investigators, defense attorneys actually spend much of their time attacking the motives and methods of the detective.

In a sense there are three tests of a detectives skill that emerge more clearly at this time. *Clearance,* or the closing of a case by an arrest, has already been resolved in order to bring the case to the prosecutor. It would appear to many investigators that clearance is the only important test; they have made the arrest and accumulated their statistic and future outcomes are in the hands of others. But another important goal is *conviction*, the main statistical measure for success of the prosecutor. A conviction rate is the number of cases ending in a finding of guilt as compared to the total number of cases the prosecutor takes to court. To think that a detective is satisfied only with clearance misses a very large point; after months of work on a case an investigator does not want to see the suspect back on the streets because the prosecutor could not secure a conviction. Another quest is to do all of the above in keeping with the United States *constitution*, or the appropriate process along commonly accepted American democratic values. As competent craftsmen, out of ignorance or design, many investigators may twist the due process privileges of the suspect to such an extent that though he is factually guilty the courts may him legally innocent.

To better understand this enormously important activity this chapter will discuss the relevant notions having to do with the Rules of Evidence, which should shape the earlier investigative process and minimize problems with the prosecutor, and the performance responsibilities of the officer in the courts. It will then turn to a discussion of the officers role in the court room as a witness.

Rules of Evidence

Order of Proof and Corpus Delicti

Perhaps, at the outset, a few vocabulary words are in order. "Evidence" is used to mean facts, be they artifacts like physical evidence or eye witness accounts. Evidence will have various "weights" or degrees of believability and persuasiveness. For example, the "best evidence rule" suggests that copies of documents do not have the weight as the originals. This evidence is presented to the court by "testimony," usually given orally, or by exhibit or display of the objects. This accumulated evidence constitutes a "proof."

There is an *order of proof*, or a priority of things that have to be done. For example, one of the first orders of proof is to establish *corpus delicti*, or that all the legal elements of the crime are present. Before we used the term in a narrow sense, that is "has a crime been committed?" Now in a much more legalistic environment the phrase takes on expanded meanings that still impact upon the investigative process. As any elementary textbook in criminal justice would indicate there are several aspects of corpus delicti. They are:

First, *legality.* The so-called criminal act under question had to violate a legally constituted written law. That law had to be conceived by people having the legitimate right to make law, a representative body such as the national Congress, a state legislature or a city council.

Second, *intent.* There has to be an evil intent behind the act under question. That is not to say that an accidental and unintended acts cannot be irresponsible and negligent. But it does mean that different degrees of culpability will occur. *Mens rea* or guilty mind therefore is an important part of corpus delicti.

Third, *act.* One cannot be found guilty of thinking about bad behavior. Since the close of the puritan colonial times the United States has wanted to avoid any "thought police." Consequently, corpus delicti demands that some act has been committed or omitted. Obviously, the act of attacking and raping is wrong. So is neglecting to file and pay your income tax, an act of omission. Furthermore, failed or interrupted and thwarted acts, under the legal guise of "attempt," will carry a sanction or punishment. To kill is a wrongful act, but so is to attempt to kill even if you fail to be successful. Other issues of "accessory," (knowing of a crime and substantially helping a criminal either before or after the event), and "conspiracy" (actually planning the crime even though you may not have been actually on the crime scene during its commission) are examples of indirect acts of criminality that might carry considerable sanctions. On the other hand, doctrines of "compulsion" and "necessity" might offer legal defenses. That is, a person may be forced to commit a crime under threat from other persons and conditions.

Four, *concurrence.* In addition, there needs to be a connection, a casual relationship, between the act and the harm done.

Five, *culpability.* A person may intend to carry out a criminal act and indeed perform the act that has been defined as illegal and still not be totally culpable. Several examples come to mind. Age may be a determinate. People under a certain age, most likely under seven years generally in the United States, may be excused for many dastardly deeds. Those between seven and seventeen who may commit the same act may fall in to the juvenile justice system and receive special attention. Those over eighteen, of course, would be judged and adjudicated as adults. Mental capacity — whether it is under the McNaughten, Irresistible Impulse, Durham, Substantial Capacity, or Guilty but Insane rules — provides various defenses for those with mental illness. Self-defense also may be used to reduce ones culpability. Of course, the investigator earlier in the investigation has determined corpus delicti by simply asking has a real crime been committed. Now it takes on more elaborate legal definitions. Only once the prosecutor has proven corpus delicti does the notion of order of proof allow the proceedings to progress to matters of guilt.

Admissibility

A very important principle of the rule of evidence is admissibility. Basically, this concept is in place to protect the court — the jury or judge if it is a bench trial — from hearing improper evidence or misleading information. Obviously, it may be actually heard in court but if objection is raised and sustained by the judge the improper evidence can be stricken from the written record which binds the jury during its deliberations. There are four important elements in this concept of admissibility: relevance, materiality, competence, and privilege.

Relevance addresses the issue of information having a connection to the case. Evidence must have bearing on the issues of the case otherwise they are irrelevant. A tricky issue, probably raised by lawyers but left to the judge to settle, might be a given defendants prior criminal history. To what extent is that information relevant to guilt or innocence now? In a trial over a crime committed in Chicago, the prosecutors introducing of evidence that the defendant lived prior to the crime in Cleveland is irrelevant.

Materiality deals with the degree of importance of the evidence. Indeed, it may be relevant but it is so insignificant that it would not change the outcome of the case. For example, in a trial over the shooting of a person at close range with a shot gun it is immaterial that the defendant was an expert skeet shooter.

Competence issues are important because they lay the foundation for other evidence. Consequently, they frequently relate to the investigation because they might address a host of possible procedural problems. For example, if the chain of custody has been broken an objection might be raise about the competency of the evidence. The implication is that the evidence could have been altered and adulterated during the period for which it was unaccounted. Taped voices would be incompetent if notation of date, time, place of the taping, and circumstances of the recording had not been established. In other words, the inappropriate carrying out of the investigative method earlier on might negate the evidence at this stage. Another example might be in a child molestation case. The judge might want to interview the victim to see if the child was reliable in terms of knowing right from wrong in telling the truth or if there was adequacy in memory.

Privilege is an admissibility rule that allows certain information sources to be banned from the court. The theory behind privilege is that certain relationships and confidentialities are so important that evidence must be sacrificed in order to preserve them. Marital privilege quickly comes to mind. Spouses must not be forced or even encouraged to testify against their mate. Of course, if a wife wants to do so she cannot be forbidden, but the state cannot force such a break in that special relationship. There are a series of professional relationships that have been sacrosanct as well. An attorney and client is a special relationship historically protected by privilege. Physician-patient, priest-penitent, and journalist-informant are other examples of evidentiary privilege. It should be added that there are legal attacks against such privileges but generally they have held up. Such privileges can be waived but only by the defendant.

Prejudicial issues might play a large part, as well. For example, the simple presentation of a colored photograph of a murder victim might be seen as prejudicing the jury just because of the graphic and gruesome nature of the lethal wounds.

Types of Evidence

In previous chapters the various types of evidence were noted and discussed. They were: physical evidence be it associative or trace. Then there were those distinctions used by forensic scientists to aid interpretation: class and individual. Now we need to see evidence as the courts see it. This exercise, though draped in the language of the court, is important because most categories have a direct connection to the investigative process.

First, is the distinction called *real evidence*. Real evidence simple means physical evidence, the hard and tangible objects of the crime that can be produced in the courtroom. The revolver or knife of a murder scene or the semen stained under garment from a rape scene fall into this category. As mentioned in previous chapters, judges and juries are tremendously impressed with a case that has a lot of real evidence. Naturally, its presence and purity is dependent upon the skill of the investigators and forensic scientists.

Second, there is *direct evidence* or eye witness accounts and first hand knowledge by victims/witness to the crime. All the work , as discussed in the chapter on witnesses and interviewing, is reflected here at this time. Not only the original interviewing but the way the witnesses have been brought along over time will reflect upon the investigator as the witness takes the stand.

Third, is *demonstrative evidence,* some times called illustrative evidence, consists of those things — sketches, maps, photos, charts etc. — that elaborate and clarify otherwise obtuse and hard to understand points of a testimony. Investigators will be either directly or indirectly responsible for the creation of such exhibits. The difference may be between a rough crime scene sketch and a finished one specially created for the courtroom presentation.

Fourth, is *opinion evidence*. Generally, in the court of law witnesses can only relate facts. Interpretations and opinions are not permissible. However, there is room for a small number of expert witnesses whose job it is to analyze and interpret to the court information that otherwise would be too difficult for the lay person. It is their job to assist the court to understand complex things. For example, forensic scientists, such as the medical examiner or crime lab technician, might be called upon to explain to the jury the markings on a body or on a spent slug from a gun. On some cases these expert witnesses are indisputable. At other times — such as psychiatrists for the state and for the defense who disagree over issues of insanity of the defendant—they may side track the proceedings with controversy. It should be noted, however, that perhaps the most expert witness in the court—the investigating police officer—is not allowed to offer opinion as evidence.

Fifth is _circumstantial evidence._ Sometimes referred to as indirect evidence this type of information has to do with inference. Evidence in the courtroom resembles a link in a chain, each one being forged to finally lead to a proof. Of course, the tighter these links the easier it is to create the proof. But some times there are missing links, the chain appears to be broken. If there are too many links missing then a proof is impossible. However, if only a small number are missing then a leap of logic may be possible. Seen another way, circumstantial evidence deals with the possibility of coincidence. One or two facts may be attributed to coincidence. But the more circumstantial facts present the more likely a proof will be accepted. In spite of popular notions on the worthless nature of circumstantial facts many cases are built and won based upon them. Of course, this an important principle for the investigator. Detectives, in the name of completeness, may be criticized for over collecting of evidence; so much of it seems so insignificant. It is the collection of many tangential pieces of information that might lead to circumstantial proof. The following diagram might be helpful:

Direct

Evidence Presented	>————>	Proof
1. Photograph of Jack hitting Jill		1. Jack hit Jill
2. Eyewitness of incident		
3. Jack admits hitting Jill		

Circumstantial Inference

Evidence Presented	>————>	Proof
1. Weapon had Jack's fingerprints.		1. Jack hit Jill
2. Jack heard to say "I'm going to hit that girl."		
3. Photograph of Jack near Jill.		

Sixth, there is _hearsay evidence._ This is second hand information in which the witness in court has no personal knowledge of the facts; they are heard said. It is recognition that a story told often changes substantially. An interesting experiment for the classroom might be to begin a story told at some length to a person at one end of the classroom and then let it circulate throughout the class to the opposite end of the room. Very likely the story — while keeping some elements — will have changed substantially by the time it gets to the last person. Such informational sources are seen to be unreliable and untrustworthy and have little place in the court. However, there might be a few exceptions to this general hearsay rule. Confessions and admissions — though corroboration through signed statements is important — are hearsay that are generally accepted in court. Former testimony — either written or oral in one trial — may be entered into a second retrial of the same offender for the same offense. Spontaneous and excited utterances are frequently admitted based upon the notion of _Res Gestae._ It is assumed that people instinctively speak the truth and any blurting out of information before a person has had time to think about it is reliable. For example, Jack is stabbed in the back. As the assailant flees a witness who saw the stabbing yells out "that fellow did it!" The witness then gets into a car and drives away and is never seen again. A police officer overhears the witnesses statement and chases and apprehends "that fellow." At the trial the officer can testify as to the unknown witnesses exclamation. It is an excited utterance and is considered trustworthy enough to be admitted. Finally, dying declarations — those statements made by persons soon to die — are exceptions to hearsay. The theory here is that people without hope to recover are more likely to tell the truth than lie and even though they are gone their hearsay statement is admissible. Of course, this is important to the investigator, because the officer will be near the dying person and ready to take down any final statements. That officer becomes the spokes person for the deceased in the court room.[1]

Officer in the Courtroom

Importance

When one thinks of criminal investigators images of sleuths discovering clues and making arrests come to mind. But a very significant part of an investigators job is acting as a witness in the court trial. On one hand this calls upon a different set of skills then those that have been outlined

---

1. George T. Felkenes, _Constitutional Law for Criminal Justice_, 2nd ed. (Englewood Cliffs, NJ: Prentice-Hall, 1988).

in this text thus far. On the other hand, however, public witnessing in the court room must be seen as another step of documenting and the presenting of research findings that many different types of investigators must do as part of their professional obligation. Unfortunately, research indicates that investigative officers have been weak in this part of their methodology. Surveys of judges and juries indicate that investigators hurt their cases when they appeared to be unprepared, cynical or biased. As competent craftsmen they have many cases competing for their time. The case at trial is already weeks old for the investigator who has worked on several new ones since the arrest. Furthermore, they are sure—even if the court is not—of the guilt of the defendant and they might come across as over confident, over bearing and impatient.

In addition, the jury is a very unpredictable group of people; they have their own psychology. Clearly, the jury looks to the words and actions of the main actors in the court. Some juries—particularly in those days and places where make up of juries leaned towards older middle class Americans—might be pro-police. They look to the detective as a positive re-enforcement of their biases. The smallest mistake or sign of weakness by the detective who is held in high regard will result in greater disillusionment by the jury. Conversely, it is conceivable in some jurisdictions that a jury could be loaded with anti-police sentiment. In such a case, any mistakes are interpreted as validation of negative feelings toward the police establishment. Consequently, the activity of the investigator as witness in the courts must be seen in theatrical terms.[2]

Presentation

In any presentation there are two considerations to keep in mind: preparation and performance.

Preparation, on one level, has already been an important activity. The purpose of this text is to better prepare the practitioner of investigation. Knowing the rules of evidence, as set forth in the earlier section of this chapter, is important to inform the investigation and prevent legal complications from surfacing at this stage. More relevant to this chapter, however, this preparation takes on two additional attributes. First, in a real sense—to carry on with the theatrical metaphors—the investigator is an actor and the prosecutor is the director. In that regard, the investigator needs to establish a working relationship with the prosecutor and take direction, do what the prosecutor demands for a successful performance. Second, all drama requires rehearsal. Of course, the demands of time on

---

2. John T. Waltman, "Nonverbal Elements in Courtroom Demeanor," *FBI Law Enforcement Bulletin* (March 1984).

both the investigator and prosecutor are great and rehearsal time is precious. Nonetheless, time must be given to drawing up the questions to be asked by the prosecutor and the answers to be expected by the investigator. Surprise and uncertainty must be kept to a minimum. Even the questions and cross examination by defense counsel must be predicted and appropriate responses determined. The detective needs to be alerted and rehearsed when it comes to any open-ended questions. They are particularly dangerous because people allowed to ramble on tend to introduce contradictions and equivocations that might be discrediting.

Performance has to do with two qualities as well. First, the general appearance of the investigator in the courtroom. The detective must look detached and professional. Conservative businesslike dress is important in the imaging of the witness. Any close and friendly connection to the court personnel suggest complicity and should be avoided.

Second, is the set of activities and impressions of the officer when they are on the witness stand. Eye contact with the jury is essential in order to inspire their confidence. The answering of questions should be devoid of emotion and partiality. Of course, the officer — as a competent craftsman and skilled methodologist — is not unbiased. Investigators, at this stage, know that the defendant is guilty; in spite of the certainty the investigator as courtroom witness must act impartial. Being as positive in your answers — avoiding such phrases as "I think" or "I believe" — also inspires confidence. Officers may refer to notes to refresh the memory but excessive use of the notes would have negative reactions in the jury. There are two things to keep in mind here. Officers may call for "present memory refreshed" privilege. In this case the officer must declare that there is some haziness over the details and that a document exists that would clarify matters. After looking at that document and it does not remedy the problem of memory then the document itself might be admitted under the principle of "past recollection recorded." Finally, the officer must realize that a legitimate strategy of defense counsel is to use various tactics to undermine the witnesses for the prosecution. In larger jurisdictions, where there might be an army of public defenders and several private counsels specializing in criminal law, it might be difficult to know the enemy. However, over time, it is surprising how well prosecutors get to know the various public defenders and defense attorneys. Elaborate negotiations, called plea bargains, occur outside of the courtroom. Such information naturally would be conveyed to the investigator in the preparation stages. Obviously, the investigator would be warned and prepared against these tactics as well.

Cross examination is an opportunity for the counsel to test the accuracy, understanding, integrity, bias, prejudice and ability to recall points of events and evidence by the witness. There are several commonly used courtroom tactics to unnerve a witness during cross examination. On cross examination, therefore, the investigator must be alert to these tactics in order to neutralize them. Of course, the investigator—unlike other witnesses—has been in court on numerous occasions and is less likely to be intimidated. Consequently, the tendency for an officer to become combative is great and must be held in check. Some of these cross examination tactics are:

1. *Impeachment* is a process to undermine the witness and remove the possibility of the testimony altogether. The attorney might try to prove that prior statements inconsistent to the current testimony have been made. Or that current internal inconsistencies are so great as to impugn the witness. Of course, the character of the witness might be called into question, as well.

2. *The demand for "yes" or "no" answers from the witness* when there is a need to have longer more explanatory answers is quite common. The purpose, here, is to prevent any pertinent and damaging information to the defense's case coming into the court. In addition, it might have the tendency to unnerve the witness and provide ways for the jury to loose confidence in the professionalism of the investigator. Although the desire might be great, it would be wrong for the witness to spar with the attorney. Investigators must allow for the prosecutor to offer objections and stop such defense strategies.

3. *The reversing of the words of the investigator* is a common tactic used to confuse and distract the witness and the jury. By remaining calm and collected and offering the corrected version the investigator might turn the tables and actually make the attorney to look as incompetent.

4. *Rapid and repetitious questions* are a favorite ploy by cross examining attorneys as well. There is a reason for this to be used especially for investigators. It is felt that any overly rehearsed and memorized testimony can be disrupted by asking questions rapidly and out of logical sequence. The same question, only slightly altered, fired at the witness rapidly is a strategy that seeks to inspire inconsistency and confusion. Another way defense counsel might use this concept is to ask: "How many discussions did you have about the answers that you have given?" As defense tries to show the jury the investigators ineptitude it hopes to dazzle them with brilliance of defense counsel. In this situation the witness can capture control and even exasperate the attorney by purposely giving slower answers—prefaced, perhaps, with a statement that "I have already answered that but if you did not understand I will be glad to go over it again more slowly."

5. A more theatrical pose would be for the defense attorney to have *long periods of silence accompanied with long penetrating stares* at the witness. The stare/silence routine sends a message that more is expected and

if it is not forth coming the implication is that the witness has failed some test. This is a difficult situation, one that can only be successfully won by the prosecution by being prepared to wait it out. Even though defense attorneys like to establish eye contact with the witnesses, it is a good idea of the investigator to establish eye contact with the jury. By doing so some of the discomfort of stare/silence ploy might be overcome. People dislike long silences and the natural tendency is to fill them in with language. Sometimes the filling-in leads to things said that would have been best left unsaid. If the officer can muster the determination—knowing that all eyes are upon the witness stand—to be silent and continue the eye contact with the jury, in time the judge will turn the ploy back on to the attorney to the embarrassment of the defense.

6. Sometimes *defense counsel will appear to be overly friendly*, with abundant politeness, in an attempt to lull the witness into a false sense of security. Of course, this always works best on the unexpecting, but the investigator must assume a latent hostility by the defense counsel and distrust any overly friendly gestures.

7. On the other hand, *defense counsel may take an overly condescending attitude* giving an impression that the witness is inept and unreliable and that the defense counsel will interpret all information. Investigators should overlook this and maintain a firm and decisive posture.

8. *Badgering and belligerent questions* shouted out are intended to make the witness loose their composure and return the answers in the same way. By staying calm, however, the witness can look more professional and leave the jury feeling that the defense counsel is a bully.

9. *Suggestive questions*, ones in which the question itself has a wrong answer or demeaning connotation imbedded in it, are another favorite tactic. For example, if the answer coming from the witness is not what was desired or expected, the counsel might respond to you (but really grand standing to the judge and spectators) that "I did not ask you that question!" Or if there is a feeling that the witness is trying to evade the question the counsel might respond by saying" Then I take it that your answer is no!"

In all cases the investigator as witness needs to remember the four C's for court room performance. Concentrate on the task at hand not allowing the defense counsel or the public nature of the proceedings to be intimidating. Remain *c*alm even when the hurly burly of the court seems to get out of hand. And always remain in *c*ontrol even though the very nature of answering questions seems to be a defensive role. Based upon the prior investigative process and the rehearsals with the prosecutor always remain *c*orrect.[3]

---

3. Devallis Rutledge, *Courtroom Survival* (Flagstaff, AZ: Flag Publishing, 1979).

Conclusions

The investigative process is like many research methods: investigators address a problem, seek out information, analyze the data and then present it in meaningful ways. Certainly, it is in the courtroom where that methodology is going to receive its greatest test. In a democratic society that is appropriate. Americans do not want a gangster state, nor do they want a police state. It is in the courtroom where guilt and innocence of the suspect turned defendant is determined. But in larger ways it is also the place where the propriety of the investigative method is tested. To safeguard against being found wanting it is necessary not only to know the steps of the investigative process but to understand them against the backdrop of appropriate legal rules. Furthermore, even if the investigation was done thoroughly and appropriately, the investigator might do the case harm in the individual performance in the witness stand. The case is not settled with the arrest but with the conviction.

SPECIFIC CRIMES
INVESTIGATION

Chapter 10

Death Investigation

Introduction

A very important responsibility and activity of the criminal justice system is the investigation of situations resulting in death. This chapter is mainly concerned with homicide and suicide investigation. But before we can turn to those specific concerns some general comments are in order.

The investigation into death is important for several reasons. First, in terms of corpus delicti there are a number of considerations to be kept in mind by the investigator. Is this death a homicide, suicide, accidental, or natural? And as the following table suggests death comes in a variety of probabilities.

Cause of Death	Odds for the average American
Disease	1 in 1.3
Heart Attack	1 in 3
Cancer	1 in 5
Automobile Accident	1 in 42
Suicide	1 in 81
Homicide	1 in 84

Second, historically death investigations had high degrees of success. Indeed, detective work had high status in policing in general, and within the detective ranks homicide investigators had even higher status. But as death rates increased the ability of the police to clear them decreased. Once homicide was the result of dramatic activity between loved ones and acquaintances whose relationship had gone sour; the killer was physically and logically ascertained. Now many stranger perpetrated and random killings have taken the competitive edge away from the investigator. Once a "walk-through," now many death investigations have become "whodunits." For example:

Homicide rates in America	Clearance rates
1971 = 8.5 per 100,000	84%
1981 = 9.8 per 100,000	71%
1990 = 9.4 per 100,000	67%

Consequently, there has developed for many death investigators an operational axiom: MAKE THE ARREST WITHIN 72 HOURS OR

173

Who Has Guns

Estimated percentages of homes with guns, based on telephone surveys.

Japan†	1.0
Netherlands*	1.9
England and Wales*	4.4
Germany	8.9
Australia*	15.1
Canada*	24.2
Switzerland	27.2
Norway	32.0
United States	48.0

† from 1995 survey; * from 1992 survey; all others from 1989 survey

CHANCES OF EVER MAKING IT PLUMMET. Commonly after this three-day window the case goes to a "cold case squad."

Issues

Furthermore, several larger societal issues are important to understand for background to this topic. A reminder is in order. The reason that these following points are framed as issues is that they are debatable, they are at this writing unresolved and remain critical in the national debate.

First, the role of alcohol in death—whether it is natural death due to disease, accident, suicide or deadly assault—seems to be present. Consumption of alcohol lowers inhibitions and raises temperament levels in many people. Of course, thousands of people consume alcohol and do not become part of a national statistic on violence. Nonetheless, for many the correlation is just too strong. But temperance and prohibition movements of the past had only limited success, and basic freedoms of America seem to get in the way of any national policy on alcohol. As a corollary here, another substance category, narcotics, seems to be responsible for the increase in crime in the last twenty years.

Second, firearms have a disproportionate place in the role of death. Quantitatively, most homicides and suicides in America are done by guns. In 1990 there were 13,035 deaths in America related to guns; other civilized countries, such as Japan, Germany, Canada, France, and England, had below 100. The old saying that "Guns don't kill, people kill" is certainly true. But people kill more effectively with guns than without them, and the United States has refused to create any meaningful gun restriction policy. Studies show that people who keep guns in their home for self-protection— and 48 percent of Americans have guns in their homes—do not use them against criminal threats but do have higher rates of accidental, suicidal, and homicidal incidence than those who do not own guns. A handgun is 40 times more likely to kill a family member or friend than a criminal. Conservatives remain concerned, however, that by taking away the right for honest law abiding citizens to have guns will leave them in the hands of the criminals. Any national policy seems stymied at present and the criminal justice system will be called upon to do impossible tasks.

Furthermore, there has been a remarkable change in the quantity and type of guns on the streets since the early 1990s. For example, the gun of preference up to the 1990s was some sort of revolver, such as a .38 caliber. Now it is a 9 mm semiautomatic, called "The Nine" in street language. This lightweight assault pistol has a magazine load—called "para-bellum," Latin meaning "for war"—with 20 to 32 bullets that can be fired rapidly in what may be called a "pray-and-spray" fashion. The potential for collateral damage and victimization is great. Finding themselves outgunned the police have sought to change their weaponry to "nines," as well. Alcohol, Tobacco and Firearms agents, for example, abandoned their .38 caliber revolvers as early as 1984 for a German made Sig Sauer 9 mm weapon that carries 16 bullets. The escalation of gun use and abuse continues.[1]

Third, violent behavior, whether it is inflicted upon oneself or others, raises other interesting issues. To what extent can it be deterred? For example, there are two forms of deterrence: specific and general. Specific deterrence means that a criminal's behavior might be changed by a specific punishment policy. The death penalty inflicted upon a killer certainly stops him from ever killing again, but so might life in prison without hope of parole. On the other hand, in terms of general deterrence, does the execution of a killer keep others from killing? That is a more difficult research question to address and answer, but the evidence seems to suggest that it does not. Then what value, besides some visceral desire for revenge, does capital punishment have? One of the few modern industrial countries of the world that has the death penalty also has one of the highest murder rates; that country is the United States.

Fourth, why do some people become violent while others do not? Several notions have sought to address this problem and by doing so the answers have become issues themselves. For example, for several years many have been concerned with the violence portrayed in the media and in entertainment. Cries for government or industry censorship periodi-

---

1. *Chicago Tribune* (June 13, 1993).

cally arise but get entangled in constitutional issues. Clearly, violent pornography seems to be under constant attack. Even the serial killer, Ted Bundy, on the night before his execution, lay much blame for his behavior on violent pornography. Of course, his history of honesty and forthrightness leads to some skepticism on that issue. In addition, some researchers have found that childhood abuse increases the odds of future delinquency and adult criminality by 40 percent. This "cycle of violence" hypothesis suggests that a childhood history of neglect and violence predisposes the survivor to a life of violence later in adulthood.[2] Lastly, Scandinavian studies in 1993 suggested that mutations in genes might explain violence in certain people. Many social scientists feel uncomfortable with such determinism.[3]

Fifth, the topic of death must give rise to an otherwise unpopular and unfashionable question about the responsibility of the victim in victimization. Of course, many victims are truly innocent of the circumstances leading to their demise; it is wrong to ever blame a child caught between warring gangs. But a very large number of those people meeting accidental, suicidal, and homicidal deaths are responsible in part for what happened. People can be pugnacious — turning an argument into a fight into a homicide — inattentive, or careless. A gang member killed in a shoot-out, unfortunate as it is, must take on some of the responsibility for his own death. Not all victims must be blamed for the plight in which they find themselves, but a significant number are responsible. That is not to say that investigators should pass judgement. But it is a necessary notion to keep in mind as an investigative strategy is formulated.

Death and Bodies

Before an in-depth discussion about the investigation of homicide and suicide is presented, some general words about the investigator's role in discovering bodies and the various types of wounds that might be found are in order. Refer to the chapter on Forensic Science for those aspects of dead bodies in terms of the pathologist.[4]

---

2. Cathy Spatz Widom, "The Cycle of Violence," *National Institute of Justice: Research in Brief* (October 1992).

3. *Chicago Tribune* (December 15, 16, 1993).

4. Dan Morse, Jack Duncan, and James Stoutmire, eds., *Handbook of Forensic Archaeology and Anthropology* (Published by the editors, 1983).

Discovery of Bodies

Bodies in the Outdoors

Frequently bodies from accidental, suicidal, and homicidal demise may rest in the outdoors. The most obvious detection of their location is smell; in time these bodies are capable of sending off a pungent odor. More likely, however, there is the gathering and compromising of the cadaver by animal life. Such activity may be seen in two ways. First, observation of focused animal activity might suggest where a body rests. Animal feeding is such that only parts of a body may be found. There are patterns or stages of animal feeding on a body.

Stage 1 — The face and arms are attacked initially
Stage 2 — Legs are eaten or removed
Stage 3 — Remaining flesh over the entire body is gone.
Stage 4 — All parts of the body have been attacked and bones are missing or widely scattered.

Second, insect infestation occurs early and thoroughly. Location of a body might be ascertained by observing insect activity. The first invader will be a blowfly that will be attracted to blood and decaying tissue. Blowflies prefer soft tissues such as the eyes, nose, and mouth, but they will cluster on exposed wounds as well. A female blowfly can lay up to three hundred eggs at a time, each turning to a maggot, then a pupa, then a fly that will feed off the corpse. Generally, maggots can destroy 60 percent of the corpse in a week. Maggots prefer darkness. Therefore, they will eat up to just below the surface of the skin. If the body is wrapped in a cloth or plastic, the maggots come closer to the skin surface. Flies will be followed by beetles and other bugs. Forensic entomologists studying the life cycles of bugs on bodies can determine the person's time of death with considerable accuracy. In fact, as more time passes since death the more likely determinations will be made by studying insect invasions and life cycles. Generally, forensic entomologist's can determine time of death accurately out to 15 to 20 days after its occurrence. Even after several months, death can be dated to within a week by these scientists.[5]

Buried Bodies

Although it is not absolutely necessary, any investigation of death is aided tremendously with the presence of a body. Of course, most often

---

5. *Chicago Tribune* (January 15, 1995).

the body is on the crime scene, the focus of the investigation. But frequently the first stages of any death investigation is the search and discovery of a body.

Some bodies that are lying out in the open can be discovered by disagreeable smells and strange animal activity. Smells emanating from a home or apartment alert neighbors to notify the police. Out in the countryside animal gathering and frequenting specific locations alert officials.

But sometimes bodies are buried and they pose a set of unique problems and procedures. Once again, such a problem might be best helped by the scientist, in this case the archaeologist. There are two phases in finding a buried body.

First, there is the issue of finding the burial location. *Discovery* may be aided if the following is kept in mind. Common search patterns as discussed in earlier chapters might be formed. Searchers should look for signs of *distress* in foliage and soils; the implication is that the dragging or carrying of a body and the digging up of the soil naturally disrupts and scars the landscape and point to the burial site. Furthermore, the discovery of *mounds* or *depressions* are suggestive. A mound indicates that a quantity of dirt was removed, that foreign volume was introduced, and that excess soil formed a hill on the site; this is a good sign of fresh graves. A depression indicates that the grave digger took the excess soil and removed or scattered it; and as the body decomposed there was an unnatural settling. This is an indicator for older graves. Once the general burial location has been ascertained, a *probing* might occur to narrow down the eventual dig. A probe is simply a long, sharp instrument that is forced into the ground to determine any texture differences. Undisturbed soil would maintain its toughness and resistance to puncture, while aerated soil, soil turned over by digging the grave, would allow greater ease to penetrate. Careful use of a probe—an ordinary one or one with vapor detecting capability—allows the investigators to outline the grave for the next step. A trial trench, a confined dig going down to initial contact with the cadaver, is the next likely step. Care should be taken to prevent destroying or disfiguring the cadaver further.

Next is the *exhumation* and recovery of the body from the grave.[6] Once the general location of the grave has been determined there are four zones or areas of investigative concern. First, there is the general area around the grave. Using the grave site itself a search pattern might be developed to discover evidence of the grave digger's entrance and exit from the area. Paths of entry would show the burden of transporting a large amount of

---

6. William M. Bass and Walter H, Birkby, "Exhumation: The Method Could Make the Difference," *FBI Law Enforcement Bulletin* vol. 47, no. 7 (1978).

dead weight. Avenues of exit, due to physical and emotional relief, might be rich with physical evidence. Second, as the official dig begins, the area from the surface to the point of first contact with the cadaver is important. A stratum search occurs. Layer upon layer is carefully removed. *Sieving*, an archaeological technique of putting all dirt from the grave dig through a fine sieve or mesh screen to discover small items would be useful at this stage. Third, the level of the cadaver itself is important. Care must be exercised at this stage because this is where one can expect the greatest amount of evidence to be found, and the decay of the body makes the body delicate and difficult to handle. Without emblaming a body in a grave, depending upon heat, humidity, and insects will be a skeleton in ten days. Fourth is the area immediately under the body. If the body has been in the grave for some time, the chances of valuable evidence, like a bullet, working its way through the remains and being deposited on the floor of the grave are increased.[7]

Taphonomy = the study of death assemblages by archaeologists and anthropologists.

Water Graves

Some bodies, due to accidental drowning, suicidal choice, or intentional dumping by a killer, may be found in watery locations. Several things must be kept in mind here. First, there are different types of watery locations each posing problems to the searcher. A pasture pond is relatively shallow, more susceptible to climatic changes, and free of predatory life. On the other hand, lakes are larger, deeper, and more difficult. Rivers have strong currents that might carry the body some distance. And oceans have vast tides and abundant predatory life to feast upon the cadaver. Second, climate will have an impact on the decomposition of the cadaver. Of course, coldness and warmth are related to the type of body of water. Clearly, a lake in the winter will impact differently than a river or ocean in the same season. Third, bodies have a particular reaction to a water grave. In the first stage the body will have some neutral buoyancy because of air in the lungs and clothing. A victim of a homicide may need to be weighted to get it to sink. Those who drown, however, will fill their lungs with water

---

7. William D. Haglund and Marcella H. Sorg, *Forensic Taphonomy: The Postmortem Fate of Human Remains* (Boca Raton, FL: CRC Press, 1996).

and sink more readily. During the second stage when a person drowns, the lungs, which are normally full of air, collapse and compress and the body sinks to the bottom. As any SCUBA diver knows, a body of water has atmospheric changes, called atmosphere, in increments of every additional 33 feet in depth. Such pressures will have an impact on a body in terms of collapsing remaining air pockets on or in the cadaver. As the tissue begins to decompose, however, it creates gases that fill those cavities and the body comes to the surface. In police language, they become "floaters." In very cold water this process of decomposition is slower. Conversely, in warm water it occurs more rapidly. A rule of thumb is that bodies in water decompose about four times faster than those on land. A body in warm water will most likely become a floater in about six days, whereas it will occur in about eighteen days in cold water. That is, of course, if the body has not become snagged and caught on an underwater obstruction.

The discovery and recovery of a body from a watery grave is difficult but might be expedited in the following ways. First, a rough estimated location of the body must be made. This estimate, based upon other investigative leads, may be broad or narrow, although, the narrower the estimate the better. Second, the conditions of the bottom of the body of water should be determined. Many locations, for navigational purposes, perhaps, have subsurface conditions mapped. If they are sufficiently detailed they would alert the searchers to valleys and snags that could hook a body and keep it submerged longer than normal. Third, to ascertain surface and subsurface currents, a trial sinking might be done. This would entail creating a weight similar to that of the missing person and casting it overboard from a boat. A rope connected to the weight would allow the investigator to conceptualize the rates of sinking and subsurface traveling possible for the cadaver. Fourth, various devices called grapples and draglines may be used in the vicinity to search the water. A boat traveling slowly would pass these grapples over the bottom of the water in hopes of hooking the cadaver or at least disrupting any features that might be clinging to the body. Fifth, as experienced in recovering downed airlines in oceans, sonar devices may be used to find wreckage and bodies. Sixth, if necessary, divers might go below the surface for an eye search of the area. Many bodies of water, however, are murky with limited possibilities for vision, but trained divers have remarkable records of recovering bodies submerged in watery graves. Divers might use a variety of search patterns similar to those used ashore. In addition, some dogs have been trained to pick up the scent of matter decaying in water and they may be used as well. A plume of scent from a decaying body rises in the water and is discernable to a dog up to one foot above the surface after which general atmospheric conditions dilutes it. A trained dog in a boat or swimming with a life preserver might pick up the scent and direct a recovery dive.

Some Typical Underwater Search Patterns

1. General surface control pattern in which a boat is trailed by two or more swimmers snorkeling on the surface who are watching and monitoring two or more underwater SCUBA searchers.

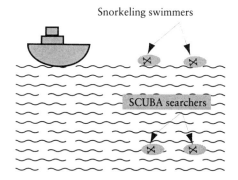

2. The "U" pattern is used once the search area has been determined.

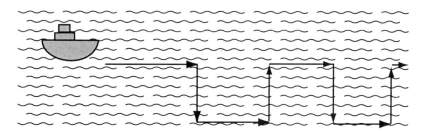

3. Tow Search

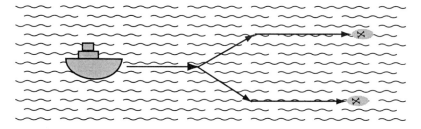

4. The "Circular Search" uses two divers in team. One holds a line while the other swims in a circular pattern around the stationary diver. After completing one circle, the searching diver extends the circular pattern.

5. The "Surface Control Pattern" uses a four-member dive team with two swimmers at surface control and two or more divers at the bottom.

River Dynamics For Dive Recovery

Velocity Differences in Curved Sections of Rivers

In curved sections of a river, water levels and speeds tilt toward the inside of the bend.

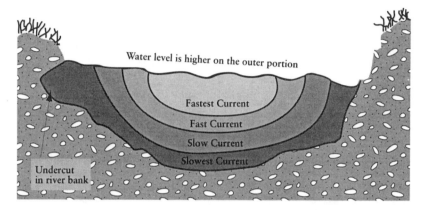

Surge and Hydraulics

Boulders and submerged obstacles can alter the flow, hang up bodies, and provide hazards to divers.

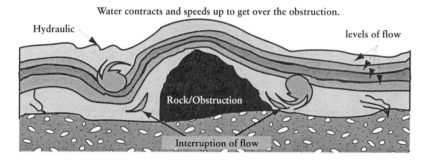

Eddy Obstruction

Boulders and other obstructions create eddies and laminar and helical flows that may hang up bodies and present hazards to divers.

Wounds on Bodies

Certainly, one of the most important activities is the discovery and study of wounds that might have caused the death. Of course, forensic scientists are the experts but the types and features of various wounds might have investigative value.

Firearms

Gunshot wounds are very common in America.[8] The killing rate—accidental, suicidal, or homicidal—with guns in America is one of the highest in the world. Their appearance will be dictated by whether they are an "entry" or an "exit" wound.

Generally *entry wounds* to the torso are deceptively clean. Of course, other factors will dictate the shape and damage of gunshot wounds. For example, the closeness of the gun to the victim may be classified into three categories:

1. *Contact wounds* are those that occur when a handgun is 0 to 3 inches away or 0 to 6 inches for rifles.
2. *Near discharge wounds* are those that occur when a handgun is 3 to 24 inches away or 6 to 24 inches for rifles.
3. *Distant charge wounds* are those that occur when a handgun or rifle is beyond 24 inches away.

At a point-blank firing the wound will take a star-like appearance as gases drive into and split the skin tissues. Tattooing, the burning around the wound, will be the next feature, and the degree of the abrasion collar varies as the gun was about three to six inches away. Smudging, the gray and grainy powdery soot and powder residues, will halo around the wound when the gun is fired from six to ten inches away. The closer the gun within this range, the more constricted the halo. If the gun is fired too close, the smudge will be consumed by the tattooing process. The greater the distance, the broader and thinner the smudge until aerodynamics take over and prevent its occurrence.

In slug entry wounds the blood and tissues, due to the elasticity of the skin, will be forced inward. Unless a major artery has been hit causing an "Old Faithful Geyser" effect, the amount of blood will be less than expected. If an artery is hit a spurt of blood reaching several feet is possible. The wound will often appear as clean and circular. However, many entry wounds will not be perpendicular. Those entering at an angle will leave a skid-like tattoo before final penetration occurs. The wound would have a

---

8. Vincent DiMaio, *Gunshot Wounds: Practical Aspects of Firearms, Ballistics and Forensic Techniques* (New York: Elsevier, 1985).

tear or comet-like appearance. Wounds from a shotgun will be similar except a spray pattern will exist. The closer the shotgun the more concentrated the spray; whereas the further the gun, the more dispersed the pattern. Generally, the pattern will be tight up to an 18 inch distance from a shotgun. The spray will be fully open if the gun is 30 inches or more away from the victim.

Of course, head wounds will be different due to the general brittle nature of the skull and the likelihood of large fracturing of bone. The investigator might expect a messier wound to the head. There are places for relatively clean wounds, however. The base of the skull at the rear and the temples would be cleaner. Many fastidious professional hit men are aware of this and pride themselves "on a clean delivery of services." They even use a smaller caliber gun, such as a .22 caliber, which enters cleanly and does not have the velocity to exit, so the slug bounces around inside the skull causing enormous damage but not exiting. They can have therefore a relatively clean but sure kill.

Exit wounds on the torso are much nastier than entry wounds. Not only the bullet, but bone and tissue will spill out causing larger exit holes than entry. The likelihood and amount of blood will be greater here, as well. Unless the shotgun was fired extremely close to the victim the possibility of exit wounds are slight. Of course, if there are shotgun exit wounds they will be very destructive and disfiguring. Exit wounds to the head by a slug will be very damaging as large pieces of bone will come out with the slug causing even greater destruction. Shot gun exit wounds to the head may be of a decapitating sort.

Of course, after entry the path of a bullet may take a meandering course depending upon the hitting and deflecting power of bone and tissue. Nonetheless, if a bullet does enter and exit, a crude trajectory might be established. It may be possible, for example, to determine if the shooter were high up and sniping downward or low down and shooting upward.

Knife

Knife wounds occur in two types. First, there are the *cut or slash* type of wound. Generally these are less lethal unless they cut into an artery. Cut or slash wounds as killing wounds suggest a more motivated and frenzied killer. Also, one might look to the wrists and forearms of the victim for "defensive wounds." These are slashes the victim might have received as he or she tried to fight off the assailant. The amount of defensive wounds, their extensiveness or absence, might help the investigator conceptualize the criminal encounter. Another kind of slashing wound that might be found on a victim's wrists are called "hesitation wounds." These are earlier cuts done by a person preparing for a suicide. They are little bites of

Hesitation wounds

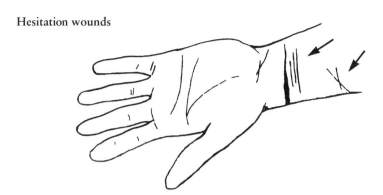

the blade to help the victim to take the final cut. Care must be taken to not confuse defensive and hesitation cuts.

Second, there are the *stab and puncture* wounds. These are more likely to be lethal because they penetrate more internal organs and arteries. These entry wounds will be a little cleaner than the slashes discussed earlier. If the wound follows the general "skin tension lines" it will be a small gash. On the arm, for example, the skin tension lines run from the shoulder to the hand. Any blade that enters in the same way will provide a clean-

Wounds Involving Sharp-Edged Instruments

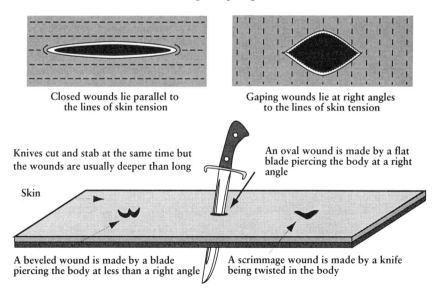

Closed wounds lie parallel to the lines of skin tension

Gaping wounds lie at right angles to the lines of skin tension

Knives cut and stab at the same time but the wounds are usually deeper than long

An oval wound is made by a flat blade piercing the body at a right angle

Skin

A beveled wound is made by a blade piercing the body at less than a right angle

A scrimmage wound is made by a knife being twisted in the body er cut. If the blade enters perpendicular to the these lines, the wound will be more beveled and gaping.

Blows

Blows from weapons come in three varieties. "Abrasions" are superficial scrapes and generally are not lethal. "Lacerations" cause tearing of tissue. "Contusions" cause breaking and hemorrhaging below the surface of the skin. Lethal wounds of this nature are particularly messy. Evidence of, or lack of, a dramatic struggle might guide the investigator.

Poisons

Poisons also provide some interesting wounds that might expedite the investigation. There are two possible sources of poisoned death. First, there are those connected to food poisoning. These are fairly easy to detect due to the diarrhea and fevered illness that accompanies food poisoning. Second, there are poisonings connected to chemical agents. As of 1978, according to the National Clearinghouse for Poison Control Center, over 12,000 people had died of poison, but of that number only 39 cases were documented homicides. There are two types of poisonous applications leading to death. The acute poisoning kills in one small dose. The accumulative poisoning is several small non-lethal doses that need to reach a certain point to cause death. The ingestion of a poison is very acidic to the system. Many victims will regurgitate some bile resulting in a burn or scorch around the mouth, on the chin, and in the throat. Furthermore, different poisons and lethal mixtures may color the vomit. There might be other telltale signs of poison. While arsenic itself is odorless there might be a slight garlic-like odor on the victim after ingestion. Cyanide has a slight bitter almond odor and tends to turn the blood and tissues of the victim cherry red. Strychnine poison is particularly violent causing the victim to go into prolonged and furious convulsions. The victim literally dies of muscular exhaustion and will likely be found in the convulsed position with an agonized grimace. Because of the muscular energy expended in the dying process, rigor mortis will set in faster than normal. Carbon monoxide poisoning may come from fires, automobile exhaust, and defective heaters. It is like cyanide and the victim will take on a cherry red complexion. Many heavy metal poisons—such as arsenic, mercury, lead and copper—can be found in the victim's remains years after ingestion.

Strangulation

Strangulation wounds are found around the throat and they take two forms. First, if the means of strangulation were an assailant's hands, considerable struggle probably occurred. This means that the assailant prob-

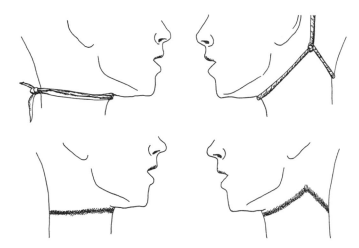

Strangulation marks vs. Hanging marks

ably used more force than necessary and there would be accompanying wounds, such as a fractured hyoid bone at the base of the tongue and severe deep bruises and contusions on the throat. If a chord or rope were used, the bruise on the neck would be a straight line. This is called a "ligature." An additional misshapen bruise would be at the point on the neck closest to where the killer cinched or knotted or exerted more leverage and pressure on the rope. Strangled by a hanging results in another type of wound ligature, a "V" shaped bruise generally just behind the ears. Often in these strangulation deaths petechiae, or the filigree red marks of ruptured capillaries on the cheeks and chin, might be found. In addition, bulging eyes, protruding tongue and elongated neck are wounds due to hanging.

Drowning

Drowning death is a form of suffocation. Water filled lungs would not necessarily be an important feature. Actually there are two possible drowning occurrences. A "wet drowning" accounts for 85 percent of drowning deaths; it is caused when large amounts of water fill the lungs. A "dry drowning" accounts for fewer than 15 percent of such deaths; it is the result of a sudden constriction and closure of the airways due to water in the throat. In these laryngospasms no water actually gets to the lungs. Dry drowning, therefore, can occur in very small amounts of water. In terms of wounds, an immersed body will take on a variety of features due to natural animal feeding, current travel and obstructions, and natural deterioration. The most indicative wound is the white foam that forms as a result of the mucous in the body mixing with the water giving a white, lathery appearance in the mouth and wind pipe. This exudate spills out of the mouth and nostrils of most drown victims. In one half to a full day the finger tips will begin to swell. Hand swelling will occur between three and five days of immersion followed by the separation of the epidermis. After a period of "washer woman skin" (a general wrinkling of the skin), a "gloving" will occur. Gloving is the shedding of the skin on the hands and feet. Finally, adipocere (saponification of the fat) will occur in two to three weeks.

Fire

Fire wounds are hard to detect particularly if the body has been consumed by the flames. It should be noted that bodies are rarely consumed. A very high temperature and long duration of flame is needed. For example, cremations use a fire of 1500°F for one and one half hours to render a body to ashes. However, in ordinary fires there are four phases. First, the body dries out. Humans consist of 70 percent water. Second, fatty tissue burns. Those areas, such as the torso, that have more fat will burn more quickly. Third, the body smolders. Fourth, the fire goes out. However, one characteristic wound is the "pugilistic position" assumed by most victims. They tend to draw up their muscles and look like a boxer in a self-protective position. If a person were dead before the conflagration, there would be the absence of smoke and soot in the lungs. While most people die of smoke inhalation some burn types are noted here:

1. First degree burns, the large engorgement of blood vessels causing redness.
2. Second degree burns, the blistering between two layers of the skin epidermis and dermis.
3. Third degree burns, death of the full thickness of the skin.
4. Charring stage, in which the body has come close to complete destruction. It is here that the pugilistic posture is most likely to appear.

Explosions

Explosions frequently are connected to many fires, and, depending upon the closeness of the person to the blast, they can cause many wounds:

1. Sever wounding with the body greatly dismembered. Recovery of these might help understand the type of explosion or bomb.
2. Intact body with missile and shrapnel punctures.
3. For the intact body there is likely to be burst eardrums for those alive at the time of explosion.

Suffocation

Suffocation resembles other types of death, such as certain poisons. Some might declare the cause of death to be a heart attack or stroke; however, small pin-mark or filigree ruptures, called petechiae, on the cheeks would suggest suffocation. In addition, there often is hemorrhaging in the eyes and under the tongue with suffocation.

Falls

Falls or leaps from high places produce terrible wounds. These wounds, however, might be shaped by the nature of the fall. For example, a "controlled fall" is one in which the person lands directly on their feet. The legs, pelvis, and back absorb the trauma, and, while significant internal injuries may occur to produce death, survival from very high fall up to 100 feet or more is possible. On the other hand, an "uncontrolled fall" is when a person lands on a part of the body other than the feet, such as the back, stomach, or head. These types of falls can be fatal from very short distances in the range of 10 to 15 feet. Of course, the wounds in an uncontrolled fall are more pronounced and noticeable.

Depending on the violent nature of the death a "cadaveric spasm" might be present. This death grip occurs if death happens in the midst of a struggle. The hand clings desperately to the last item, hair or fibers of an assailant or a gun in a suicide, preceding the demise.

Homicide

Introduction

Homicide is one of the ten leading causes of death in the United States. As stated earlier, not only are murder rates increasing or leveling off, but clearance rates have been declining. Great fanfare resulted when the homicide rate began to drop in 1996. This indicates an interesting social dynamic. In the past estranged friends and loved ones killed each other. In the last decade random/recreational and killings perpetrated by strangers have increased, frustrating the police. Many explanations are offered for the drop in homicide rates, none of them compelling. They include more aggressive policing, more people put in prison for minor offenses thereby stalling any more aggressive behavior, a demographic shift with fewer people in crime-prone age groups, to name a few.

The demographics are revealing. The age category for those most likely to be victims has been between 25 and 29. Recently, however, there is considerable evidence to suggest that these victims are becoming younger. The age category for those most likely to commit the homicide was between 18 and 24. So there was a turbulent decade or so between 18 and 29 in which a majority of homicides occurred. Since 1990, however, the general mean age has become younger.[9] More and more young killers are increasingly killing younger people. Of course, it is the poor, black male who dispro-portionately makes up the numbers in both categories. For example, stud-ies in 1985 showed that black men had a 1 in 21 lifetime chance of being mur-dered compared with a 1 in 131 lifetime chance for white men. The numbers for females are 1 in 369 for white females and a 1 in 104 for black females. Figures for black men have gotten even worse since 1990; black men have become an endangered species.[10] Many of these killers and their victims are unemployed or are gang members connected to the illicit drug industry.

Furthermore, there are some highly dangerous occupations. Taxi dri-vers in large cities top the list and have a 40 times greater chance of being a homicide victim than ordinary occupations. The second most danger-ous occupation is any in which the person is alone in a store or tavern and has the responsibility of handling large amounts of money. Third most dangerous is law enforcement.

Several explanations have been offered in an attempt to understand why some people resolve their real or imagined problems with violence. One collector of trivia estimates that in any given day an average person encoun-tering 1,000 persons will be in contact with one person who has killed. Such attempts may be called "violent person profiles." Some of these pro-filing efforts will be addressed shortly in the discussion of serial killers. One profiling attempt looked at behavioral patterns in the more immedi-ate history of the person. For example, the violent predator has:

1. Been imprisoned more than half the time in 2 years before the current arrest.
2. Had prior convictions.
3. Had a criminal conviction before the age of 16.
4. Used drugs in the immediate two years before the current arrest.
5. Been consistently unemployed for the two years prior to the cur-rent arrest.[11]

Other profiling explanations are more Freudian in their approach. For example, violent persons have:

1. Had poor identification with their fathers and a weak sense of their maleness.

---

9. *Newsweek* (December 2, 1985).
10. *Chicago Tribune* (May 6, 1985).
11. *Chicago Tribune* (October 6, 1982).

2. Been victims of abuse and violence themselves.
3. Experienced a sense of humiliation, of being powerless and with-drawn. They demand an expanded body buffer—that area around themselves in which unwanted intimacy makes them uncom-fortable—than most people.[12]

Another approach is that they fit into the "classic homicide triad." This triad of development and characteristics is that the person was a:

1. Late bed wetter as a child.
2. Torturer of animals and other small children.
3. Youthful fire setter, first with parents and neighbors property than moving on to school facilities.

Homicide Types

One way to study homicide is placing these events into one of three cate-gories such as:

1. Intimate events. For example:
   a) Domestic, planned, or spontaneous killings of family members.
   b) Conflict or dispute between friends or neighbors not related.
   c) Retaliation or revenge killing for a real or imagined past wrong.
   d) Power or the desire to obtain and retain power over an indi-vidual or a group.
   e) Mercy killing of a suffering loved one or acquaintance.
   f) Sadistic killing for the pleasure of inflicting pain, suffering, and death.
2. Group
   a) Cult killings connected to a zealous group.
   b) Terrorist killing to make a political statement.
   c) Frenzy of a group as in a lynching.
3. Criminal
   a) Contract killing by a professional hit man.
   b) Street gang killings.
   c) Organized crime killing to intimidate another group.
   d) Kidnaping and killing.
   e) Connected to another crime like a burglary or holdup.
   f) Product tampering or injecting deadly substances into legit-imate products.

---

12. Stephen G. Michaud, "The FBI's New Psyche Squad," *The New York Times Mag-azine* (October 26, 1986).

Of course, these lists are suggestive rather than comprehensive.

Homicide Motives

There are any number of reasons why some people kill. The following categories are meant to be suggestive. Generally speaking, the popular culture might think in terms of the five L's as motivation: love, lust, loathing, lunacy and lucre.

1. *Emotional or spontaneous killing* is perhaps one of the larger categories. An angry friend at a local tavern, an abused wife who cannot take any further physical and emotional trauma, or a jilted boyfriend who is blindly jealous are just a few examples. According to FBI statistics, in 1993, 1,530 women were killed by their husbands or companions. Frequently, because this murderer is still on the scene or is known to be closely connected to the victim, these homicides become a classic "walk-through." However, some of these, such as "hate crimes" or those driven by racial or homophobic desires, become more difficult. Another recent development in this category is related to workplace stress violence. The National Institute for Occupational Safety and Health estimates that an average of twenty workers are slain and 18,000 are assaulted each week in the United States. Another example of these types of killings is the classic "barroom brawl." Up until the 1960s and 1970s barrooms were a very common killing ground. Men drinking and conversing together frequently ended up in a fight resulting in a killing. A change in the economic and social nature of the saloon showed a decline in this type of violence in the 1980s and 1990s. There are less factories with hard working and hard drinking workers to frequent the bars. In addition, bars now became frequented more by women and middle class professionals. In 1994 there were 4.7 homicides per 100,000 adults 25 years or older, compared with 8.1 in 1981. Of course, this drop-off is being offset by increases by those under 25.[13]

On Friday, August 16, 1996, at San Diego State University, a thirty-six-year-old graduate engineering student, Frederick Martin Davidson, stepped into a testing room. He was to be confronted and defend his graduate thesis for the second time. Previously, his thesis had been rejected and he was reportedly depressed over his progress. The head of the thesis review panel, Cheng Liang, moved forward to greet Davidson. Without any hesitation Davidson went to a place in the room where he had earlier secreted a gun, then he

---

13. *New York Times* (August 19, 1996).

turned and shot Liang dead. Professors D. Preston Lowery III and Constantinos Lyrintzis were then murdered as well. A total of 23 shots were fired from the 9 mm Taurus handgun. The police found a dazed and bewildered Davidson wandering the halls and made the arrest.[14]

2. *Removal of an impediment* accounts for a large number of homicides, especially with the rise of drug gang related killings. The impediment might be a competitor in a business or a gang, or it could be a philandering mate who wants to marry someone else.

3. *Killing for a financial gain* is quite common. On one level, of course, there are professional hit men. Historically, these killers are a fairly recent occupational development in America, probably emerging with the establishment of Murder Inc. in the early 1930s. It is a well-developed profession today. Killing someone for their insurance falls into this category as well. So does killing someone during a holdup.

4. *Homicides for self-protection* are possibilities as well. The elimination of a witness to another crime falls into this category.

5. *Political killings* may be done by a lone individual with a particular gripe or psychosis. The assassins of Presidents Garfield, McKinley, and Kennedy were like that. Or political killings might be part of a conspiracy as that in the killing of President Lincoln. Generally in the latter cases, unless the perpetrators are particularly inept, are harder to find than the former.

6. *Motiveless murders*, those random and recreational types, are particularly difficult because of their inexplicable nature. In Illinois, for example, there were a series of Expressway shootings in which the killer or killers simply picked out a passing car and fired at it.

7. *Sexual murders*, largely connected to serial killers, have apparently increased in the last two decades. A more complete discussion of the serial killer is provided below.[15]

Coverup Strategies

Killers have several coverup strategies. Of course, the classic and most dependable coverup is anonymity; keeping one's identity and connection to the homicide a secret is the most desirable strategy. Second, there is the plausible alternative ploy; that the death was not a homicide but an acci-

---

14. *The San Diego Union Tribune* (August 17, 1996).
15. Lester Adelson, *The Pathology of Homicide* (Springfield, IL: Charles C. Thomas, 1974).

dent or even a suicide. Third, there is the justifiable or excusable killing; one acted in self-defense, for example. Fourth, there is the diversionary tactic; the killer calls in and reports the death in hopes that the police do not expect the murderer to do such a thing.

Multiple Killings

Definitions

One of the more perplexing and sensational types of homicide is multiple killings or the taking of two or more lives. Their occurrence automatically enhances the perpetrator's sentence in most jurisdictions.[16] Multiple killings may be classified into two large categories.

One type is the taking of many lives at *one event*. It might be a double homicide at a robbery. Or it could be a homicide-suicide. It might be a family affair with a husband going wild and killing a wife and several children. Or it might be a disgruntled employee, as in many incidents in the last several years of postal workers who come to the workplace and randomly kill numerous fellow workers.

Another type is the taking of several lives *over time*. Here there are two subtypes. For example, the spree killer will take several lives but there is little cool-off period and no evident psychological qualities that establish a pattern style killing. On the other hand, the serial killer not only kills many over time but demonstrates several distinguishing qualities that set this type apart from others.

Serial Killers

Serial killers are a particularly interesting group, not because of their number but because they have achieved a pop-culture status.[17] They will be discussed further because of the contributions of social science, particularly psychology, in establishing the principle of profiling.

There is disagreement over the number of kills that warrant the designation of serial killer. The Justice Department's FBI prefers the number being placed at six. Of course, that might be a self-serving bureaucratic

---

16. J. Levin and J.A. Fox, *Mass Murder: America's Growing Menace* (New York: Plenum, 1985).

17. Steven A. Egger, *Serial Murder: An Elusive Phenomenon* (Westport, CT: Praeger, 1990).

reason to avoid being inundated with large numbers of multiple killers. Such a designation would have left out the infamous Jack the Ripper as a serial killer. Scholars tend to make the designation at four.

There have been serial killers throughout history everywhere in the world. But it was not until the 1970s and 1980s that America apparently discovered the serial killer. Names like David Berkowitz, John Wayne Gacy, Ted Bundy, Wayne Williams, Henry Lee Lucas, and Jeffrey Dahmer became headlines. The FBI responded in the mid-1980s by creating the National Center for the Analysis of Violent Crime, or NCAVC. The Center is directed by the Behavioral Science Unit of the FBI Academy at Quantico, Virginia. It consolidated research and provided expertise to law enforcement agencies confronted with unusual, vicious, or repetitive violent crime. The NCAVC's Violent Criminal Apprehension Program, or VI-CAP, provides a national clearinghouse for unsolved violent crimes. It is also largely responsible for profiling serial killers.

Some Notable Serial Killers

1. John Wayne Gacy, executed in May 1994, was convicted in 1980 for killing 33 young boys from 1972 to 1978.

2. Patrick Wayne Kearney confessed in 1977 to killing 32 men. He was convicted of 21 murders and sentenced to life in prison.

3. Dean Corll, Elmer Wayne Henley, and David Owen Brooks killed 27 boys and young men in a torture-murder ring in Houston from 1969 to 1971. Henley fatally shot Corll in 1973. Henley and Brooks are serving life terms.

4. Juan Corona was found guilty of killing 25 farm workers whose bodies were found buried near Yuba City, California, in 1971. He is serving a life term.

5. Joel Rifkin, who admitted killing 17 women in the early 1990s is serving a life term.

6. Jeffery Dahmer confessed to killing and dismembering 17 persons from 1978 to 1991. He was murdered in prison as he was serving a life term.

7. William Bonin is serving a life term for the murder of 14 boys between 1979 and 1980.

8. Richard Ramirez was convicted in 1989 and sentenced to death in the California Night Stalker killings of 14 people in 1984 and 1985.

9. Albert DeSalvo confessed to being the Boston Strangler who had killed 13 persons in 1962 to 1964. He was murdered in prison while serving a life term.

10. Angelo Buono and Kenneth Bianchi, the Los Angeles Hillside Stranglers in 1977 and 1978, killed 10 people. Both are serving life terms.

11. David Berkowitz, known as the Son of Sam, killed five women and the male companion of one of them in New York City in 1976 and 1977. He is serving a life term.

12. "Zodiac" killer claimed in a series of letters to San Francisco newspapers and police to have killed 37 people in the 1970s but the case was never solved.

13. Theodore Bundy was convicted of three Florida slayings. Shortly before his execution in 1989 he confessed to 36 other murders.

14. Wayne Williams is serving two life sentences for his 1982 conviction in the slayings of two young black men in the Atlanta area. Police blamed him for the killings of 22 other young blacks, but he was never charged in those deaths. This case was the first utilizing profiling techniques developed by the FBI.

15. Green River Killer in the Seattle area murdered 49 persons from 1984 to 1988 and was never apprehended.

Although, in the world of homicide, serial killers play only a small role, they have become a national fascination. Knowledge of the extent of serial killers is scant, but is estimated that between 3,000 and 5,000 people a year are victims to a serial killer. In any given year there are probably 35 to 40 serial killers at work. Most of these are men, and there appears to be a sexual agenda connected to their killings. There is one exception, however, and that is Aileen Carol Wuornos, a Florida hitchhiker in the early 1990s, who killed at least 7 men after they stopped to offer her a ride. Some claim that she is the first documented female serial killer in the United States. Such a phenomenon as serial killers has excited Hollywood, and countless movies and books have come out with serial killing as theme. The FBI has helped with the centers and programs focusing on these murderers. In 1983, the Violent Criminal Apprehension Program was established. Then, in 1987, the National Center for the Analysis of Violent Crime was begun from which profiling procedures came.

Profiling is the establishing of a series of psychological and personality characteristics of a serial killer.[18] It is a general picture of expectation drawn from empirical studies of apprehended serial killers. It is based on the assumption that the crime scene reflects the personality of the offender.

---

18. Ronald M. Holmes, *Profiling Violent Crimes: An Investigative Tool* (Newbury Park, CA: Sage, 1989).

Furthermore, the offender will not or cannot change their personality. In addition, the killer's method of operation will remain the same.

Geographically, serial killers may be broken down in to three groups: about 60 percent of them are purely local in their predatory patterns, 35 percent may be considered more regional, and 5 percent are national. The implications are that a national or regional predator has a job that allows him to travel vast distances without being suspicious. The infamous "Red Ripper" in Russia, for example, is illustrative. Andrei Chikatilo during the 1980s traveled in his capacity as securer of goods for his Soviet factory to kill around fifty young women and boys. He was apprehended and executed in 1993. Some serial killers graduate from one group to another. For example, Ted Bundy went from local (northwest) to regional (Utah) to national (Florida) geography in his career development.

Analysis of Serial Killers

In the analysis of a serial killer, it might be helpful to divide the killing act in three ways: pre-event, event, post-event.

Pre-event analysis is concerned with the personality development of the killer. Most are white males, though Wayne Williams of Atlanta, whose case actually was one of the first in which profiling was successfully used, was an exception. Other personality characteristics seem to be present. First, many come from a broken home, are an only or oldest child, and are dominated by their mothers. Second, though they have average to above average intelligence, they are socially inept. Sixty percent have never been married. Friendship networks are scant and superficial. Third, they have an exaggerated fantasy life, increasingly fusing the real with the fantasy world. A part of this fantasy life is fed by an obsession with violent pornography. Fourth, they are part of the culture of violence, most likely being a victim of violence as a young person. Fifth, they have easy access to and affection for weapons. Sixth, the average age of serial killers is 30, but the "trigger year" seems to be 25. In other words, all the stuff percolating throughout youth and young adulthood comes to head in the mid-twenties.[19]

In addition, there seem to be one of four motives commonly used by serial killers. First, there is the "power killer" who gets gratification due to control. The "hedonistic killer" is one who gets pleasure due to the act of killing; this type is the ultimate power killer. The "visionary killer" hears voices encouraging him to do these deeds. Finally, the "mission killer" who feels he is doing society a favor by removing a particularly obnoxious element, such as prostitutes.

---

19. C. Wilson and D. Seaman, *The Serial Killers: A Study in the Psychology of Violence* (New York: Carol Publishing, 1990).

In addition, it must be assumed that a serial killer is always on the prowl. The time of prowling, however, might be suggestive. For example, the season of the year or time of day might suggest migratory or employment patterns. If possible the events surrounding the initial encounter might be helpful. For example, the brandishing of a weapon might occur to command compliance. Most serial killers are highly personal murderers, they like to strangle, suffocate, and knife their victims. In that sense a gun might be used only to force the encounter into a more isolated location. Many serial killers use ploys such as being in the need for help. Others might use their charm as when picking someone up at a bar.

Event analysis is more extensive. First, there is the *nature of the victim*. Serial killers might be known by their selection of low risk versus high risk victims. Generally there are two types of victims that are very low risk for the killer: prostitutes and hitchhikers. Both types have one thing in common — they are highly vulnerable. Particularly vulnerable is the prostitute, who has an occupation that is personally very risky even in the best of situations. Prostitutes establish very private and intimate relations with strangers. Such low risk victims for the killer might suggest a conservative, less desperate and immature killer. High risk victims might be children and other females known by casual contact. Ted Bundy in his final killings went to high risk victims when he killed some college students in Florida, which suggest his experience and confidence levels. Another way to look at this is in the use of weapons. In other words, the possession, display, and use of a gun or knife suggest a low risk endeavor. The killer's use of the hands to beat or strangle has a higher risk taking component.

Second, there are some *geographic considerations*. An investigator needs to study the "encounter sites," those places the killer finds his victims. One way to look at this is the "zone of comfort concept." This means those areas in which both the killer and victim have a high degree of comfort. The more comfortable the potential victims are the less alert and more vulnerable they become. For the killer it will be those places with which he is both most familiar and yet retains anonymity. This might be local areas within three to five miles from where the killer actually resides. Or it might be along avenues of familiarity such as routes taken to work. Serial killers, in a sense, are always on the prowl; and the more successful they are the more embolden they become to spread and broaden their selection of encounter sites. Conversely, the less successful they are the more likely they will return to areas of past success. But even the selection of an encounter site may be seen in terms of low risk versus high risk. Obviously, a "sin strip" where prostitutes frequent is low risk because men are always stopping to talk and proposition the women. Prostitutes always, for short periods of time, disappear from view. Others, such as the Red Ripper, who used bus stops and train terminals are a little more risky.

"Event sites" may be difficult to find because the killer may remove the body and deposit it some place else. Those event sites that have been discovered have allowed students of the problem to create two categories: organized and disorganized sites. Organized, or controlled, sites are neater and more orderly than disorganized sites; they suggest greater planning and less spontaneity. Probably, there was more conversation, even scripted ceremony, at this site. Restraints were used and any sexually aggressive acts occurred prior to the killing. Most likely the body was hidden or transported to another dump site. Disorganized sites are more randomly selected and are sloppy and disorderly in appearance. The act is more spontaneous with little conversation, and most aggressive sexual acts are done after death. The body is left at the site. This brings up another aspect of the event, that being the "ceremonial rituals" expected by the killer. Many of these killers want control, and they create fantasy scenes they expect to be played out by the victim. Consequently, the time element becomes important. The more scripted the event the more time the victim and the killer will spend together and the greater likelihood that physical evidence will be left behind. On the other hand, less ceremony means less time.

"Dump sites" are those places the victim has been placed after death. As suggested above, sometimes the body is left where the crime occurred, but often it is dumped some distance from the killing place. The dump site is important for the killer because it gets the investigation away from the event site, and it allows the killer to return to the killing area to vicariously relive the event. Determining dump sites is also important because if the killer always returns to the same general area it allows for surveillance stake-outs to be used. Another aspect of the dump site is its message value. For example, if the body is haphazardly left one message is given. But sometimes the body is placed in ways to shock the public and police who encounter it; that sends another message about the mind and motives of the killer.

"Activity sites" may be determined by connecting the event and the dump sites. The killer traveled from point A to point B, and there might be evidence and witnesses along that path. Once suspects have been determined, activity sites are working areas, living areas, transit areas, and recreation areas. In connection to this activity concept the determination of the time of activity may be important. For example, if most crimes occurred in the daytime this might mean the person was unemployed, worked a night shift, or had a job that allowed him to prowl. Night crimes suggest that the person had a conventional day job or was unemployed.

Other considerations about the event stage are the time spent with the victim. Some serial killers establish a relationship keeping the victim for prolonged periods. Others prefer a quick kill. Likely there will be considerable ritualization involved. Victims will be forced to play out a prearranged script. Victims may mistakenly believe that compliance might lead to mercy, but they are wrong. These scripts are part of the killer's gratification, and the ultimate and inescapable last act is death.

Souvenir collecting is another import aspect of this type of killer. A piece of clothing or part of the body will be taken to fondle and fantasize over later.

Many serial killers simply leave or dump the body. A few, however, display the body. There are several likely purposes for this. At the basic level there is the aesthetic value, the modeling of a murder victim extends the quest for power that drives so many of these killers. Then there is the shock value. Serial killers might feel more power knowing that the people discovering the body and then the police investigating the scene are shocked and shaken over the posed body.

Post-event behavior is also patterned. For example, most serial killers are obsessed with their crimes; they follow the news and keep clippings and diaries. Furthermore, they are souvenir collectors, and keep mementos of the crime. This ranges from an article of clothing to a piece of the anatomy to the entire body. Considerable fantasy and masturbation occurs over these relics. Very often the killer will return to the scene of the crime, either alone or with a loved one, to have a vicarious thrill. Finally, the more egotistical killers will play a "cat-and-mouse" game with the police by taunting them for their inability to make a capture. This was done by the "Zodiac" killer in San Francisco in the mid-1970s.

While their numbers might not seem to justify such concerns, serial killers remain a fascination to the public and a perplexing problem to the police.[20]

Serial Killers and the Organized Personality

As children and adolescents

1. School problems—including lots of truancy and suspensions, and violation of rules. Low grades contrary to apparent intelligence.
2. Delinquency shown by running away
3. Persistent lying and fabrication of fanciful stories
4. Early and repeated sex in casual relations
5. Substance abuse
6. Vandalism and theft

Eighteen and young adulthood

1. Inability to sustain work
2. Inability to sustain relationships

---

20. D.K. Rossmo, "A Methodological Model," *American Journal of Criminal Justice* vol. 17 (1993).

3. Irritable and aggressive
4. Failure to honor financial obligations
5. Impulsive
6. Chronic lying
7. Reckless

Personality

1. Lack of remorse or any sense of guilt
2. Quest for immediate satisfaction, little self- restraint
3. Inability to learn discipline from punishment
4. Lack of fear
5. Excessive rationalization and a tendency to blame others
6. Copes with stress by abuse
7. Braggart
8. Likes to be noticed. May have tattoos
9. Weak mate—girlfriend or wife
10. Likes weapons
11. Average or above average IQ
12. Can "pass" polygraph
13. Constant need for excitement
14. Manipulates people
15. Fits well into society
16. Is a CHAMELEON
    C = cunning
    H = habitual criminal
    A = actor
    M = macho
    E = egotistical
    L = low key appearance
    E = experimenter
    O = operator, a wheeler-dealer
    N = no guilt

As a killer

1. Selects intraracial victims and victims close to own age group.
2. Manipulates victim, will have victim remove clothing.
3. Cruises to select victim, travels with ease and frequency.
4. Plans out the crime.
5. Works in a skilled job.
6. Kills and moves the body.
7. Uses a weapon.
8. Collects trophies, personal clothing from the victim or a piece of the victim.
9. Disfigures cadaver, to shock, hinder identification, or hinder the investigation.

10. Mutilates or displays female genitalia to humiliate victim and shock society.
11. Returns to event site.

Serial Killers and the Disorganized Personality

Childhood and adolescence

1. Low birth order status, youngest of a large family.
2. Father's work unstable.
3. Harsh discipline as a child.
4. Childhood bed wetting extended longer than average
5. Cruelty to animals.
6. Childhood fire setting.

Eighteen and young adulthood.

1. A loner, becoming secluded and isolated.
2. An underachiever with a poor self-image.
3. Poor personal hygiene habits; clothes and body are dirty and messy.
4. Few acquaintances he has consider him odd.
5. Is a nocturnal person.
6. Has no close friends.
7. Internalizes hurt and humiliation.
8. Lives alone or with a significantly older female relative.
9. Minimal use of alcohol.
10. Minimal interest in the news media.
11. Likely to be thin with some physical malady that contributes to an unattractive appearance.
12. High school drop-out with a below average IQ.
13. Lower to lower middle class economic position.
14. Unskilled job or unemployed.
15. No military service or discharged as unsuitable.
16. History of voyeurism, fetish thefts, exhibitionism.
17. Some history of mental illness.
18. Social aversion, rejects society.

As a killer

1. A blitz killer—surprise attack, renders victim unconscious or dead quickly.
2. Weapons will be those handy.
3. Body generally left at the scene of the assault.
4. There may depersonalization of the victim with much disfigurement of the face.
5. Crime scene will be sloppy and random.

6. Postmortem bite marks to breast, buttocks, neck, thighs, and abdomen are likely to be present.
7. Postmortem dissection of body. Possible evidence of anthropophagy, the consumption of the victim's flesh and blood.
8. Postmortem sexual activity may be present. Generally this killer will use foreign objects rather than the penis.
9. No effort to hide the body.
10. The body may be positioned is some sort of symbolic way.
11. Might be evidence of ritualism.
12. Very likely to take some souvenirs, particularly parts of the body.[21]

Suicide

Introduction

Another death situation with which police investigators might encounter is suicide, or the taking of ones own life. Along with accidental, natural, and homicidal death, suicide must be dealt with in establishing corpus delicti. Suicide has had a curious place in the justice and the religious systems of the United States. For years the taking of ones life, or "the rushing into God's presence uninvited," was against the law. Religious leaders saw it as a prohibition to the entrance to heaven. Of course, it was impossible to punish a successful suicide so the attempt of the act rather than the act itself was stigmatized. Now, of course, the issue largely revolves around assisted suicides by friends, loved ones, "angels of mercy," and well-meaning doctors.[22]

Some disturbing developments in suicide have occurred lately and make the investigation even more problematic. One has to do with the age factor. For years suicide was seen to be a middle-age male problem. But two new age cohorts have come into the picture. The number of elderly persons taking their own lives has increased rapidly in the last thirty years. The national suicide rate is 12.8 per 100,000; the elderly suicide rate, however, is 20 per 100,000. Elderly white males living by themselves have the highest likelihood for suicide. The reasons for this are connected to larger social issues to be sure. For example, loneliness, financial problems, bad health, and fear of moving into a rest home were the common reasons determined.

---

21. See a series of articles published by the Federal Bureau of Investigation in the *FBI Law Enforcement Bulletin* (August 1985).

22. *Newsweek* (April 18, 1994).

The other growing group are the young. Numbers of stressed and distressed young people commit suicide every year. In 1992, the most recent year for which figures are available, 1,847 teens killed themselves for a rate of 10.8 per every 100,000 teens. Disturbingly, many of these young people seem quite normal, even "All-American" types. In 1995, Scott Croteau, age 17, committed double suicide; he hung himself and then, in the process, shot himself in the head. He had been a star athlete and scholar at his Lewiston, Maine high school.

What are some of the causes of these teen suicides? First, there are natural changes, tensions, and depressions that are part of puberty. Certain biochemical changes occur that make young people more vulnerable at this time. But two factors stand out as causes of suicide among teens. They are: the presence of long-standing disturbing family issues, and a long-time hidden depression. In addition, there appears to be a "copy-cat" factor as one suicide sets off several more. Sometimes in a frenzied friendship pattern, two teenagers will make and consummate a suicide pact. Another concept that needs to be considered is the "pseudo-suicide." Many suicide attempts are not meant to be successful. Some people, and young people are important here, are calling out for notice and attention. One way to get that notice is a failed suicide attempt. Unfortunately, sometimes the pseudo-suicide, inadvertently, becomes successful and ends in a death. There are some indicators that a young person contemplated suicide over time. They are useful for the investigator to know so as to conceptualize the case. Some are changes in eating and sleeping patterns, withdrawal from friends and family, rebellious or violent behavior, or sometimes there will be a reoccurrence of running away. There might be disregard for personal hygiene, frequent headaches, fatigue and boredom. Toward the time of the suicide act, the young person might start giving away favorite personal possessions.

Motives for Suicide

For most people death is a fearsome thing to be avoided. Consequently, the desire to take ones own life seems to be a puzzle for most.[23] Some suicides explain their reasons, and make the investigation easier by leaving notes. However, many do not. Perhaps Sigmund Freud had it right when he said that anger turned towards others is aggression, anger turned against the self is depression.

There are a variety of reasons for suicides to leave or chose not to leave a suicide note. For example, for those who do leave notes there is a desire

---

23. David Lester, *Why People Kill Themselves* (Springfield, IL: Charles C. Thomas, 1972).

to explain themselves and their action to loved ones. In addition, there is a desire to put things in order by imparting last minute practical information, such as where important documents are stored. There might be a desire to take off or place blame for the act as well. But most suicides — those more resolved, perhaps — do not leave notes, and it becomes important for investigators to determine that it is indeed a suicide and to try to understand the reasons why the person took his or her own life.

So it might be useful for the investigation of this type of death to ascertain any particular motives for a suicide. One way to do this is to consider the concept of Life Crisis Units. This notion was set forth by Dr. Thomas H. Holmes, a psychiatrist at the University of Washington in Seattle, who has drawn up an illness predictor scale. The theory behind this analysis is that certain stressors have profound impacts upon humans and if they are present in certain quantity the person will be more susceptible to disease, accident, and thoughts of suicide. Forty-three emotional crisis, or Life Crisis Units(LCUs), are ranked in order of severity. Of those people with over 300 LCUs for the previous year, almost 80 percent get sick in the near future: with 150 to 299 LCUs, about 50 percent get sick in the near future; and with less than 150 LCUs, only about 30 percent do so.[24] The top ten stressors are:

Rank	LCU value	Event
1.	100	Death of a spouse
2.	73	Divorce
3.	65	Marital separation
4.	63	Jail term
5.	63	Death of a close family member
6.	53	Personal injury or illness
7.	50	Marriage
8.	47	Fired at work
9.	45	Marital reconciliation
10.	45	Retirement

Methods for Suicide

One way to understand the death scene and determine it as a suicide is to think in quantitative terms. Below are listed common suicide methods based on their occurrence:

---

24. *Chicago Tribune* (November 6, 1996).

1. Firearms
2. Drugs and chemicals
3. Hanging
4. Carbon monoxide
5. Jumping
6. Cutting/stabbing
7. Drowning
8. Poisons

Such a list, however, is deceptive because of the accidental and homicidal possibilities. Consequently, a new priority list might be constructed, and degrees of investigative certainty be established, based upon factoring in those variables. A new ranking might be:

1. Hanging
2. Jumps
3. Carbon monoxide
4. Poisons
5. Cutting/stabbing
6. Firearms
7. Drugs and chemicals
8. Drowning

Such a ranking may be explained in the following manner. While, in terms of quantity, hangings do not seem to be large in number they do take a certain style that is informative. Most suicides hang themselves in a slumping way, that is the victim ties something around the throat and slouches down decreasing the flow of oxygen until conscience is lost leading to greater relaxation and weight exerted on the hanging device. In addition, there might be some disruptive furniture, such as a chair that has been kicked over, that suggests the person suspended themselves. There are some accidental hangings, such as sexual asphyxiation (a masturbation practice in which a person ties a restraint around the neck to enhance the ejaculation pleasure), but they are rare enough to warrant the investigator a high degree of certainty of this not being a suicide situation. Homicidal hangings are rare.

Intentional jumps are generally so theatrical that there is little doubt with a suicidal leap. Whereas accidental fall, such as at work or during recreation, are witnessed by co-workers and friends. While certainly present, and a possibility, homicidal falls are rare enough to not warrant too much concern. Also, intentional jumps are likely to be of a controlled variety as discussed earlier.

Accidental carbon monoxide poisoning certainly can occur but suicides do take precautions by plugging up air vents and doorways so the event is easily conceptualized.

There have been a large number of accidental poisonings due to poorly obtained or prepared foods. Unlike other countries, such as England, the United States has never been too homicidal with poisons.

Hesitation wounds would be a giveaway when it comes to suicides with the knife. These must not be confused with defensive wounds obtained by fighting off an attacker. Generally hesitation wounds are not as deep and dramatic as defensive ones. In addition, suicides are not likely to make a self-inflicted wound through their clothes while a knife homicide would do so.

Certainly guns are the most frequently used suicide weapon, but the number of accidental and homicidal gunshot deaths is so great as to arouse suspicion. Several indicators are helpful. First, the placement of the wound; very few suicides aim for the body. It should be noted, however, that women who use guns for suicide tend to shy away from disfiguring wounds and might go for a body shot. Second, the distance of the gun; contact or near contact wounds suggest suicide while distance shots do not. Third, the number of shots; suicides and accidental deaths rarely have multiple wounds while homicide victims do. Fourth, the angle of the shot. Fifth, the handy presence of the firearm and residues on the hands of the cadaver.

The large number of accidental overdoses—from Marilyn Monroe to John Belushi to River Phoenix, to name a few celebrities—of drugs is such to overshadow or weaken this as a conceptualization device of certainty in suicide.

While homicidal drowning is rare so are suicidal ones. On the other hand, the number of accidental drownings is large. In terms of bathtub drowning it is almost axiomatic, for vanity's sake, perhaps, that a suicide will do so fully or partially clothed. While an accidental (or disguised homicide) will present a nude body.

Conclusions

Of course, there are other forms of death that might meet the criminal investigator. Child killing has increased at alarming rates. The 1995 Report by the U.S. Advisory Board on Child Abuse and Neglect claims that about five children are killed a day by parents or caretakers. About 30 percent of abuses end in fatalities. Others estimate that nearly 5,000 children are killed each year. These killings almost always cause a local, if not national, sensation.

It appears that the most vulnerable are those under four years of age. Frequently, these killings are the product of months or years of abuse. Forty-six percent of abuse cases that lead to death are connected with neglect; children are locked away and left alone, and not fed or cared for. Forty-two percent of deaths have resulted from beating or dramatic shaking and burning. A common thread throughout these abuses is that the killer is young, poor, and addicted to drugs. A common catalyst here appears to be the inability to tolerate excessive crying, the child's refusal to eat, or excessive soiling of diapers. A trail of visits to local hospitals and trauma units likely has been laid. Wounds of another nature might be present. For example, there might be burn or whipping wounds. Healed broken bones might be revealed by X-ray.

Frequently, these characteristics are present in the investigation of child abuse turned to homicide. The act has been done by an unconnected significant other such as a single mother's boyfriend. There is a cycle of violence present with the abusive parent having been a victim of child abuse when young. The female tends to protect and rationalize the abuser. And there has been an ongoing coverup of abusive activities. Consequently, canvassing of neighbors who might have heard or seen examples of abuse becomes important. School officials might have seen physical and emotional signs of abuse. Finally, local hospital personnel might be aware of suspicious wounds on children who have been brought in for care.

Hit-and-run automobile killings are frequent. Either for felonious reasons, such as the driver was a fleeing felon or driving a stolen car or wanted to use the car as a weapon, or for mischievous ones, operating a vehicle without proper papers or being drunk, hit-and-run is an investigative problem of increasing importance.

Although this chapter is not comprehensive, it did set out to discuss the two most important causes of death investigation: homicide and suicide. From the standpoint of society in general, and criminal justice in particular, unnatural death always takes preference over other aspects of societal misdoings. Another very important one has to do with criminal sexual behavior.

Chapter 11

Sexual Offenses

Introduction

Definitions

Sexual offenses consist of a wide range of criminal activity in which sexual appetites and perversities are prevalent. In addition, sexual offenses may be a series of violent acts in which sexuality—either with the weapons used or the objects at which the aggression is aimed—is a component. Sexual crimes may derive from normal sexual drives and curiosities manifested in abnormal ways. Sexual criminals take highly personable, private, and loving human activities and distort them with what prevailing culture determines as criminally bizarre.

This wide range may be seen by trying to categorize them and suggest their place and impact in the criminal justice system.

Mutual Consenting activities are those done by agreement of the parties directly involved but are deemed inappropriate by larger society. They are interesting because they show a wide range but also how public attitudes and police procedures change over time. Some examples are:

1. *Fornication* or sexual relations out of wedlock by unmarried persons. In a more Biblical or Puritanical society this was viewed as a sin/crime with the sanction of expulsion or some sort of stigmata.
2. *Adultery*, or sex outside of wedlock by married persons. Even more than fornication, this act was seen as an insult to God, community, and family, and was often punished by death.
3. *Homosexuality* or sexual relations between members of the same sex. The more Biblical-oriented saw this as a perversion, likely a cause for the fall of Sodom, Gomorrah and Babylon. Beginning in the 1960s a Gay Rights movement took off some of the stigma as gay and lesbian lifestyles were largely legalized.
4. *Statutory rape* is the carnal knowledge of a consenting female who has been designed as a victim because she falls under a certain age category. This takes on particular importance if one remembers that so many single parent welfare mothers are very young girls who are pregnant due to the actions of an older boy. In Illinois, for example, if a girl is under 17 and has consented to

sex with someone who is at least five years older, it is considered statutory rape.

5. Of sex activities of mutual consent, *prostitution* remains criminalized. Many but the more fundamentalist Christians acknowledge that prostitution cannot be completely ended. It frequently, incorrectly, is given the sobriquet "the oldest profession" linking it to antiquity. Nonetheless, prostitution remains a crime in the legal codes, forcing the police to enforce the unenforceable.

Prostitution takes on many forms that illustrate law enforcement and investigative patterns. Perhaps at the top of the vocation is the *call girl* operation. These prostitutes develop and keep a book of steady customers generally adding to it by personal referral. Frequently, there is a madam or facilitator, but generally these young women are individual entrepreneurs who gain business by personal beauty and sexual skill. They charge large amounts of money and, unless there is some other crime, these prostitutes are left alone. A less prestigious type of call girl might belong to an *escort service*. A glance at the yellow pages of any large city's telephone directory will show the pervasiveness of this business activity. While a few are legitimate services for providing escorts, the vast majority are solicitations for prostitution. Further down the status order, and further up the enforcement priority, are massage parlors, dance halls, hotel lobbies, and strip joints. The latter have become so notorious that a counter-entertainment called "gentleman's clubs" have arisen to promise nude dancing with guarantees of no prostitution.

At the bottom of the occupational ladder is the *street walker*. This prostitute solicits on the streets and is seen as a public health menace who not only disrupts the public sphere of society but is the cause of much petty crime. Any police crusades against prostitution center here. In America's gender confusion over these crimes, it is the female prostitute rather than the male customer who is generally persecuted and prosecuted.

Nuisance sexual behaviors have a wide range of activity as well as moving up the ladder of seriousness. Some are:

1. *Transvestism*, or sexual excitement by dressing as the opposite sex.
2. *Zoophilia*, the use of animals for sexual arousal.
3. *Mysophilia*, the sexual arousal by filth.
4. *Urophilia*, excitement given by the presence of urine.
5. *Coprophilia*, pleasure gained from the presence of feces.
6. *Fetishism*, the use of nonliving objects for sexual arousal. Favorite objects, to name a few, might be high heels, boots, whips, leather clothing, corsets, uniforms and women's undergarments. Fantasies of "bad-boy" scenarios and desires for female domination and bondage are common as well.

7. *Necrophilia*, sexual pleasure from once living but now dead humans.
8. *Masochism*, or pleasure from being humiliated, bound, or beaten.
9. *Sadism*, pleasure obtained from inflicting pain.
10. *Frotteurism*, or the getting of sexual pleasure from touching or rubbing against a non-consenting person generally in a crowded public place.
11. *Cannibalism*, or the need to eat parts of human flesh to achieve sexual pleasure.
12. *Exhibitionism*, or displaying oneself to get pleasure.
13. *Voyeurism*, watching others in the act of sex or nudity. A "peeping Tom" would fall into this category. This would also include listening to sexually arousing conversation, such as the proliferation of "phone sex" in every major city.
14. *Scoptophilia*, sexual enjoyment from obscene phone calls.

Serious sex offenses are threefold and will constitute the remaining part of this chapter. They are: forcible rape, child molestation, and incest.

Rape and Sexual Assault

General

Forcible rape, or carnal knowledge of a woman against her will, is an important crime because it raises several issues. First, it is a fearsome assault in which the likelihood of permanent physical, emotional, and psychological damage is present. Second, it places the act of sex in the larger context of power motivation. In fact, recent reforms of rape law have used such terminology as sexual assault or sexual battery to show this interpretation. Third, it places traditional police procedures and assumptions on trial. For example, the practice of determining that an actual crime has been committed, a practice done at all crime scenes, has been interpreted as "blaming the victim" or questioning the integrity of the victim. Finally, this crime has shown the impact of the feminist movement since the 1960s. There has been a rearranging of the stigma off of the victim and on to the system. This can best be seen in history and the reforms of rape law.

History and the Law

The history of rape goes far back into the Judeo-Christian era. Genesis 39:7–20 recounts the story of Joseph in Egypt being falsely accused of rape by a high official's wife. The phrase "Potiphar's Wife" was used to characterize the vindictive woman who wrongly accuses a man. In Deuteron-omy 22:23–29 the law of Moses set forth more clearly the nature of rape. For example, if a man raped a betrothed woman in the field far out of hearing distance for rescue the penalty would be death. If she were not promised to another, the rapist would have to marry the female and pay a fine to the father. Clearly, the father rather than the female was seen as the main victim in this early law. If the rape occurred in the city within hearing of rescue and the woman did not cry out, then both would be put to death. Much the same kind of law might be seen in the Code of Ham-murabi, the oldest existing written law at 17th century B.C.

Similar traditions might be seen in the early Anglo-Saxon laws of the late tenth and early eleventh centuries A.D. Precise fines were calculated based upon virginity and class standing. Apparently, unwarranted sex was the damaging of goods and fathers were seen as the main victims. Common law definitions developed over the next several centuries to identify rape as "carnal knowledge of a female against her will." Some sort of proof had to be evident to show that resistance was present, frequently this meant that physical wounds needed to be present. Furthermore, as Lord Matthew Hale articulated in his *History of the Pleas of the Crown* (1736), "The husband cannot be guilty of a rape committed by himself upon his lawful wife, for by their mutual matrimonial consent and contract the wife hath given her-self in this kind unto her husband, which she cannot retract."[1]

Much of this law and tradition carried over into colonial America. Case law soon added to the common law assumptions coming to the new nation. For example, a minister in New York was acquitted of a rape in 1838 claiming that the woman had a bad reputation. The courts felt that in order for the woman to be believed she had to meet three conditions: (1) she must be of good reputation; (2) there must be evidence of physical resistance; and (3) attempts at calling out for help must have been demon-strated. An unmarried sexually active woman was already on the road to prostitution and was not to be trusted when claiming a sexual violation (*People v. Abbott*). Fifteen years later the New York courts further defined resistance to be that of using all of her physical abilities (*People v. Morri-son*, 1854). In 1874, the courts declared that the woman had to resist to the point of being overpowered. The cessation of resistance at any point of the attack was seen as consent.[2]

Much of the same attitudes existed until the 1960s and 1970s when the impact of the feminist movement was felt. It was clear that over the histo-ry of rape legislation, case law and attitudes that the victim, not the defen-

---

1. Quoted in Rob Hill, *Rape in America: A Reference Handbook* (Santa Barbara, CA: ABC-CLIO, 1995), p. 47.
2. Ibid., p. 48.

dant, was the one on trial. Criticism mounted as numerous police departments simply "unfounded" many rape cases. Embarrassed over the criminal act, intimidated by the legal requirements of proof, and fearful of the police investigation of the incident, many victims simply failed to report the incident. In 1972, in an attempt to counter these historic trends and prejudices, the Bay Area Women Against Rape opened a rape crisis center in Berkeley, California. Within eight years there would be over 400 centers across the country. But the most important development was in legal reform.

Four areas were of concern in the reform of rape law. First, there was the redefining of rape and replacing it with a series of offenses based upon the presence or absence of aggravating conditions. Historically the essential elements of traditional rape laws called for (1) force, (2) absence of consent, and (3) vaginal penetration. They made no allowance for male victims, acts other than sexual intercourse, sexual assaults with an object, or sexual assaults by a spouse. Many states passed gender-neutral laws even substituting sexual assault, sexual battery, or criminal sexual conduct for the term rape. Other sex acts such as fondling, cunnilingus, fellatio, and anal intercourse were included. Emission of semen was no longer a requirement. These new crimes were determined by the seriousness of the offense (whether there was penetration or other sexual contact), the amount of coercion involved, the degree of injury to the victim, and the age and incapacitation of the victim.

Second, there was a desire to change the consent standard by eliminating the necessity of a victim physically resisting the attack. Under the common law the victim had to demonstrate physical resistance to the utmost. Such a requirement was contrary to common sense that suggested that the greater the resistance the more likely injury to the victim would occur. Some states, like Pennsylvania, simply removed the resistance requirement altogether. Others, like Illinois, tried to define consent more clearly by saying it was "a freely given agreement to the act of sexual penetration or sexual conduct in question." Still others tried to define more clearly what constituted resistance.

Third, there was a desire to remove the requirement that the victim's testimony needed to be corroborated. Historically this was essential, it was thought, to protect males from false accusations. It was believed that such accusations were very difficult to disprove so the burden was placed upon the victim. Critics attacked it as sexually discriminatory "protecting the male defendant against the mere word of a female." A number of states eliminated corroboration requirements and by the 1990s only six maintained them.

Fourth, was related to admitting evidence about the victim's past sexual conduct. Under the common law the sexual history of the victim was allowed to undermine her credibility. Prior sexual activity was seen as a sign of her character; presumably unchaste women might lie about rape. This was called the "loose woman" defense. Reformers criticized this practice as placing the blame upon the victim, that past sexual activities had no relevance on present circumstances. Throughout the 1970s and 1980s a series of "rape shield laws" were enacted in most states. By 1985 the federal government had such a law. These laws were designed to keep out of court any evidence of a victim's past sexual history. Of all the rape law reforms, these shield laws have been the most controversial. Some feel that they infringed on the rights of defendants to confront hostile witnesses. Many states, trying to maintain a balance of the rights of the victim and the accused, wrote some exceptions into their shield laws to give the court some flexibility to admit evidence of prior sexual conduct when it was directly relevant. For example, a history of prior consensual sexual activity between the victim and accused is generally admitted.

Another area of concern in the history of rape was spousal attack. Under the common law husbands could not rape their wives. National attention was focused on this issue in 1978 with *State v. Rideout*. This was the first test of Oregon's revised rape law, which eliminated the exclusion of husbands from the charge of rape. John Rideout was acquitted and temporarily reunited with his wife, but the nation-wide attention was great and the notion that husbands could be prosecuted for raping their wives was firmly established in the law by 1993.

Finally, date rape particularly on college campuses became an issue. As early as 1987 California representative Tom Hyden got the legislature to be the first to address sexual assault on college campuses. That same year North Dakota became the first state to pass a date rape law. Two years later Wisconsin required the university system to include information on sexual assault and harassment in student orientation programs. In 1990 the Student Right To Know and Campus Security Act made this nation-wide. The Campus Sexual Assault Victim's Bill of 1991 further required colleges to develop and publicize their sexual assault policies.

These changes in the law have not had the desired effect. One study of the legal reform found that the system had prejudices against women who did not rigorously resist attacks. Many still believed that prior sexual conduct was important in their determinations. The new laws did not produce an increase in reporting of the crime nor conviction of those accused.[3]

The intellectual community has not come to an agreement of why this crime occurs. Frequently, it becomes involved with the various ideological agendas that are current. Three theoretical constructs might be mentioned.

Feminist theory places rape in the context of male dominance and exploitation. Pornography and prostitution are reflective of this tendency to see women in degrading ways condoning their subjugation in aggres-

---

3. Cassia Spohn and Julie Horney, *Rape Law Reform: A Grassroots Revolution and Its Impact* (New York: Plenum Press, 1992), pp. 159–175.

sive ways. Rape is a tool of domination and is reflective of sexual dispar-
ities. For example, women of lower socioeconomic standing are raped by
men of even lower status. Even in spousal rape, the husband is likely to
be threatened by the growing economic and social status of the wife. Gains
in social and economic equality of females increases the number of rapes
by those males left behind, it is believed by this perspective.

Social learning theory suggests that repeated exposure to the act of rape
promotes positive feelings towards it. Such aggressive behavior is learned
from three sources:

1. Family members and peers,
2. One's culture or subculture that condone it,
3. Mass media, particularly television.

The media has particular impact by providing models to imitate, equat-
ing violence with sex, perpetuating myths such as "no really means yes,"
and desensitizing the viewer to the pain and humiliation of sexual aggression. In some ways this perspective is similar to the feminist theory. It dif-
fers, however, by looking at cultural rather than socioeconomic factors.

Evolution theory suggests that rape is part of human biological development in which different reproductive tendencies arose over time separating males and females. Females gestate on a limited basis and then
become preoccupied with nurturing and protecting the species. The record
of the largest number of offspring for a single female is 69. Females become
conservative in their sexuality in the name of conserving and preserving
the species. Males seek to spread their sperm and fecundity. Since they
take a smaller part in the postbirth period, they have a vested interest in
finding their evolutionary place in having multiple sex partners. The record
number of offspring for a single male is 888. Males become liberal and
risque in the name of spreading and preserving the species. As the female
turns from reproduction to caregiving the male still makes reproductive
demands which might take the dimensions of rape.[4]

Problem

No matter what you call it, rape remains a major problem in modern-
day America. In 1990 a Senate investigation into the problem concluded
that rape had increased four times as fast as the overall crime rate over the
previous decade. The 1992-1993 National Crime Victimization Survey, a
yearly study of 100,000 people to uncover those crimes that otherwise go

---

4. For a general discussion of these theories see Lee Ellis, *Theories of Rape: Inquiries
into the Causes of Sexual Aggression* (New York: Hemisphere Publishing Corporation,
1989), pp. 10–16.

unreported, found that 310,000 rapes occurred in one year. That year, the Justice Department reported the number to be 155,000. A series of seven large-scale studies done between 1979 and 1991 concluded that 15 to 25 percent of the women in the United States had been raped.[5]

The ages of rape victims range widely too. The 1991 National Crime Victimization Survey found that women aged 16 to 19 were at greatest risk (3.5 per 1,000), followed by ages 20 to 24 (1.7 per 1,000), ages 12 to 15(1.1 per 1,000), and ages 25 to 49 (1 per 1000).

In addition, opposed to the conventional wisdom that strangers are largely responsible for this crime, the survey found that 80 percent of the rapes were committed by someone known to the victim. More than one-third of that number were done by a relative. One survey conducted by the University of Arizona in the early 1990s discovered that one out of four women of college age reported having been raped. A 1993 study published by the National Association of College and University Attorneys declared that campus acquaintance rape has reached epidemic proportions.

Finally, there is every indication that there is a racial disparity in rape with young African-American women of the lower socioeconomic classes being raped more often. The U.S. Bureau of Justice Statistics estimates the chances that a white victim will be raped by a white man is 78 percent and the chances that a black victim will be raped by a black man is 70 percent. So rape is largely an intra- rather than an interracial activity.[6]

Types of Rapists

Outwardly, rapists seem to be normal, average people. Some demographic information might be gleaned from data taken from the *Uniform Crime Report*. For example, in 1991 a total of 29,964 men and 386 women were charged with forcible rape of females. For both sexes, 33 percent charged were between 25 and 34 years of age, 18 percent were 25 to 29, and 15 percent were between 30 and 34. On the national level, 55 percent were white and 44 percent were black. These percentages were much closer in city arrests. On one hand, rapists appear to be of average intelligence, to have been married at least once, and to have an income well above the poverty level. On the other hand, they appear to have some personality dysfunctions, such as the inability to form or maintain emotionally intimate relationships. They have little ability to trust, sympathize, or empathize with others. There is some evidence to indicate that many experienced some sort of sexual abuse as children from a family member, teacher, neighbor, or friend. Alcohol abuse is another common denominator

5. Rob Hall, *Rape in America*, p. 89.
6. Quoted in *Newsweek* (July 23, 1990), p. 48.

among convicted rapists. Finally, there is some evidence that many rapist are actually sexually dysfunctional in the form of impotence, premature ejaculation, or retarded ejaculation.

The Rapist

Some have argued that there is even a pre-act process, an "anatomy of a sex crime," that a sex offender goes through. It is a five step evolution:

1. Emotion, or feelings of anger, loneliness, or depression.
2. Fantasy, or sexual fantasies arise to offer a sense of relief from these emotions.
3. Distorted thoughts, or rationalizations that might justify carrying out the fantasy.
4. Planning, or starting to put the fantasy into action by looking for victims and likely places to commit the act.
5. Acting it out.

In terms of prevention or therapy, a rapist caught in any one of these stages might be frustrated in ever acting it out.[7]

After the approach has been made, control by the rapist is established and maintained first by surprise. Then four other means of control might be used by the rapist. Although these are discussed in context of the serial rapist they might be applicable in any rape scenario:

1. Mere presence. The physical presence of the rapist might assert control over the victim.
2. Verbal threats of a dirty and menacing way might be used.
3. Display of a weapon, such as a knife or gun.
4. Physical and painful force. Ripping of clothing and hitting the victim.

Reactions of resistance to a rape might have any number of effects. If the victim aggressively resists the rapist may:

1. Cease demands,
2. Flee,
3. Compromise his demands,
4. Use greater verbal threats,
5. Use greater force.

Types of acts will vary, as well, from ordinary sexual activity such as kissing, fondling, and vaginal penetration to anal and oral sex. Verbal activ-

---

7. See *New York Times*, Science section (April 14, 1992).

ity during the act itself will vary too. There might be compliments and pseudo wooing. More likely, there will be pejorative and insulting comments, demands, and threats.[8]

Since 1979 scholars have tried to create typologies of rapists. Some of these are described below:

The Anger Rapist seeks revenge on women for perceived wrongs and injustices done to him in the past. These types of rapes are more likely to have been committed by strangers than acquaintances. Such rapists consider sex to be dirty and use the act to humiliate and degrade the victim. Language and acts are abusive and obscene. These rapes are impulsive, sudden, and of short duration. The assailant is generally not sexually aroused by the attack and will likely experience impotency. Consequently, the rapist generally requires the victim to perform oral sex in an attempt to achieve an erection. Emotional and physical exhaustion rather than sexual gratification brings the assault to an end.

The Power Rapist seeks to validate his masculinity with a conquest. These types of rapists feel inadequate and are compelled by fantasies that, although the act begins in resistance it will evolve into "happy" compliance and pleasure. They use only that force necessary to obtain and maintain control. Overt bodily harm is minimal and unintentional. Generally, their fantasy is not fully realized and the frequency and intensity of attacks will increase. Language is instructional and inquisitive, seeking to gratify and validate their fantasy. Some of these rapists might even try to establish a post-rape relationship. Many of these power rapes are committed by acquaintances in a social context called "date rapes."

The Sadistic Rapist seeks to abuse and torture. His motive is to punish and destroy. He has blended the attributes of anger and power into a more horrifying act. These acts are planned and calculated with victims being kidnaped and held for prolonged periods of time. Initially, these rapists seem normal and even charming, but once revealed they become commanding, excitable, and degrading. These assaulters have a greater interest in anal intercourse than other rapists. Victims may be tortured with bites, burns, mutilation, and even death. In fact, an important subset of this category would be the sex killer.

These murderers are different from regular killers in that they use strangulation rather than guns to prolong the control over and suffering of the victim. In addition, unlike the common killer, these people are generally strangers to their victims.

---

8. Robert R. Hazelwood and Ann Wolbert Burgess, "The Behavioral-Oriented Interview of Rape Victims: The Key to Profiling," in Robert R. Hazelwood and Ann Wolbert Burgess, eds., *Practical Aspects of Rape Investigation: A Multi-disciplinary Approach* (New York: Elsevir, 1987), pp. 151–168.

The Serial Rapist, since the mid-1980s, has become an object of considerable study. These are people who have committed between 10 to 60 rapes each. Demographically, they seem to be average with 71 percent being married at least once. An equal percentage were living with a wife or girlfriend at the time of their crimes. Eighty seven percent were average to above average in intelligence. Any abnormalities could be seen, however, in their youthful development. Most of the convicted serial rapists had disturbed childhoods having lived in either a detention or mental health center. Three-fourths had a history of stealing that ranged from shoplifting to burglary. A favorite activity was voyeurism. Sadistic masturbating fantasies were an important part of the serial rapist's early development. Generally, the rapist was a stranger, but the event likely took place in the home of the victim. They may be divided into "minimalists" with 75 percent of the serial rapists using minimal force. The remaining 25 percent increased the use of force over time. These "increasers" drifted to anal intercourse as part of their activity. Those with "increaser" tendencies started younger (20 years rather than 22) and continued their activity longer (30 years rather than 28). They assaulted more victims (40 victims each rather than 22.4) in a shorter time interval (19.7 days rather than 55.2) than other serial rapists.

The FBI has identified three methods of operation used by these serial rapists. However, such categories might be useful in thinking of other rapists as well, such as:

1. *The Con*, in which the rapists poses as someone who is helpful or in need of help, such as a policeman, a good Samaritan, a lost motorist, etc. The assailant at first appears friendly and charming; suggesting that this type of rapist has confidence in his ability to interact with women. When the victim is in his power the rapist turns dramatically to hostility.

2. *The Blitz*, in which the rapist randomly and impulsively selects, attacks, and overpowers the victim. There is little or no real planning involved. The victim has little or no opportunity with which to cope with the attacker. Often gagging and blindfolding are done immediately as part of the assault. This rapist probably has poor interaction skills with women and any relationships are one-sided and stormy.

3. *The Surprise*, in which the rapists selects out a victim, observes her over time to see when she is most vulnerable and then overpowers her when she does not expect it. Likely, the offender does not have the confidence to approach the victim either physically or by subterfuge.[9]

---

9. Ibid., p. 155.

It is found that serial rapists do change their attack style over time. For example, 50 percent used the surprise style for their initial rape. The other styles were equally divided. Although the surprise approach remained the prevalent one, over time the blitz gave way to the con as the second most favorite.

The Acquaintance Rapist is a rapist who is known by the victim. The woman trusts the perpetrator and her guard is down. Generally attacks occur in "friendly" environments such as the victim's own home. Clues to aggressive behavior are missed or overlooked by the victim. One study found that one third of the victims of a stranger-related rape screamed for help but only 11 percent of the acquaintance-related ones did. A subcategory of this would be "date rape" in which the victim not only knows the perpetrator but the attack takes place either in a romantic or social situation. College women are particularly vulnerable because they are in an environment intensely populated by unmarried males and females, and where alcohol plays an important social role. In addition, these women generally are single and actively dating. Fraternity and other social gatherings may even play insidious games such as "pulling train." This would be targeting a vulnerable young women, getting her drunk, isolating and victimizing her in multiple rapes. In one major study of college women and rape, 89 percent knew their attacker. Of these, 60 percent were assaulted in a dating situation (25 percent were casual dates, 35 percent by steady dates).[10] Many of these kinds of rapists have a particular mindset. They may even deny that they committed rape. Instead, they talk in terms of sex being a male entitlement. That being male implies being aggressive and masterful. Females must play at being coy. Force and resistance are part of the seduction game. Those who try to excuse themselves place the blame on the female, claiming that she was seductive, provocative, and got what she deserved.[11] Some of these attitudes might be seen in spousal attack.

The Marital Rapist is the spouse of the victim. Marital rape is forced sex by the victim's husband. Historically, it was impossible under the law for a husband to rape his wife. As late as 1985 over half of the states exempted the husband from responsibility of such an act especially if he still lived with the victim. It was not until 1993 that such exemptions were disallowed. In many ways this rape is more traumatic than others. Not only is there the violation, loss of control, and violence of other rapes, but there is the sense of betrayal by a loved one. Some think that this the most common form of sexual assault. The National Women's Study declared that

10. Ibid., p. 84.

11. Diana Scully and Joseph Marolla, "Convicted Rapists' Vocabulary of Motive: Excuses and Justifications," *Social Problems* 31 (1984), pp. 530–544; and Diana Scully and Joseph Marolla, "'Riding the Bull at Gilley's': Convicted Rapists Describe the Rewards of Rape," *Social Problems* 32 (1985), pp. 251–263.

61,000 women are raped a year by their husbands or ex-husbands.[12] Estimates vary that between 3 to 14 percent of married women are raped by their mates.[13] The numbers are even higher for battered wives. Some studies indicate that victims of this crime tend to be in the lower socioeconomic class. For example, high school dropouts are four times more likely to be victims. Those sexually abused as children are three times more likely to be victims of marital rape. Frequency is high as well, with over 70 percent in one study reported being victimized on numerous occasions. Often this type of assault happens as the relationship is coming to an end; it is as if the offender is trying to reestablish control over the wife.

The Opportunist Rapist is one whose primary motive may not be sexual. This kind of rape is an afterthought during the commission of another crime such as a burglary or kidnaping.

The Gang Rapist is one who gets caught up in the activity of a group and goes along out of peer pressure as much as out of anger or power issues.

Investigation of Rape

Besides the above typologies, there are several other areas of information of which the investigator must be aware and which shape investigations.

Sexual Assault Units are those investigators in a criminal investigative police who specialize in sexual offenses. The presence or absence of these units reflect both the political and police attitudes over the importance of this crime. The larger the department the more likely this unit will exist. It would have, by experience and specialized training, a more professional approach to this crime. New York City's sex unit established in 1973 was the first in the country and became a model for others that followed. Chicago created its unit in 1980. But these units had a hard time. Budgetary cuts forced the New York unit to reduce from 125 detectives in the mid 1970s to 70 officers ten years later. In Chicago an administrative reorganization took the sexual assault unit and put it with the homicide and robbery units to form a new violent crimes bureau. Police chiefs and superintendents are reluctant to over specialize their officers. In addition, detectives who might have a choice would pick homicide investigations over that of sex offenses. Another problem is that these units have been filled with white, middle-class males who might be impatient and insensitive to the needs of a victim of a sexual attack. In addition, some jurisdictions like

---

12. D.G. Kilpatrick, C.N. Edmunds and A.K. Seymour, *Rape in America: A Report to the Nation.* (Arlington, VA: National Crime Center, 1992).

13. D. Finkelhor and K. Yllo, *License to Rape: Sexual Abuse of Wives* (New York: Holt, Rinehart & Winston, 1985).

New York City set up Sex Crimes Analysis Units (SCAB) that collected data, prepared public awareness programs, and trained detectives in rape investigation. In New York it was initially made up entirely of females and there was some male resistance. At cost cutting time these units were the first to be eliminated.

The Dark Figure of Crime refers to not reporting a crime. It is believed that historically and even today many rape assaults went unreported. Estimates vary widely from 40 to 90 percent of the rapes go unreported. There are three reasons why a victim does report the incident to the police:

1. To prevent further crime by the offender to the victim;
2. To punish the offender;
3. To prevent the offender from harming others.

More importantly are the likely reasons for a victim to not report the crime:

1. The private and personal nature of the crime. This a crime in which the invasion of body and soul is literal and profound.
2. Embarrassment over the crime. There is the feeling that people, such as husbands, boyfriends, acquaintances, and co-workers, will think differently of the victim. There may also be a feeling that there is a stigma attached to the victim of sexual assault.
3. Feeling that the police would be indifferent, biased, or ineffective. They did not want to deal with a male police officer; some were afraid that the police would not believe them.

Physical Ramifications of Rape are numerous and far reaching. Besides the obvious problems of sexually transmitted diseases (STD), such as venereal infections and AIDS, there are long-term problems. For example, victims even ten years after their victimization have reported poorer physical and mental health.

Psychological Ramifications of Rape are even more important to the victim and the investigators. Most victims of any crime go through several psychological phases. Rape victims do too, but perhaps in even more dramatic ways. These include:

1. *Phase 1, the non-acceptance stage.* This occurs at the onset of the attack in which the victim cannot believe it is happening and may be nearly paralyzed. Shock, disbelief, and inability to accept the reality of the attack may extend even into the immediate post-event stage. Such a feeling might explain the lack of resistance to the assault and a lack of cooperativeness in the early stages of the investigation.
2. *Phase 2, the detachment stage.* This occurs during the attack when the enormity of the event overwhelms the victim and she

removes herself from the reality. It is like she is watching the incident happen to another.

3. *Phase 3, the disturbed stage.* After the event a wide range of emotional and nervous reactions might occur. Uneasy sleep and frightening dreams are common. Many victims of sexual assault have rape trauma syndrome at this time.

4. *Phase 4, the integration stage.* This involves the victim regaining personal power and control by integrating the event into their lives and trying to move on to establish a sense of normalcy in their lives.

While these steps are characteristic of all victims of all crimes they are powerful enough to form a psychological profile called rape trauma syndrome (RTS). For the investigator these features are important to see because they explain behaviors that might seem incongruent with expected behavior and better inform the investigative and interview process.

There are four elements characteristic of posttraumatic stress syndrome, and RTS seems to be closely connected to them:

1. The source of the stress is of sufficient magnitude to affect almost anyone.
2. This stress must generate intrusive imagery, such as recurring memories, daydreams and nightmares.
3. The victim will experience a "numbing" feeling about the environment and daily activities.
4. At least two of the following symptoms will be manifested:
    a) hyper-responses such as crying spells and fits of paranoia.
    b) disturbed sleep patterns such as insomnia and dreams. Victims have three types of dreams following an attack:
        i)   nonmastery dreams in which the victim relives the event and remains powerless to stop it.
        ii) symbolic dreams which introduce surrealistic themes drawn from the attack.
        iii) mastery dreams that replay the attack but in ways in which the victim takes control.
    c) feelings of guilt over the event and the victim's possible contributory behaviors.
    d) difficulty remembering or concentrating.
    e) avoidance of activity that might recall the event such as sex.
    f) flashbacks of the attack during normal sexual activity.

Unfounding of rape is the number of accusations determined to be false or without sufficient evidence to support the claims of the offense. All too often the police, in the name of bureaucratic competence, are looking for the "ideal rape case." If the case falls out of this ideal it is more likely to be unfounded.[14] The unfounding rate for Crime Index offenses, excluding rape, was 2 percent in 1991. The unfounding rate for rape was 8 percent. There have been several reasons for this unfounding of a rape complaint; these include:

1. *The character of the victim.* Those with a shady past, such as a prostitute, historically have been given little credence. Although prostitutes can be raped, many officers feel such reports are due to an angry hooker whose customer has refused to pay for her services. Or perhaps it is an argument between a hooker and her pimp.

2. *The character of the offender.* One that has a prison or arrest record makes the police more eager to peruse the case. Interracial rapes, particularly if the victim is white, are likely to anger and inspire the police. Conversely, those "respectable" persons accused of rape, people of property and standing, are likely to be given a favorable hearing.

3. *The relationship of the victim to the perpetrator.* Boyfriends and husbands can be guilty of rape but police have been weary of false complaints based on the possibility of a lover's quarrel.

4. *The victim's condition*, both physical and psychological, have been used in the past to determine unfounding.

5. *A sensible story.* The primary basis of unfounding today has to do with the inconsistences of the story by the victim. The quality and quantity of information are seen as having critical importance.

6. *Timeliness of the story.* Although trauma and doubts might make rape victims delay reporting the crime, the length of time between the event and the accusation casts doubt in the minds of many investigators.

7. *Likelihood of Munchausen's syndrome* or the desire to manipulate medical and criminal justice personnel to obtain attention.[15]

Some of these attitudes and procedures have been reshaped since the reforms of the law but many old-timers remain entrenched in detective squads and in the name of "craftsmanship" still follow older notions of when to unfound the crime of rape. They remain suspicious of victims

---

14. Ann Wolbert Burgess, "Public Beliefs and Attitudes Concerning Rape," in Robert R. Hazellwood and Ann Wolbert Burgess, eds., *Practical Aspects of Rape Investigation: A Multi-disciplinary Approach* (New York: Elsevier, 1987), p. 9.

15. Charles P. McDowell and Niel S. Hibler, "False Allegations," in Robert R. Hazelwood and Ann Wobert Burgess, eds., *Practical Aspects of Rape Investigation: A Multi-disciplinary Approach* (New York: Elsevier, 1987), p. 281.

that meet certain criteria such as previous and willing sex with the assailant, or who "provoke" rape through their appearance or behavior.[16] Nonetheless, recent studies have indicated that police attitudes towards rape are not so stereotypical and insensitive as previously believed. Furthermore, a famous recanting of a rape charge by Catherine Crowell Webb in 1985 released Gary Dotson after he spent six years in jail, pointed out that the possibility of false complaints was ever present.

Physical evidence of rape comes in many forms. The first officer on the scene, besides caring for the safety of the victim, needs to secure any samples of physical evidence. If the crime was done in the victim's home then such items of value might be bedding and clothing that might have hair, fibers, and semen. Search for fingerprints, tool marks, footprints, and tire marks would be appropriate. The victim becomes a major source of evidence as well. If the assault occurred some place other than the domicile of the victim, attempts to collect evidence might be more difficult. Victims with overpowering feelings of "dirtiness" due to the crime may take a shower and throw away clothing. The victim should be seen by health care personnel immediately and medical protocol will dictate retrieval of much of this evidence. For example, blood samples will be taken for typing and enzyme work. An oral wash might be necessary for a saliva sample. Head and pubic hair will be combed to obtain foreign hair or fibers. A number of hairs from the head (from 25 to 100) and pubic area (from 10 to 50) will be pulled from the victim for comparison study. Several swabs of the external genitalia (both cervix and anal) will be taken for semen samples and to check for possible venereal infection. A colposcope may be used to ascertain and document internal injuries. Attention is paid to the hands, such as the fingernails, to recover evidence as well. All of this seems intrusive and insulting to the victim, but it does help in obtaining evidence. This is especially true in the last decade as DNA evidence has grown in importance.

Beginning in the 1990s many states set up DNA data banks of all known sex offenders. Semen and salvia samples would be taken of all those convicted of a sex crime. Such a data bank would allow a match of a sample taken from a victim to that of offenders on file. One of the interesting repercussions of the advent of DNA in investigations are the large number of accused and even convicted men being released after being proved that they could not have committed the act.

Interviews of the victim are important and sensitive issues in any rape investigation. The victim has been physically assaulted and psychologi-

---

16. John C. LeDoux and Robert R. Hazelwood, "Police Attitudes and Beliefs Concerning Rape," in Robert R. Hazelwood and Ann Wolbert Burgess, eds., *Practical Aspects of Rape Investigation: A Multi-disciplinary Approach* (New York: Elsevier, 1987), p. 57.

cally traumatized. The emotional suffering might be even greater than the physical. The police, largely made up of male officers with all the insensitivities and biases that implies, make the interview process very uncomfortable by asking highly detailed and personal questions.

Of course, one of the initial desires is to establish the identity of the perpetrator if it is not known. One such way is to create a sketch or picture from the memory of the victim. In fact, the largest number of criminal investigations using composite sketches are rape inquiries. Forensic artistry goes back to the late nineteenth century and grew to 300 certified artists by the mid-1990s. In the mid-1980s the FBI established the first formal school for composite artists. Today there are three general methods in which these images are produced. First, there is the general artistry produced by hand sketching. This is a long laborious process that relies on total recall by the witness. Richard Speck, the infamous Chicago killer of eight student nurses, was caught due to a sketch inspired by the memory of one of the surviving victims. Second, there are foil composite kits consisting of transparencies of facial features that are layered to build an image. Smith & Wesson was one of the first to create an Identi-Kit foil system in the 1950s. This system relies less on rote recall of the victim/witness and more on recognition factors. Third, are computer systems that allow the artist to bring up images and then make slight alterations as dictated by the witness. In the last analysis, however, the success of the sketch as an investigative tool in rape investigation depends on the memory and psychological state of the victim.

While the quest of the interview is to get as much useful information as possible, the investigator needs to remain aware of the fragile state of the victim. The interview atmosphere and style, therefore, becomes very important. The following are some guidelines in establishing the best interview environment:

1. Physical comforts of the victim must be addressed.
2. Downplay any personal acts or postures that might be interpreted as aggressive or forceful. The interviewer's body language should be positive and supportive and not easily interpreted as anti-female.
3. Avoid being judgmental and impatient.
4. Use gentle approaches. Use active listening techniques by paraphrasing the story back to the victim in supportive ways. Use the "I" message— "I understand" or "I see," for example. Use the "eye" approach if appropriate by establishing and maintaining eye contact.
5. Conduct the interview in the most comfortable place for the victim.
6. See the victim in private unless she needs the emotional support of family.
7. Deal with the family of the victim with care, concern and courtesy.

8. Allow the victim to ventilate.[17]

Literal questioning needs to gain enough information to identify or profile the offender and to understand the event. Generally the questions should be structured thus:

1. What method of approach was used by the offender? For example, was it a "con," "blitz," or "surprise"?
2. How did the offender maintain control? For example, was it mere presence, threats, or force?
3. What amount of force was used? For example, was it minimal, moderate, excessive, or brutal force?
4. Did the victim resist the offender, and if so, in what manner? For example, was it passive, verbal, or physical? Sometimes women might use subterfuge such as claiming they are pregnant or have venereal disease. They may try to repel the attacker by vomiting, urinating, or defecating.
5. What was the offender's reaction to resistance? For example, did he cease demands, compromise or negotiate, flee, threat, or use increased force?
6. Did the rapist experience a sexual dysfunction? For example, was there erectile insufficiency, premature ejaculation, retarded ejaculation, or conditional ejaculation?
7. What type and sequence of sexual acts were required? For example, were there other acts besides vaginal penetration? Was oral sex required? Anal sex is particularly interesting for interpretive reasons. For example, it might suggest one of four conclusions about the rapist. First, it might be part of a fantasy fulfillment. If fellatio occurs it generally precedes anal sex. Second, it might be an experimentation. Third, it might be part of the punishment and humiliation process. Almost always the rapist will demand fellatio after anal sex. Fourth, the rapist might be an ex-convict.
8. What was the verbal activity of the rapist?
9. Was the victim forced to say anything?
10. Did the rapist use a condom?
11. Did the victim have consensual sexual intercourse with another prior to the attack?
12. Was there any sudden changes in the offender's attitude?

---

17. Mary L. Keefe and Henry T. O'Reilly, "Changing Perspectives in Sex Crime Investigations," in Marcia J. Walker and Stanley L. Brodsky, eds., *Sexual Assault: The Victim and the Rapist* (Toronto: D.C. Heath, 1976), p. 163.

13. What precautionary actions were taken by the rapist? A more experienced rapist might require the victim to bathe and douche after the attack.
14. Was anything taken?
15. Did the victim have any experiences that would suggest her being targeted?[18]

Rape remains one of America's more fearsome crimes. It is particularly interesting because it places enormous burdens upon the police in general and the investigators in particular to find ways to be efficient, appropriate, and sensitive to the needs of the victim. As bad as rape is, it assumes even greater concern when the victims are children.

Child Molestation

General

Sexual abuse of children in America is widespread. The American Humane Association announced that there were 2,000 reports of sexual abuse of children in 1976. this abuse doubled in the next twelve months, followed by a fivefold increase in the next five years. One study in 1978 found that one-fourth of all females experienced sexual abuse before the age of 14; one-third did so before age 18. One in nine boys had been sexually abused. In 1992 another study of twelve states found that 51 percent of all their rape victims were under age 18. By comparison, in 1992, 25 percent of the total female population was under age 18. Sixteen percent of victims were under age 12. This age group was 17 percent of the total female population. This problem became so fearsome by 1995 that many states considered passing laws requiring former sex offenders to register and announce their presence to the community within which they resided. Conservatives felt that this was necessary information for families to have in order to protect their children. Liberals wondered whether the civil rights of former sex offenders were being violated.

Those molester-rapists who are attracted to prepubescent children, those whose victims are 12 years of age or younger, are labeled pedophiles. If the rapist attacks older age groups he is a hebephile. The latter term remains largely out of the national vocabulary and incorrectly all child molesta-

---

18. Robert R. Hazelwood and Ann Wolbert Burgess, "The Behavioral-Oriented Interview of Rape Victims: The Key to Profiling," in Robert R. Hazelwood and Ann Wolbert Burgess, eds., *Practical Aspects of Rape Investigation: A Multi-disciplinary Approach* (New York: Elsevier, 1987), pp. 154–167.

tion has been called pedophilia. These rapists prefer to have sex with children. They can and do carry on sexual relationships with adult females, but they prefer children. Adult relationships are difficult for these offenders. Often they maintain an adult relationship to disguise or acquire access to children.

This activity might be seen in a variety of ways. It might be the individual attack of a child. It might take the form of producing or participating in a child sex ring, child prostitution, or child pornography.

In addition, though treated separately in many studies, incest falls into this group of child molestation. Incest is having sexual relations with a child but that child may be directly or indirectly related to the molester. Although there may be many variations, it is largely a daddy-daughter abuse. This is a very serious problem with estimates of around 90 percent of sexually abused children being victims of a family member. For purposes of discussion, the stranger and family member as molester will be treated as the same with occasional highlighting of any differences.

Typologies

For analytical and investigative purposes a typology of molesters can be drawn under two large categories: situational and preferential.

Situational

Situational child molesters do not have a sexual preference for children, but for a variety of reasons come to rely upon a child for gratification. He may victimize a child once or have a long history bordering upon the next type, the preferential child molester. Several notorious revelations of child molestation most likely are connected to this category. For example, molestation in a day care institution is likely done by this type. In the early 1990s, 11 friars at a California seminary were accused of a twenty year history of molesting at least thirty-four boys. This was a situational act of molestation. Probably there are more situational molesters than preferential, but they are likely to molest fewer victims. These situational molesters can be further divided:

Regressed molesters turn to children as a sexual substitute for a preferred peer partner. They have low self-esteem and poor coping skills. Victims are chosen because of their availability and many of these people molest their own children. Coercion is their main mode of operation. This type of situational molester may or may not collect child pornography.

Morally Indiscriminate abusers must be seen against the backdrop of a general pattern of abuse in their lives. He uses and abuses, manipulates, and controls all kinds of people: family, friends, and any others who by chance cross his life. Choice of victim is dictated by vulnerability and opportunity. He obtains victim by lures, manipulation, or force. He is likely to prefer pornographic literature of a more sadomasochistic nature not limited to children.

Sexually Indiscriminate abusive behavior is done by otherwise normal appearing people who are sexual experimenters. He moves toward children out of boredom with other sexual experimentation. Children are simply new and different. He may use his own children as part of some wife-swapping scheme, group sex, or satanic ritual. Of all situational molesters, he is most likely to collect child pornography, but it would be just a small part of a larger more varied collection.

Inadequate molesters are social misfits. They are those suffering from some psychoses, mental retardation, or senility. They find children to be non-threatening. They exploit their size and appearance of adulthood to obtain and control the victims. They have difficulty expressing their feelings and may build up to dangerously explosive situations in which a child victim might be tortured or killed. They are likely to collect a wide range of pornography.

Most of the sexually motivated child killers profiled by the FBI have been the situational child abusers, especially those exhibiting the morally indiscriminate and inadequate patterns of behavior.[19]

Preferential

Preferential child molesters are different. They are the classic pedophile. They have a definite preference for children as sex objects. Even though they may range across wide age categories, there is a preference for young people between the ages of 10 and 12. These youngsters are still children but are at that age when parents are granting greater freedoms; they are at a time of greater vulnerability. While fewer in number these violators tend to molest at greater rates. They will be the chief collectors of child pornography. They might be divided into three subcategories.

Seductive molesters obtain victims in a courtship fashion; they give attention, affection, and gifts to achieve their sexual desires. Frequently, the child arrives at a point that they are willing to give sex for the benefits they have been receiving. Frequently, these offenders have multiple victims even operating a child sex ring. This seducer has the ability to relate to children, he knows how to talk and listen to them. He may pick out those most vulnerable, those victims of emotional and physical neglect.

---

19. Kenneth V. Lanning, "Child Molesters—A Behavioral Analysis for Law Enforcement," in Robert R. Hazelwood and Ann Wolbert Burgess, eds., *Practical Aspects of Rape Investigation: A Multi-disciplinary Approach* (New York: Elsevier, 1987), pp. 201–256.

Introverted molesters do not have the social skills necessary to seduce children. Of all the molesters this one fits more closely the old stereotype of the person hanging around the play park or school yard. He engages children in nonverbal ways. Sometimes he will publicly expose himself or make obscene telephone calls. He might marry a female with the sole desire to gain better access to her children. Of course, he will have collections of child pornography and will visit child prostitutes.

Sadistic molesters prefer children too, but sexual gratification comes only after inflicting pain or suffering. They generally use lures or force to obtain victims. Their tastes in pornography runs to the sadomasochistic.

Profiling the Pedophile

Since these preferential child molesters are considered the classic pedophile, it would be more profitable and easier to profile them. This might be done by considering several large topic areas. While no one indicator must be taken as conclusive evidence, the accumulative effect of indicators is important for the investigator's consideration. The indicators are:

1. *Personal characteristics.* Although not all victims of child sexual abuse become offenders as adults, a large majority of known offenders have been abused. As teenagers they exhibit little interest in the opposite sex of their own age and their dating experience remains limited. As young adults they remain unmarried and live a longer time with their parents. Dating remains rare. If there is a marriage, it is generally a special relationship with a domineering female or a weak passive woman-child in which the sexual content is limited or nonexistent. There may be a history of being fired from a job or released from a military obligation with no official explanation. There might be frequent or unexplained moves or changes of employment.

2. *Youth focus of behavior.* There will be a limited number of peer relationships and an excessive interest in children. His associates and circle of friends are young, and he tends to hang out where young people congregate, such as school yards, arcades, and shopping centers. Any activities with children tend to exclude adults. His hobbies and interests appeal to children. For example, he may collect toys or dolls, build model planes, perform as a clown or magician, or some other behavior attractive to children. His domicile may have a youthful or fanciful look in its decor. There may be frequent photographing of children.

3. *Access to children.* Most of these pedophiles have age and gender preferences. The older the age preference the more exclusive the gender desired. Those who prefer toddlers and the very young tend to choose males as much as females. A pedophile attracted to teenagers tends to specialize on females or males exclusively. There might be an age category

that is preferred. For example, they may like boys between ages 8 and 10, or girls between ages 6 and 12. There are several ways to gain access to children. First, hanging out where children are likely to be. Second, by marrying a woman with children to gain access to them. Third, pose as neighborhood "nice guys" who like to take the kids on trips and excursions. Fourth, they may seek occupations that give them access to children, such as a teacher, day care worker, camp counselor, baby sitter, scout leader, or foster parent. They may seduce children with attention, affection, and gifts.

4. *Sexual fantasies will focus on children* particularly in the collection of child pornography. This is such an important indicator of pedophilia that it warrants further discussion.

Child erotica and pornography are a very important part of any pedophile activities. Also, it becomes valuable evidence in any investigation. An important sidelight here is that it is collected and maintained with loving care.

Child erotica is any material relating to children that might be used for sexual gratifications. They might include toys, games, drawings, sexual aids, books about children, and nonsexual explicit photographs of children. The child was not abused in the production of such materials.

Child pornography is the sexually explicit reproduction of a child's image, voice, or handwriting. The only way to produce this material is to molest and abuse a child. They have been shamed by sexual poses and activities. Furthermore, they may be blackmailed later by the pedophile on threat of public exposure. There is a permanent record of their sexual abuse. It can be commercially made or produced for sale. This is illegal in the United States but many foreign countries still allow such activity. Another source is the homemade variety of pornography. This homemade genre is more widely produced and distributed than the commercial. In either commercial or homemade production, the prepubescent child most likely was not abducted but seduced into the activity. The pubescent model, however, is likely to be missing or a runaway child exploited by a pimp or profiteer.

There is a fine distinction in child pornography. *Technical* pornography is sexually explicit renditions of anyone under the age of 18. *Simulated* pornography is the sexually explicit rendition of anyone over 18 made up to look as if they were under that age.

A very important concept in pornography for pedophile is that they are collections.

Motives for collecting. There are several reasons for collecting such material. First, they are a source of fanciful gratification. Second, some believe that it is also an attempt to validate their behavior. For example, many pedophiles collect, publish, and distribute information to rationalize and justify their behavior. Third, it might satisfy the need for camaraderie. As one author noted, pedophiles swap pictures like others swap baseball cards. Third, the object of lust will grow up and lose the interest of the pedophile. A picture captures the victim for a long period of time. Fourth, they might want souvenirs of past conquests for future fantasy.

Uses of the collection. Obviously, a collection can be used to aid in personal arousal. It might be used to lessen the inhibitions of a victim. It might be used for blackmail. A pornographic collection might be used as a medium of exchange with other pedophiles and as a means of profit, sharing it with others for a price.

Characteristics of Collection. First, the pedophile's collection is very important. Considerable time, money, and effort have gone into the collection. Second, it is constant. He rarely throws anything away and he regularly adds to it. Third, it is organized, detailed, neat, orderly, and maintained. Fourth, it is permanent and very rarely will the pedophile destroy it. There are some cases in which one pedophile willed his collection to another. Fifth, it is concealed and secret, but it must be accessible as well. If the pedophile lives alone this is no problem. But if he lives in a marital or familial situation considerable pains must be taken in concealment. Sixth, many pedophiles feel the need to share their collection with others. They brag over the extent and quality of the collection.[20]

Another recent development for pedophiles has been the advent of the computer as a means to store information such as addresses of victims, communicate with other molesters, and locate individuals with similar interests on electronic bulletin boards.

Event Styles

There are basically two general types of molesters when it comes to thinking of the style of contact and abduction. One group might be called "wolves." They are aggressive but have different ways of making contact and conquest. First, they may just out-in- out attack and take away. They may do this physically or threaten with a real or imagined gun. Second, they may act as an authority figure, a policeman or teacher. Third, they may present a fabricated crisis to the child, such as telling them that their parents are ill or have been in an accident and that the child must come with the molester.

Another group might be called "lambs," or wolves in sheep's clothing. First, they may try to court the child with money, toys, candy, or other gifts. Second, they may use name recognition to lower defenses. Children are told not to talk to strangers, but someone who knows his or her name

---

20. Ibid., pp. 224–239.

may not be seen as a stranger. And molesters may use a variety of ways to obtain names. Names of children may be overheard at a playground or be affixed to clothing and lunch boxes. Third, a very popular ploy is to lure the child in a variety of ways. For example, the classic search for the lost puppy might be used. In this case a molester may have a photograph of a dog and ask the child to help find it. Or the molester might give a job offer to the child. Fourth, they might use the nice guy approach by using ego flattering or false caring of someone in distress. They may pose as creating a game they would like the child to play or have the proposed victim come to the molester's home to play with his supposed child. Many children stereotype molesters as monsters. These so called nice guys counterbalance that image by appearing very ordinary.

Investigation

Investigation of child molestation is very difficult. There are several reasons for this:

1. *Nature of the crime.* It seems like common sense to state that this activity is universally condemned. Not only rape, but consenting sexual relations between adults and children seem widely disapproved. However, there is some support for the practice of consenting adult-child sexual relationships. There are a few organizations that support this mutual consenting sexual activity between adults and children. The Rene Guyon Society, the North American Man-Boy Love Association (NAMBLA), the Pedophile Information Exchange (PIE), the Child Sensuality Circle, the Pedo-Alert Network (PAN), and the Lewis Carroll Collector's Guild are groups that advocate adult-child sexuality and work to change laws that make it a crime. They might argue that laws against adult-child sex are puritanical and should go the way of those against masturbation, fornication, and adultery. These people leave the door open to the fact that actually the child is the seducer; this comes into the psychology and popular literature as the "Lolita Complex."

Another area of concern in this area is defining what constitutes sexual activity. Of course, blatant sexual intercourse is easily defined. But hugging, kissing, and appearing naked in front of a child, especially in cases involving incest, may be a little more difficult to investigate.

2. *The child is an ideal victim.* Children are naturally curious about sex which often is presented to them as a taboo topic by their parents. They are easily led by adults, particularly those who have dramatic authority such as a teacher. For many there is a natural desire to defy their parents. Finally, children are not very good witnesses. They may not understand exactly what has happened to them and do not have the vocabulary or understanding with which to explain it. Incestuous victims have an addi-

tional problem; their attacker is a member of the family. They carry the extra burden of knowing that their cooperation ultimately will do great damage to family arrangements. In addition, recently the phenomenon of repressed memory has come to light. This is when the act is so traumatic that the victim pushes it out of consciousness for years and then due to some stimuli it comes to memory. Of course, this means that many accusations come forth years after the event and places the word of the victim against that of the accused.

Those incest victims who report their victimization can be placed into three groups. First, those telling their parents of the incident were likely to be young children. Second, those telling friends, other family members and marital partners were likely to be in early adulthood. Third, those telling a therapist did so at a later point in their lives.[21]

3. *Nature of parents.* If the molestation took place by a family member there might be a tendency to cover it up or deal with it in other ways. A neighbor or stranger molestation might call upon over reactions by the parents. This is natural and understandable but might get in the way of the investigation. In an incestuous incident the wife might react in a way to hamper the investigation. For example, at first she might deny it ever happened. It is an attack upon her place, biologically and socially, in the family constellation. This will be followed by rage toward the father. Then this rage might turn to the daughter for perceived seductive behavior. At last there will be the reconciliation stage and renewed denial. Of course, in many of these stages the wife would be less cooperative.

4. *The nature of molesters.* As discussed above molesters generally seem quite ordinary. They may be pillars of the community or of a profession. Incestuous fathers have been profiled; the incestuous family tends to be reclusive, secretive, and very private. The father is likely to be authoritarian, dictatorially demanding his wishes to be carried out at all times. He is likely to be middle-aged and have a lower degree of education than average. There is likely to be some dysfunction within the family. The father may be unemployed and alcohol will likely be a problem. Sexual abuse is historical within the family with the relationship going back for some time. Some marital discord is likely. The wife may be preoccupied having a consuming job outside of the home, or she may be a passive person, little noticed as the daughter increasingly assumes her role. Attitudinal studies made of incest offenders suggest that they have three mindsets in common. They endorse attitudes supportive of male sexual privilege, perceive

21. Thomas Roesler and Tiffany Wind, "Telling the Secret: Adult Women Describe Their Disclosures of Incest," *Journal of Interpersonal Violence* 9 (1994), pp. 327–338.

children as sexually attractive and motivated, and tend to minimize the harm caused by taking sexual advantage of children.[22]

When child molesters are apprehended they tend to have predictable reactions, such as:

a) *Denial.* This is the general first reaction. There will be expressions of surprise, shock, and indignation. Claims that a mistake has been made will be forthcoming.

b) *Minimization.* The molester may try to minimize what has been done in quantity and quality. There will be claims that it was only done once or rarely. Accusations of victim compliance and cooperation might be made.

c) *Justification.* There might be claims of ignorance of the age of the child, or that it would be better to learn these things from a loving parent or relative than out on the streets. There might be considerable effort in blaming the victim. The child might be accused of seduction or being a prostitute. This is the ploy used most often by the pedophile.

d) *Fabrication.* The creating of fabulous stories to explain such behavior is common. A doctor might claim he was doing research. An incestuous parent might claim that he was giving sex education to his child. Collectors of pornographic pictures might claim they are doing anatomical studies.

e) *Mental illness.* Many molesters when confronted with irrefutable evidence play the "sick card." They claim some sort of illness and that they cannot control their behavior. Many pedophile manuals advocate such tactics.

f) *Sympathy.* Some try to play the "sympathy card" as well. They use the nice guy defense. They claim they are sorry and sick and go on to show they are a pillar of society, a family man, or a good man gone astray. Since so many continue to stereotype molesters as evil and dirty old men, this tactic sways judges and juries a great deal.

g) *Attack.* Some molesters become quite aggressive. They bribe and threaten victims to keep them quiet. They may attack the procedures of the investigative officers. If they have any wealth and influence it will be brought to bare to alter and affect the process.

22. Karl R. Hanson, Ricco Gizarelli, and Heather Scott, "The Attitudes of Incest Offenders: Sexual Entitlement and Acceptance of Sex With Children," *Criminal Justice and Behavior* 21 (1994), pp. 187–202.

h) *Bargain.* Many molesters may try to redeem themselves in some way by giving important information about child sex rings, prostitution, and pornography activities.

i) *Suicide.* A few molesters, especially those from respectable middle-class backgrounds, may be so shamed by the accusations that they take their own lives. Investigators might feel some guilt for this and must place it in perspective.

5. *Nature of investigations.* Many times investigators have very little to go on particularly from incest. Victims of incest rarely report it. Instead, suspicious relatives, neighbors, teachers, and health care workers bring it to the attention of the police. These victims give some signs; for example, they might have an inordinate knowledge and interest (positive or negative) in sex for their age group. They may have very strong and negative feelings toward their parents. Fathers would be disliked for what they have done; mothers blamed for not protecting the child.

Another problem for investigators is the "isolation of affect" issue. In most cases those who work in highly undesirable circumstances divorce themselves from it by ventilating to comrades, leaving their work at work, and having hobbies that distract them. Investigators of child molestation have a hard time doing this; they take their work very seriously. Male officers are particularly troubled by this crime and these criminals. Their enthusiasm might trample upon the constitutional rights of offenders and damage the investigative process.

The interview becomes problematic as well. Children who have been sexually abused by an adult will naturally feel uncomfortable relating that information to adults who are strangers. They may not have the vocabulary to describe the event. Many investigators have turned to anatomically correct dolls to help the victim point out what exactly went on.[23] Often there is an effort to recruit female officers to handle these kinds of interviews. In addition, the child might need the support of parents at this time, but their emotions might be so strained that parents might be a disruptive feature at the interview. Of course, in cases of incest this problem is even greater because the father will not be available and the rest of the family might feel the child is threatening the family structure.

Finally, in the court proceedings the child will be confronted by a number of new people. Officers might serve a useful transition and support role as the child moves to the prosecutors office and to the courtroom settings.

---

23. Marcia Morgan, *How to Interview Sexual Abuse Victims Including the Use of Anatomical Dolls* (Thousand Oaks, CA: Sage Publications, 1995).

Conclusions

Sex offenses are a unique and troublesome criminal activity and criminal investigative process. Males, based on physical strength, have an unusual advantage over the typical female in asserting this assault. Children are even more vulnerable. The criminal investigative system has too long been insensitive to the victim of rape. Although the system has sought to become more accommodating to females, there is much that needs to be done. Police may or may not have an impact on preventing the acts of rape and molestation, but they must not in the name of efficiency victimize the victim again.

Chapter 12

Arson Investigation

Introduction

Definitions

For the purposes of this book arson may be defined as the deliberate and illegal setting of a piece of property afire either by ignition or initiation. Initiation describes the discharging of an explosion. This is a departure from many standard textbooks, but the importance of bombs and the investigation of explosions has become so important that it is warranted here. That property in the definition of arson may be a building, vehicle, or land.

Explosions

General

This section is unique because most books on arson do not include a discussion on explosions. In terms of police work there are several possible explosive incidences that might be encountered, including:

1. Homemade bombs,
2. Transportation accidents involving explosives,
3. Bomb threats,
4. War souvenirs and military munitions,
5. Commercial explosives,
6. Sabotage devices,
7. Military aircraft accidents.

Definitions

Explosions are rapid fires that give off large amounts of energy. Unlike a fire, explosions do not need external oxygen; they have oxygen in their chemical makeup. Some are called "low explosions" or "low velocity" events, they burn more slowly and can be used to propel a bullet or rocket or automobile without destroying those nearby. They push rather than shatter the surroundings. There is no real center to this type of explosion as air molecules ignite uniformly and the blast wave goes out in uniform and concentric ways. Windows broken a long distance from the scene indicate a low velocity explosion. A gas explosion is a good example of a low velocity event.

"High explosives" are more unstable and cause more destruction. They punch and shatter the surrounding environment. There is a central point of detonation and the greatest amount of destruction occurs near the point of origin.

There are three types of explosions, all of which can occur accidentally, naturally, or intentionally. It should be noted that the term "explosion" suggests an outward thrust of power and destruction. However, implosions, in which the forces are inward, should be considered part of this discussion as well.[1] It should also be remembered when considering this crime that there are a large number of bomb hoaxes or false reports of a bomb that create considerable cost in terms of work stoppages and erodes the sense of social well being and security. Of course, the investigation of an unexploded bomb, either because it has not been engaged or because it is a hoax, is as dangerous if not more so than looking at an incident after the destruction of a bomb has occurred.

There are three types of explosions:
(1) Explosions due to steam or mechanical initiation, (2) explosions due to chemical initiators, and (3) explosions due to nuclear causes.

History

Explosives as a means of a criminal act have a long history in the United States. Particularly after the Civil War, a war that acquainted a number of people to the power and potential of explosions, many criminals turned to this means to help carry out criminal acts. As banks and railroad express cars moved to more secure safety measures by inventing "strong boxes," safes, and vaults, criminals turned to opening them with explosives. By the 1890s a series of robbers, called "yegg" burglars, introduced nitroglycerin as a means of explosive entry to a bank and its vaults and became a criminal scourge.

In addition, ideological radicals, termed anarchists, threw bombs at hated capitalists and their lackeys. Perhaps, one of the more notorious explosions in the nineteenth century occurred at Haymarket Square in Chicago. On May 4, 1886, amidst a demonstration and public rally of anarchists, a squad of police arrived to break up the gathering. A bomb was

---

1. Thomas G. Brodie, *Bombs and Bombings: A Handbook to Detection, Disposal and Investigation for Police and Fire Departments* (Springfield, IL: Charles C. Thomas, 1972), p. 30.

thrown killing several officers outright and fatally wounding others. Altogether, seven officers died. On the flimsiest evidence, four anarchists were hanged for the incident.

At the turn of the century the Industrial Workers of the World (IWW) started where the anarchist had left off. Johann Most, the intellectual leader of the American radicals, had even published a book, *Science of Revolutionary Warfare,* in the early years of the new century which became a call to arms and a handbook on how to make bombs. Shortly, political leaders and enemies of the IWW were assassinated. Harry Orchard became the notorious bomber when he blew up the Independence, Colorado, railroad depot platform on June 6, 1904. A year and a half later, on December 30, 1905, Orchard killed former Idaho governor, Frank Steunenberg, with a bomb in Caldwell, Idaho. Bombs were thrown in the Wall Street area of New York City and at the Los Angeles Times building as well.

A lull in bomb activity occurred until after World War II and then it broke out again with a series of crazed bombers. A sixteen-year career of terrorizing New York City as the "mad bomber" came to an end for George P. Metesky in 1956 when he tauntingly gave so many clues to a newspaper that his arrest followed shortly. On November 1, 1955, United Flight 629 from Denver fell from the sky; it was the first recorded case of an airplane bombing. Also, it was the first case in which the use of bomb residue as physical evidence led to a capture and conviction. But it was in the period of the 1980s and 1990s that the bomber attained ominous status in America, as the accompanying table suggests.[2]

	1985	'86	'87	'88	'89	'90	'91	'92	'93
Explosive device	575	580	600	593	641	931	1,551	1,911	1,880
Incendiary device	102	1120	104	156	203	267	423	582	538
Damage (in millions)	6.3	3.4	4.2	2.3	5.0	9.6	6.4	12.5	700
Persons injured	144	185	107	145	202	222	230	349	1,323
Deaths	28	14	21	20	11	27	29	26	49

The FALN, a radical group wanting independence for Puerto Rico, bombed the Chicago political headquarters of George Bush during the Republican

2. Federal Bureau of Investigation, *1993 Bomb Survey.*

primary races in 1979. In Salt Lake City a deranged dealer in antiquities began killing people with homemade bombs who might expose his shady dealings with the Mormon Church. One of the bombs went off in the backseat of his own car, seriously injuring him. A prominent judge in Alabama and a civil rights lawyer in Georgia were killed by letter bombs sent to their homes by Walter L. Moody in 1989. From 1990 (3,541 reported incidents) to 1994 (5,290 incidents) there has been a 49 percent increase of reported incidents of explosives.

At the same time bombs were increasingly used in the Middle East by liberation-oriented terrorists adding to the general fears in America. The world was stunned in 1988 when a Pan Am flight headed for New York City exploded over Lockerbie, Scotland, killing everyone aboard.

Then there was the strange character dubbed the "unabomber." A serial bomber, coded as "UNABOM" because his first victims were connected to universities and airlines, struck sixteen times between 1978 and 1995 killing three and wounding 23 in California, Utah, and Illinois. He inspired a nationwide hunt and became an-on-going media event.

On February 26, 1993, the World Trade Center in New York City was bombed by terrorists, six people were killed and more than one thousand were injured. The explosion caused an estimated $700 million in damage. The attack, attributed to a radical Muslim group, was carried out with a 1,200-pound bomb left in a rental truck parked in a garage under the complex. That was the worst bomb attack in the history of the United States until an incident Oklahoma City.

On April 19, 1995, a bomb weighing thousands of pounds exploded in front of the Alfred P. Murrah Federal Building in Oklahoma City killing 169 people and injuring nearly 400. Members of the far right hate groups were arrested for the bombing. America was stunned by the ease in which the crime had been committed in its heartland.

Bombers and Their Motives

There are several possibilities when it comes to motivation for crimes involving explosives.

First, there is organized crime. Historically, to cover up the crime or to minimize discovery of evidence, members of organized crime have resorted to explosions. The planting of a crippled bomb, one that will not explode, is a favorite form of frightening or extorting someone by organized crime. Another is a "stink" or "stinch" bomb, a device to scare and extort rather than destroy. Since some members have gone semi-legitimate by expanding into construction businesses, obtaining explosives has not been a problem. Furthermore, professional bombers have arose most likely out of the ranks of organized crime. The favored location for a bomb by these professional bombers would be under the hood of an automobile on the left side of the engine, so the electrical system of the car will be used to detonate. Sometimes a bomb will be placed under the gas tank so that the gas feeds the initial explosion.

Second, a deranged individual who has some personal revenge agenda or who takes delight in the act of creating an explosion and fire may be motivated to do this type of crime. For example, George P. Metesky, the mad bomber who terrorized New York City in the 1940s and 1950s left a clue when he wrote a letter to a local newspaper revealing his grudge against Consolidated Edison, where he had worked years earlier. Walter L. Moody Jr. was driven by revenge. He had been convicted for maiming his wife with a bomb in 1972. The United States Court of Appeals for the 11th Circuit later denied his appeal. In 1989, years after his release from prison, he sent two bombs packed with nails that killed a member of that appeals court, Judge Robert S. Vance and a lawyer, Robert E. Robinson.

Third, terrorist groups throughout history have used the bomb to frighten the public and call attention to their cause. In the nineteenth century the anarchists were prominent and radical labor organizations became known in the twentieth century. The Georgia-based Ku Klux Klan conducted a how-to-do-it bomb school in the 1960s. In 1969 the Students for a Democratic Society (SDS) distributed bomb information in their pamphlet *Your Manual.*

Students for a Democratic Society
Literature on How to Make a Pipe Bomb

1. Buy a piece of pipe at any hardware store; buy cap-ends for the pipe at a second hardware store.
2. Buy gunpowder at a gun shop. If any questions are asked tell them your are learning to reload your shells for "hunting deer."
3. You can buy fuse at another gun store
4. Now you are ready to construct a bomb
5. BE CAREFUL
6. First, drill a one-eighth-inch hole in the pipe in the middle
7. Second, screw one cap on pipe.
8. Now insert a three-inch length of fuse into the hole in the pipe.
9. Fill the pipe with black powder; don't spill it on the threads of the exposed pipe. Now screw on the other cap.
10. For a simple time fuse, take a long cigarette and tape the fuse along the bottom of the cigarette. Now leave quickly. You have five to ten min-

utes until it goes off. Make sure that the cigarette burns freely to insure detonation.[3]

Political groups, such as the Puerto Rican "independecia" who resented American imperialism, have been noted for their use of bombs. Muslim radicals were blamed for the World Trade Center bombing. Far-right militias, who hate the apparent oppressive nature of the federal government, have been linked to the Oklahoma City destruction.

Bomb Devices

There seems to be three ways a person might obtain explosive materials. First, they might be purchased. There are numerous manufactures of explosives and many people purchase these materials for legitimate reasons connected to construction, clearing, and demolition. The federal government has set up means to regulate the manufacture, purchase, storing and use of explosives, but such materials remain remarkably easy to obtain. Second, materials may be stolen. It has been estimated by the Bureau of Alcohol, Tobacco and Firearms that in 1993 more than 4,000 pounds of all types of blasting agents were stolen. Third, materials can be homemade and improvised.[4]

No matter the type of explosive, there are four well-defined effects of an explosion. First, there are fragmentation bombs. These send out pieces of metal shrapnel that kill, maim, and destroy. The following table suggests the safest distances away from an explosion to minimize danger from flying missiles:

Explosives (in pounds)	Safe Missile Distance (in feet)
1–27	900
30	930
34	969
38	1,008
40	1,020
44	1,050
48	1,080
50	1,104
55	1,141

---

3. Quoted in Joseph Stoffel, *Explosives and Homemade Bombs,* 2nd ed. (Springfield, IL: Charles C. Thomas, 1972), pp. 6–7.

4. See for example, David Harber, *The Advanced Anarchist Arsenal: Recipes For Improvised Incendiaries and Explosives* (Boulder, CO: Paladin Press, 1991).

60	1,170
65	1,200
70	1,230
80	1,290
90	1,344
100	1,392
200	1,754
300	2,008
400	2,210
500	2,381[5]

Second, percussion bombs rely on the air pressure created by ignition. In high explosives it is this blast wave, with 1.4 million pounds per square inch and traveling at 12,000 miles per hour, that is the most devastating. When an explosion occurs underground, this concussion effect is called "earth shock," and under the water it is called "water shock." Water shock can travel considerable distances and damage steel plates of ships, even if there is not a direct hit. Third, incendiary bombs are concerned in spreading or being a medium of fire.[6] Fourth, a combination of the above three types can also be used to create an explosion.

Sensitivity of explosives is a useful concept that refers to the ease with which explosives may be initiated. Black powder is sensitive to spark or flame but not to a blow or shock. Nitroglycerin and lead azide, an explosive used in blasting caps, are extremely sensitive. Many explosives become more sensitive with age. Because of this sensitivity or lack of sensitivity, many explosives use a "fire train," or the taking of a weaker temperature ignition and transferring it up a train of ever ascending temperature mediums to allow a greater explosion. For example, a match would easily ignite some paper, that would ignite some wood, that would in turn ignite coal. But a match by itself would be incapable of igniting a lump of coal. The same principle would be used in a detonation, here called a "firing train." For example, a firing pin strikes a detonator that stimulates a booster that leads to the main explosion. Blasting caps serve this function for dynamite.

In addition, bombs can be divide into two large categories: simple and sophisticated.

Simple bombs range widely from homemade concoctions to items obtained in the open market.

5. Drawn from Joseph Stoffel, p. 193.

6. Napalm is a classic form of this explosive. It is a liquid fuel which is gelled by the addition of a soap powder or soap chips.

1. Explosive Before Firing

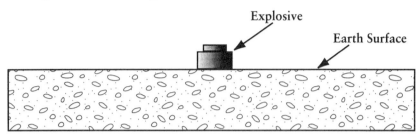

2. Explosion Starts

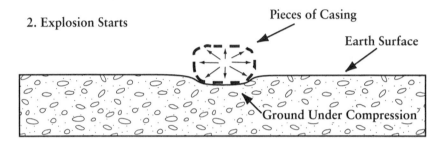

3. Crater Forms

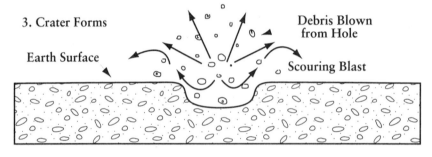

4. Final Form

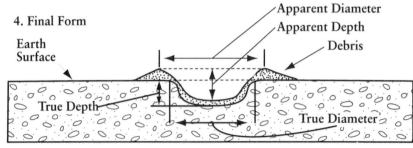

1. Mine Before Explosion

Earth Surface

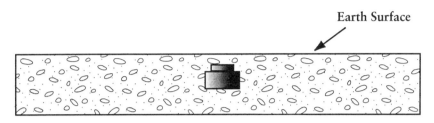

2. Explosion Starts

Surface Starts to Lift

Earth Surface

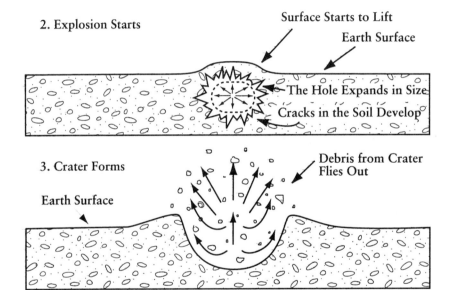

The Hole Expands in Size

Cracks in the Soil Develop

3. Crater Forms

Debris from Crater Flies Out

Earth Surface

4. Final Form

Apparent Depth of Crater

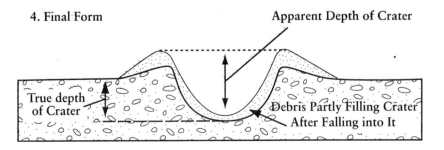

True depth of Crater

Debris Partly Filling Crater After Falling into It

- Fireworks are used to celebrate holidays and other spectacular events. While most accidental explosive incidents occur from items at the lower end of this category—firecrackers, sparklers, and fountains—the more explosive items have caused considerable accidental injury. Since they are readily available, "basement bombers" might take these items and customize them for more dangerous explosives.
- A classic is the "Molotov cocktail," flammable stuff in a bottle with a burning rag-wick top that ignites the contents when the device is thrown and broken.
- A blasting cap is actually a small explosion that is used to initiate a larger one. They were invented in the 1860s by Alfred Nobel. But even before Nobel, cannoneers used a similar concept on their weapons. Also, most rifles had a percussion cap, a small explosive device that in turn set off the main charge of the weapon. Today, commercially produced caps are copper or aluminum tubes, closed at one end and filled with several highly sensitive explosives that form part of the overall explosive train. Since blasting caps are highly sensitive, they come in small amounts. Their purpose is to explode a more stable, safe explosive. They might be placed in a letter or package and sent through the mail. Actually, automobiles with air bag assemblages have electric blasting caps and can be torn down and used for criminal purposes. Of course, there are numerous (and dangerous) ways to make these at home.[7]
- Black powder is the oldest known explosive. It is a low explosive that burns progressively as opposed to high explosives that detonate by means of a shock wave that passes through the explosive. Black powder consists of 75 percent potassium or sodium nitrate, 15 percent charcoal, and 10 percent sulfur. Commercially, it comes in two metal kegs each containing twenty-five pounds of powder. Sometimes it is compressed into pellets as well.
- Smokeless powder was discovered in 1838 and began to replace black powder as a propellent in most weapons. It is a low explosive that burns progressively. Two types of smokeless powder are used as small arms propellants; they are called single-base and double-base powders.
- Ammonium nitrate used for fertilizer (ANFO) has also been used for explosives. It was first discovered in 1859 but not used until 1867. The bomb used at Oklahoma City was made from ammo-

---

7. Ragnar Benson, *Ragnar's Homemade Detonators* (Boulder, CO: Paladin Press, 1993), pp. 1–6.

nium nitrate mixed with fuel oil—contents that almost any person could purchase at an agriculture supply store.

More sophisticated bombs require more effort and higher skill levels to assemble.

- "Pipe and powder" devices are more sophisticated than those listed above. Unconfined or loose black powder will burn, but when compacted it becomes explosive. Commercially packed black powder, also known as dynamite, is usually in cardboard with a wax covering. Homemade devices may be even more powerful when packed in a metal pipe.
- Hypergolic activated bombs are a combination of chemicals that are not explosive when alone, but become so when united. This action is called hypergolic and requires some basic knowledge of chemistry. One example is the "jerry can bomb." In this device, a large dent is put in the top of a metal jerry can. The dent should not rupture the can. The jerry can is then filled with industrial chemicals. Acid is poured directly into the dent. The acid slowly burns through the metal and comes into contact with the industrial chemical causing detonation.[8]
- Nitroglycerine or "blasting oil," first prepared in the late 1840s, is a very powerful and unstable explosive. It is an oil, slippery to the touch, with a clear or slightly yellow color when newly made; as it ages, it becomes brown with purple streaks. It is very sensitive to shock, impact, friction, and flame. Some create nitroglycerine by extracting it from commercially produced dynamite; this procedure is called "cooking." One way to cook it is to place dynamite in boiling water and skim the nitroglycerin off of the top, or by "milking" the dynamite through a silk stocking in hot water and then skimming off the nitroglycerin. Obtaining this "soup" is very hazardous and many criminals have had their basement labs blowup in front of them. Those who handle it for prolonged periods of time complain of chronic headaches. It was a Swedish chemist named Alfred Nobel who found a way to mix nitroglycerine with special clays and mold it into sticks he dubbed dynamite that produced a stable and safe form of explosive.
- Dynamite is another form of sophisticated explosive and is commercially prepared. It is always packaged in fifty-pound cases or in large cylindrical cartridges, with the diameter and the weight stamped on each explosive. Nobel developed blasting caps to

8. Seymour Lecker, *Deadly Brew: Advanced Improvised Explosives* (Boulder, CO: Paladin Press, 1987), p. 51.

help detonate these sticks. Construction companies readily purchase dynamite. Federal laws strictly regulate manufacture, purchase, and storing of commercial made explosives. Some interest groups have fought to lessen or restrict some regulations on explosives. For example, the introduction of taggants, identifiers to be discussed shortly, has been fought by a variety of groups such as the National Rifle Association and the Institute of Makers of Explosives.

- TNT or trinitrotoluene, a yellow powder, is considered to be one of the safest and strongest explosives. It was developed by the Germans in 1902. It can be melted and poured into bombs and shells and used in underwater situations as well.

- Military ordnance consists of a variety of items such as grenades, mines, mortars, and bombs made exclusively for the military and are extremely dangerous.

- C-3 and C-4 or plastic explosives (plastique) are part of military ordnance but are so powerful and dangerous that they deserve a separate notation. For example, commercial-dynamite — the most powerful grade available to the public — has a detonation velocity of approximately 19,000 feet per second (fps). Military TNT detonates at about 22,600 fps. C-4 detonates at speeds of 26,400 fps. C-3 is yellow and C-4 is dirty white to light brown in color. Both are a semi-plastic, putty-like material containing Research Development Explosive (RDX). They are produced only for the military, but can be legally sold to non-military parties under the supervision of the Bureau of Alcohol, Tobacco and Firearms. More likely C-4 will be stolen from military and naval bases. Between 1979 and May 1990, for example, the Bureau of Alcohol, Tobacco and Firearms reported over 3,500 pounds of stolen C-4.[9] In addition, many survivalist and paramilitary groups have homemade recipes.[10] Plastic explosives can be molded and stuck like a wad of chewing gum anywhere an explosion is needed.

---

9. United States General Accounting Office. Briefing Report to the Chairman, Legislation and National Security Subcommittee, Committee on Government Operations, House of Representatives: Defense Inventory, Control Over C-4 Explosive and Other Sensitive Munitions (September 1990).

10. Ragnar Benson, *Homemade C-4: A Recipe For Survival* (Boulder, CO: Paladin Press, 1990) and Seymour Lecker, *Homemade Semtex: C-4's Ugly Sister* (Boulder, CO: Paladin Press, 1991).

Types of Bombs
Used in crimes from 1989 to 1993

Explosive	Incidents	Share
Flammable Liquids	2,876	30%
Black Powder	1,430	15%
Smokeless Powder	1,449	15%
Chemicals	1,487	15%
Photo Flash/		
Fireworks Powders	1,458	15%
Commercial Explosives	250	3%
Military		
(not C-4 and TNT)	249	3%
Match Heads	149	2%
Ammonium Nitrate		
and Fuel Oil	32	1%
C-4/TNT	17	1%
Others	203	2%

Source: Federal Bureau of Alcohol, Tobacco and Firearms.
Percentages do not total 100% because of rounding

Initiation

In addition to the bomb device itself, there are three methods of initiation or ignition that must be considered. These may be known as fusing mechanisms

First, the most common form of initiation is time control. There are four types of time control and delay. The most common is burning usually with a trail of black powder or some other form of fuse. A safety fuse is a cordlike feature with a black powder interior. It burns at approximately 90 to 120 seconds per yard. Manufactures warn not to use less than two feet of fuse. Detonation cord may be used to connect explosive charges together. The material explodes at 21,000 fps. and will insure simultaneous detonation of dynamite even underground. The second most often used form of time delay is mechanical; it is found in the form of a clock or watch set at a prearranged time for the initiation. When that time period has elapsed, the clocking device sets in motion the ignition process. Third, there is the corrosive agent such as an acid eating through metal separating a chemical that explodes on contact with the acid in a hypergolic reaction. Fourth, electrical time delays generally incorporate a relay held in place by a battery.

Another form of initiation is through motion. Most often these are seen in military situations and are labeled "booby traps." Some form of pressure or motion is needed to trigger the explosion. These motions may be any one or combination of three dimensional movements: up, down, right, left, forward, or backward. In addition, explosives may be initiated by pull, tension release, pressure, and pressure release. Although rarely used in the United States, it is very likely that most letter and package bombs are initiated by some form of pressure or motion.

Finally, another form of initiation is through remote control. For example, a radio transmitter might produce an impulse in a radio receiver to explode the bomb. A battery or other power source might be used to remotely initiate. At the simplest level a long string or wire might be pulled to cause the explosive device to detonate. This is a useful method to insure accuracy since the bomber must be nearby to view the victim. Of course, being so close might jeopardize the bomber as well.

Investigation

Corpus Delicti. In any investigation of an explosion it must be determined if initiation was intentional or due to natural causes. The most likely natural explosion comes from gas, generally a gas leak. Dust or flour explosions are similar to gas in effect and principle. A mixture of approximately 2 to 7 percent fuel to air is explosive. Less than 2 percent will not explode. As may be seen the percent of fuel is low and an equal weight of gasoline will produce more explosive force than an equal weight of dynamite. Appliances and utilities service lines are likely to be the source of gas leaks. Vapors can collect in different areas due to wind and confinement in structures. Therefore, there will be inconsistencies in effects of the explosion and burning patterns. Generally, partitions and walls will be pushed over in different directions. Finally, gas explosions are labeled low velocity with all the characteristics described earlier. Victims of a gas explosion will have greater degrees of burning wounds covering larger parts of the body. Also in a gas explosion the burning will occur early; a fireball will attend initiation and lower degrees of fire will take place after. It is estimated that nearly 60 percent of all explosions are due to gas leaks.

Taggants. Some argue that investigation of explosions would be easier if regulations of the industry were greater. The federal government has established considerable regulation of the industry already, but many argue for placing taggants in commercially produced explosives. Since the early 1970s the technology has been available to add microscopic particles to explosives, some of which would survive an explosion. These particles, called taggants, may be color coded and flourescent to enable detection by ultraviolet light after an explosion. Coding could refer to a particular manufacture and sub-coding could indicate time periods of production. In this way the history of the explosive material could be traced more easily, thus suggesting who had access to it over time. In 1979, while conducting a $5 million pilot project using taggants in explosives, the firearms bureau was able to track down and convict a person who had used the explosives to make a bomb to kill one person and injure another in Baltimore. Shortly after, however, Congress called off funding of these projects largely due to the efforts of the National Rifle Association (NRA) and makers of explosives. The NRA feared that such tampering with powder would somehow impact the quality of ammunition. The Institute of Makers of Explosives felt taggants would be too costly, forcing machines to be cleaned more often, and that taggants would make their product more unstable. Clearly, the investigation of an explosion would be easier if taggants were uniformly added to all commercially produced explosives, but politics has undermined investigations.

Police Specialization and Technology. Another investigative aid has been the growing number of specialists in bomb investigation. On the federal level the Bureau of Alcohol, Tobacco and Firearms has assumed importance and expertise in the investigation of explosions. Indeed, the FBI has increasingly become involved. In local policing, the larger cities have created bomb squads. The New York City police department, for example, has America's oldest bomb squad that was established in 1903. Today thirty-six investigators are assigned to the squad and investigate nearly 10,000 bomb threats each year. By 1995, Chicago had 12 officers assigned permanently to a bomb squad.

It is relatively easy to make a bomb. Most of the ingredients can be purchased at a sporting goods and electronics stores. Half the states allow purchases of dynamite over the counter. On the other hand, the technology for detecting and disarming an explosive has become quite complex. Some technological tools as found in the bomb squad of the New York City police department include:

- *"Jerkus" rope.* This is the earliest and simplest of devices to deal with bombs. As its name implies it is simply a long rope to be looped around a device and jerked from a distance. Such a jolt, it was believed, would cause the bomb to explode. Although, more modern devices have been developed, the jerkus rope remains in the car trunks of most investigators as a last resort.
- *Portable X-ray machines.* About the size of a dust- buster, these devices can be brought to the scene of a suspicious parcel and used to determine the parcel's danger by X-ray pictures.
- *Total Containment Vessel* (TCV). A bright yellow globe that looks like a diving bell made from HY80—the same material used in the hulls of nuclear submarines— the TCV can contain

and digest a very high explosive. Sometimes such a device is larger and motorized and takes suspicious devices off of a scene to a safer place for handling.

- *Bomb Freezing.* Bomb freezing is the use of liquid nitrogen to make the components of a bomb inert. A Styrofoam container would be placed over the suspicious object. Then the liquid nitrogen would be introduced through an opening in the container, thus rendering the components of the bomb inoperable.
- *A Bomb Suit.* A heavy (up to 64 pounds) armor covering the body is worn by those trying to handle explosives. Often, in the name of dexterity, the hands are not protected. In the past, the back of the bomb suit was open, giving rise to the good luck saying among bomb squad investigators, "Never turn your back on a bomb." The most common injury to bomb investigators remains those on the fingers and hands. Most investigators dislike the bomb suit because of its discomfort.
- *Water Disrupter.* It is estimated that it takes an electrical circuit 3 milliseconds to complete circuitry. A water disrupter, a long steel tube that fires a burst of water strong enough to punch through wood, can disengage connection in one millisecond, thereby disrupting the explosion.
- *Robotics.* Robotics is the creating of machines that will encounter and handle high explosives.
- *Dogs.* Canine detection of explosive materials has become very popular, and the New York bomb squad has six dogs for such duty.

Point of Origin. Another investigative tool has to do with the point of origin, in this case the bomb crater. Craters indicate the type and quantity of explosives used and perhaps reveal remains of the bomb. Low velocity explosives on dirt will make craters of wide diameter and shallow depth. Sides of the crater will be more gradual. On cement, low velocity blasts make grooves and gouges from the metal container. Unconfined low velocity explosions will leave discolorations on cement surfaces. High velocity explosions will make craters of small diameter but greater depth. Sides of the crater will be steeper as well. Dynamite, however, may depress cement without removing much; on top of heavy steel, dynamite may dent and discolor. C-4 will dent heavy steel, pitting and tearing it. The search of a bomb site, the crater and environs, is essential to discover parts of the bomb filler, the remaining stuff that was part of the explosive material, and the parts of containers. How much area to search is an important investigative decision. One way is to go from the seat of the explosion, the place where the bomb was placed. Likely this will include the crater floor, the berm or crater slope, and the talus debris. How much further the perimeters of the search area are is a policy decision of the investigative leadership.

To be most effective bombs need to be confined, which means that fragments of the container, be they metal or cardboard, might be discovered at the floor, walls, or berm of the crater. Four things need to be considered when analyzing these fragments: the number, shape, hardness, and size. The greater the number, more jagged the shape, and the harder and smaller the elements, the higher the velocity the explosive. In addition, other physical evidence might be wire, tape, detenator parts and residue.

Witnesses to the explosion might also have valuable insight. For example, a report on the sound of the blast might be suggestive. A sharp crack will indicate C-4 or a bomb in the open. A dull thud or boom may indicate it was inside a building or it was a black-powder bomb. The color and amount of smoke might be important also. For example, dynamite and black powder give off white smoke while TNT and C-4 give off a black or gray smoke.

Explosions are a very dangerous form of arson causing considerable damage to property and persons each year. Investigation of such incidence has increased in importance in the last two decades.

Fire

Magnitude

Arsonist fire has had a long history in America. But it was not until the turbulent 1960s, with all of the urban rioting, looting, and destruction, that it was recognized as a national crime problem. Losses to arson were estimated to be $74 million in 1965. Ten years later that figure was placed at $634 million. Finally, in 1978 the FBI made it a class I crime on its index crimes.

It is estimated that throughout the 1980s the rate of arson increased 300 percent. In 1985, 103,270 arson fires were reported by the law enforcement community. Although structural arson held steady or slightly decreased, the burning of mobile property, such as trailers, mobile homes, and cars, increased 9 percent. Analyzed on a cost-per-incident basis, arson is likely the most expensive crime committed in America. For example, the losses per incident is about ten times greater than that of robbery.[11] Nationwide, in 1989, arson accounted for 25 percent of all fire service injuries; 31.6 percent of all fire service deaths were due to this crime. Across the nation 15 percent of all structure fires were due to arson. In large met-

---

11. John J. O'Connor, *Practical Fire and Arson Investigation* (New York: Elsevier, 1987), p. 1.

ropolitan areas 25 percent of all structural and 25 percent of all automobile fires were due to arson. Some states had a greater incidence of this crime. For example, 46.6 percent of all fires in Hawaii were connected to arson. California followed with 28 percent.[12]

Difficulties

The investigation of arson crimes is extremely difficult with conviction rates being less than 20 percent. The reasons for this problem are numerous:

- First, in many cases the property destroyed is undesirable. Frequently it is in a rundown area of town and the people most directly affected are powerless.
- Second, often the destroyer of the property, either directly by setting the fire or indirectly by hiring a professional torch, is a respectable property owner.
- Third, much of the property and evidence of the crime is destroyed by the fire or by the fire fighters.
- Fourth, organized and professional criminals have increasingly become involved in arson. The number of "professional torches" have undoubtedly increased and, with specialization, have made their detection more difficult.
- Fifth, local police departments have been generally slow to develop specialists in arson investigation. All states have a Fire Marshal's office to enforce fire codes and investigate fires in public buildings, but in most cases these offices are understaffed.
- Sixth, the federal level of policing has increasingly become involved with crimes having to do with fire and explosions. The Bureau of Alcohol, Tobacco and Firearms became involved in the investigation of explosives-related incidents with the enactment of the Organized Crime Control Act of 1970. In February 1978, the ATF implemented a formal arson program to assist in the investigation of arson. That same year the FBI made arson an index crime and shortly would become involved in arson incidents. Consequently, in any given arson crime it is possible for local, state, and federal officials to become involved in the investigation.

---

12. National Fire Data Center, *Arson in America: A Profile of 1989*, NFIRS (Washington, DC: United States Fire Administration, Technical Report Series, 1990), pp. 6, 21. NIFRS is the National Fire Incident Reporting System established by the National fire Data Center in the early 1980s to collect, quantify and report on the incidence of fire in America.

- Seventh, many insurance companies have a vested interest in the investigation of such destruction of property they have insured. Consequently, larger insurers will have training programs and investigators who might appear on the scene as well, thus making jurisdictional and investigative lines hazy.

Definitions

Successful investigation of crimes by fire needs to be informed with a knowledge of some basics.

There are three elements to fire that have been portrayed in the past as a triangle: heat, oxygen, and fuel. However, that historical triangle fell short in explaining true fires. Consequently, a forth element was introduced called a chemical chain reaction which made the geometric metaphor a tetrahedron. For simplicity this discussion will emphasize the three main elements.

Heat is the energy possessed by a material or substance due to molecular activity. This phenomena is measured by different scales, either Celsius(C), Fahrenheit (F), or Kelvin. British thermal units (BTU) show how much heat is required to raise one pound of water one degree Fahrenheit.

There are five ways to produce heat:

1. Chemical causes are due to the result of rapid oxidation. The introduction of certain chemicals will cause a reaction resulting in the generation of heat.
2. Mechanical heat is produced by friction.
3. Electrical heat may occur when there is a malfunction of wiring or appliances.
4. Compressed gas as in an internal combustion engine generates heat.
5. Nuclear energy results in the splitting or fusing of atomic particles and causes heat.

There three ways to transfer heat:

1. Conduction refers to the transfer of heat by way of molecular activity within a material, usually a solid. When one touches and is burned by a hot stove conduction is at work.
2. Convection refers to the transfer of heat through a circulating medium such as air or a liquid. This is the chief cause of the spread of fire in structures.
3. Radiation refers to heat moving in waves and rays such as sunlight or x-rays. Radiation travels at the same speed as visible light, 186,000 miles per second.

Oxygen is an important part of any fire. The air we breath is 21 percent oxygen. If the oxygen level drops below 15 percent, a fire may be extinguished or smothered due to the lack of oxygen. However, a fire that develops in an oxygen-rich environment would burn faster. Some materials, such as plastics (with cellulose nitrate), inspire flame because of the oxygen present. Some oxygen is changed by fire producing carbon monoxide a primary cause of asphyxiation and death at a fire scene. Carbon monoxide may be a fuel with its own ignition temperature of 1128 degrees F, and is believed to be a cause of most *backdrafts* or smoke explosions, something to be explained shortly.

Fuel comes in three states: gas, liquid, and solid. Generally all fuels are converted into gases. For example, gasoline as a liquid does not burn; the vapors rising from the liquid fuel burn. Wood, perhaps the most common solid fuel, is not flammable; it gives off resin vapors that burn. The wood itself decomposes. Gas will spread and eventually equalize its distribution in a fixed room or container. When a gas fuel diffuses into the air, the mixture may ignite or explode. The percentage of gas to air at which this occurs is the lowest limit of that gas's flammability. The upper limit is the percentage at which the mixture is too concentrated to ignite, there is too little oxygen. For example, for natural gas this range is 5 to 15 percent. It becomes flammable at 5 percent of gas to air, but it would be stifled at 15 percent.

Liquids evaporate fumes. The temperature at which a liquid turns into a gas is called its *boiling point*. Since a liquid's boiling point suggests its readiness to vaporize, and hence be more prone to ignite, it is used as a way to determine volatility. A low boiling point means high volatility and an increased risk of fire. *Flash point* is that temperature which a liquid gives off enough vapor to form an ignitable mixture. For example, gasoline has a flash point at -50 degrees F; for kerosene it is 100 degrees F. A flammable liquid is one with a flash point below 140 degrees F. Those with flash points above 140 degrees F. are classified as combustible liquids. *Fire point* is that temperature at which a liquid produces vapors that will sustain combustion; it is several degrees higher than the flash point. For example, the fire point for kerosene is 110 degrees F.

Solid fuels have a definite shape. Combustibility is due to their shape and volume. Powdered or finely cut kindling, for example, ignites more easily than larger bulky samples of the same materials.

Phases of a Fire

Normally, fire goes through four phases. Of course, these phases may be impacted upon by heat, oxygen, and fuel. These phases are incipient, emergent smoldering, open burning, and oxygen regulated smoldering.

The incipient stage is the earliest phase of a fire and may go unnoticed. It will vary depending on the type of fuel. It may last a few seconds, as in a liquid accelerant near an open flame, or it may take days, as in cases of spontaneous combustion.

The emergent smolder stage may be only slightly detectable. Heating of materials nearest the source may occur, and some slight smoke may appear, but the rest of the environment is unchanged.

Open burning is characterized as flames increasing at geometric rates. For example, the intensity of the fire will double with each 18 degree F (or 10 degrees C) increase in temperature. Heat will rapidly go from the point of origin to the uppermost points of the room or structure. As the temperature of the air molecules of a confined space reach ignition temperature two things might occur, "fairies flying" and "flashover." "Fairies flying" refers to the ignition of small pockets of flammable gases giving the ghost-like appearance of small flashes. This is a precursor to "flashover," a process in which flames flash over the entire space. The average fire reaches flashover in eight minutes.

Oxygen regulated smoldering occurs in confined areas in which the flame in the previous phase depletes the oxygen and returns to a smolder. Smoke and heat are still present at temperatures over 1000 degrees F. Such a situation reduces fuel gases and only needs their reintroduction to burst into a fire at an explosive rate. This is called a *backdraft* or *smoke explosion* and can be very dangerous to the unexpecting fire fighter.

Places of Fire

For the purposes of this book, there are three places a fire might occur: outdoors, in an automobile, and inside a structure.

Wildfires are defined as uncontrolled fires in forests and watershed areas. They become a particular problem in the late, hot, dry summer months. Any examination of such fires needs to be posed on the issue of accidental or arson. Most are accidental with causes directed at acts of nature, such as a lightning strike in a forest or prairie, or by the carelessness of campers. Of the 1,832 wildfires in 1991 it is believed that 1,305 were started by lightning. The U.S. Forest Service estimates that 26 percent of all fires of protected acreage (92 percent of all U. S. forest and watershed land is protected under the Clarke-McNary Act of 1924) are due to arson. Regional analysis finds a disproportionate numbers of such fires (56 percent of all wildfires in the area) in the South. Normal or accidental fires generally take on the appearance of a fan, the narrowest part being nearer the point of origin. Multiple overlapping fans suggest arson.

Automobile fires by incendiary causes are even more prevalent. Accidental fires may occur and the investigator has to eliminate that possibility before starting an arson investigation. There are at least five considerations when exploring the possibility of an accidental vehicular fire. Accidental vehicular fires are malfunctions due to:

1. Electrical problems in the elaborate wiring, fuses, and battery systems.
2. Fuel system problems in the tank and fuel lines.
3. Careless smokers.
4. Dragging of foreign objects that causes friction.
5. Multiple vehicle collisions.

Although, accidental fires do occur, the overwhelming majority are intentionally set by the owner of the vehicle. The primary motive is economic or "selling it to the insurance company." Several items might be examined to help document that the fire is an arson, including the general exterior and general interior of the vehicle.

General Exterior

While single car collisions can happen, any fire attributed to such an incident must document that indeed a collision had occurred.

- Generally the materials of an automobile do not lend themselves to fire destruction. Consequently, any automobile that is extensively damaged from bumper-to-bumper must be regarded as suspicious.
- Signs of accelerant splatter or splash, distinctive finger-like patterns on the surface of the car, that will point to any flow of a liquid accelerant would be suspicious.
- Tires may be changed and older or worthless ones substituted in some sort of salvaging process by the fire setter.
- Gas caps might be blown off because the arsonist introduced explosive chemicals to the gas tank. The gas plug might have been removed to allow gasoline to drain and pool underneath the vehicle to fuel the fire.
- Suspension systems might fail, a process called sagging, due to intense heat. Undercarriage springs and shock absorbers might sag only after heat is introduced by an accelerant. Generally steel will soften at 1,000 degrees F and will fail between 1,500 and 1,700 degrees F. Of course, the duration of the heat and the mass of the steel will affect the outcome.
- Glass, particularly the windshield, will crack (the term used in arson investigation is craze) at about 800 degrees F, soften at about 1,000 degrees F, and fail at 1,400 degrees F. If the heat increase is slow, the cracks and breaks will be rounded; if the increase is rapid, they will be jagged.
- Multiple points of origin of a fire on the exterior suggest arson.

Chrome fittings will discolor, due to different temperature ranges. This discoloration can be used to indicate the heat of the fire, as shown in the table below.

Chromium Discoloration due to Temperature Ranges

Color	Temperature (F°)
Yellow	450–500
Purple-Brown	550–575
Blue	600–875
Light Red	900–1,000
Dark Red	1,100–1,300
Bright Red	1,400–1,500
Salmon	1,600–1,700
Lemon	1,800–1,900
White	2,000–2,400
Sparkling White	2,400+

General Interior

There are three interior areas that are examined for arsonist activity: the engine and the passenger and trunk compartments. An accidental fire in any one of these three places tends to be confined to that compartment. On the other hand, arsonist fires do spread.

The *engine* is an internal combustion devise, or a controlled explosion. Therefore, it is highly volatile in terms of explosions and fire. But engineers are aware of this and materials in this area are not as flammable as elsewhere in the vehicle. Nonetheless, as when a valve is blown, ordinary fire can start in the engine and continue as long as it is fed by gasoline. The probability of accidental fire is greater here and is less for arson.

Passenger areas have much more flammable materials such as seat upholstery and padding, floor mats, and carpeting. Foam rubber and other plastic products used in the interiors of cars may burn at temperatures approaching those of common accelerants and may distort such indicators as sagging.

Trunk and luggage compartments are close to gas tanks in most cars in America and are a favorite place for an arsonist to begin a vehicle fire. Such an arson can expect the added booster of the gas tank.

Structural Fires. The possibility of an accidental fire must be addressed as part of the preliminary investigation of arson. There are at least five sources for an accidental fire:

1. Careless human activity, such as children playing with flammable materials and adults with items of tobacco.
2. Gas leaks either from faulty or damaged service lines or appliances.
3. Electrical malfunctions either from faulty or damaged service lines or appliances.
4. Spontaneous combustion due to the chemical energy generated by composed piles or discarded greasy rags.
5. Natural causes such as lightning strikes.

Arson fires of a structure are common enough to warrant an extended discussion of their investigation. The reader should consider much of the subsequent discussion to be directed towards fires in structures.

Motives of Arson

First, awareness of the motivation of fire setters is essential. Motives can be placed into two large categories: irrational and rational.

Irrational

Certainly, pyromaniacs, those with psychological problems that compel them to set fires, are among this group of irrational arsonists. It is estimated that about 30 percent of all arsonist fires are done by this group. The general personality type has been profiled by investigators. A pyromaniac arsonist is likely to be a white male under the age of 25. There probably was a pathologically-distressed upbringing within a family providing a father-absent and mother-dominated environment. The person was academically retarded with slightly below average intelligence. There are probably socially and sexually maladjustments as well, and the person is either unmarried or the marriage is largely dysfunctional. Some argue that these people set fires for some sexual gratification. Certainly there is some sort of sensual arousal for these "fire bugs." The pyromaniac is emotionally and psychologically disturbed with considerable feelings of insecurity and cowardice. This person starts fires impulsively and does not plan or carry combustible materials. Likely there is no connection or links between fires.[13]

Youthful vandalism accounts for upwards of 50 percent of arsonist fires. In terms of analysis, this category can be divided into two groups: children and adolescents.

Although very young children have been known to set fires, this discussion focuses on those between 6 and 12 years of age. Fires of such individuals are associated with hurtful or revengeful fantasy. Generally there

---

13. Much of this discussion of fire setters relies upon Anthony Olen Rider, "The Fire Setter: A Psychological Profile" in *FBI Law Enforcement Bulletin* vol 47, nos. 6, 7, 8 (1980).

is some learning disability and maybe even the presence of a physical handicap. Boys are likely to be enuresis or bed wetters. Some form of family-home dysfunction is likely to be present. Some forms of antisocial behavior may be evident as well such as truancy, stealing, running away, and aggressive behavior. A primary target of these young arsonist is the home or some other form of family property.

Many of the characteristics mentioned above may be useful for this category of adolescent fire setters between the ages of 12 and 16. There is likely to be a history of delinquency. The young person has a poor academic record. There is likely a pathological personality with manifestations of aggressive and disruptive behavior. Sexual immaturity is characteristic as well. Although revenge is a common motive, these arsonists shift their targets from homes to schools and churches. In addition, having found-like-minded cohorts, they tend to do it in pairs or pacts.

Another group of irrational arsonists are those ordinary people caught up in a "mob mentality" during a riot or chaos connected to some other civil disturbance. These arsonists-looters may have a revengeful attitude due to perceived racial, economic and social wrongs. Events in Los Angeles after the Rodney King incident and trial illustrate this point. Similar events in Miami in 1980 can also be recalled. Perennial "Devils' Nights" in Detroit during Halloween also are indicative.

Finally, there are those who in a crazed revengeful state set a fire. They may be angry with an employer or former employer and come back to vent their feelings. Recently separated or divorced persons may want to get revenge for the martial disruption. Or perhaps it will be a spurned lover, such as in the event that occurred in a Hispanic social club in New York City, in October, 1976. A jilted boyfriend set fire to the club and 25 people were killed.

Rational

There are those who calculate and in very rational ways determine to set fires. Nationally, only 9 percent of all arson cases are cleared by arrest, and only 2 percent result in convictions. In short, arson appears to pay as a criminal activity. Some examples of these are:

Terrorists are those people motivated by political or religious reasons to cause widespread insecurity through intimidation and dramatic damage. FALN (Fuerzas Armadas de Liberación Nacional Puertorriqueña or the Armed Forces of Puerto Rican National Liberation) was known for starting fires in New York City department stores. Fires at abortion clinics might be put into this category as well. The Animal Liberation Front (ALF) and People for the Ethical Treatment of Animals (PETA) have targeted stores in the past that sell fur products. Of course, these groups want to be discovered, frequently calling and laying claim to the deed. Their motive is to call attention to their particular cause and tactics.

Crime is another reason for many arsonist activity. Rather than political motives these arsonists are driven by economic ones, such as crime, business fraud, insurance fraud, and professional arson for profit.

- *Crime concealment* is one motivation for arson. A burglar might set a fire to remove evidence of his breaking and entering. A murderer might burn the victim and surrounding area to minimize detection. Stolen automobiles and getaway cars may be torched to destroy evidence.
- *Business-related fraud* is another motive for arson. Some business persons might want to eliminate competition. Perhaps a nearby competitor has become a threat and needs to be undermined. In a variety of ways organized crime has become involved in arson. They may use it as a means of extortion and intimidation. Various demolition and rehabilitation scams result in arson. For example, an owner of a large tract of land covered with old buildings might have trouble selling because of the vacant structures. Not wanting to suffer the cost of demolition, the owner burns the buildings down. In large urban areas there may be problems with building strippers as well. These people come into abandoned buildings to salvage various plumbing fixtures, pipes, and tubing to sell as junk. Since so many of these items are in the walls this is an arduous task. Some strippers have been known to set many small fires to bring in the fire department who not only quash the fire but partially demolish the building, thus exposing various items for the strippers.
- *Insurance frauds* are a common motive for arson. A business or home might be set afire to get rid of an expensive piece of property and receive reimbursement from the insurance company. "Steal and burn" cases have to do with reporting a car stolen, or taken to a place where it is likely to be stolen, and then later finding it gutted with fire.
- *Professional torches* are those career criminals who have taken up arson as their specialty. While they probably have a longer history, public awareness of this type of criminal probably dates to the late 1960s and early 1970s when the careers of Angelo Monachino of Rochester and Willie Noriego of Tampa Bay became known. Some profiling of professional arsonists has been done to inform any investigation. Of course, the prime motive for such a criminal is profit. They are generally white males of 35 to 55 years in age with slightly above average intelligence. They have antisocial personalities which manifest as ego centered,

manipulative, exploitative, deceitful, and scheming. They have a high-risk lifestyle characterized with high alcohol consumption, irregular work record, and living beyond their means resulting in frequent debt. They have not been married or are divorced and live a solitary life. Their arsonist behavior can be broken down into three phases: (1) Pre-event—in which there is considerable time spent in planning and preparation. In fact, numerous visits to the site might occur in which much of the arsonist preparation takes place; (2) Event—in which little time is spent; it may be a matter of coming only to provide ignition; and (3) Post-event—very little time is further spent on this business; the arsonist departs the area to establish alibi and begin negotiating new business.

Mechanisms of Arson

Basically, there are three broad considerations or investigative levels of analysis when it comes to the mechanisms of arson. They are: ignition devices, plant, and trailer.

Ignition devices set the spark of the fire. Their purpose is to insure the ignition will take place and provide the setter enough time to retreat to safety. Ignition devices range from simple to sophisticated.

The simplest ignition devices are those related to "direct ignition" or the applying of the flame directly to the kindle. The most obvious is the match and it can be expected at the most amateurish skill levels, such as the youth. The match provides very little time for the arsonist to escape his own fire. A more thoughtful arsonist might use the cigarette delay. Several matches might be attached by a rubber band half way down a burning cigarette. Once the smoldering cigarette burns down to the matches, a dramatic ignition occurs thus insuring a good ignition and a time delay for the setter. A lit cigarette can provide a 10- to 12-minute fuse when used this way. Burning candles might be used in a similar fashion, allowing the flame to work its way down to a more flammable medium. For example, a seven-eighths-inch diameter candle will burn one inch in 57 minutes in a draft-free environment. Therefore, a six-inch candle can provide nearly a six-hour departure allowance for the arsonist.

More sophisticated ignitions are "indirect" in nature. Some examples include the following. Gas appliances or services might be used to set a combustible atmosphere. Gas would fill the room reaching those levels needed for an ignition at which time a burning candle placed in the corner of the room might provide the ignition. Mechanical devices, such as kitchen timers and alarm clocks, might be wired to set a spark ignition. Electrical wiring, appliances, and fuses may also be used. Hypergolic action might be used to bring together chemicals, that when standing alone are not combustible, to form an ignition. For example, phosphorus and air will ignite. Phosphorus might be placed in a watery form in which the water is allowed to drip out; once the water has depleted the phosphorus that is also exposed to air, an ignition would take place. Any number of chemicals might be susceptible to hypergolic action.

Plant is material, kindling, placed around the ignition device that takes the initial spark and allows it to grow into a longer lasting flame. Plant can be divided along the spectrum from simple to sophisticated items.

The simplest plant, sometimes called ordinary plant, would be newspaper, wood shavings, rags, and clothing. Such stuff is generally favored in home and business fires because it is natural, things that might be found around the place ordinarily. Of course, the problem is that such plant will not be sufficient to stimulate the flame.

More sophisticated plant, sometimes called booster, would be accelerant such as kerosine and gasoline. Although more reliable, they often leave behind evidence of their use.

Trailer or streamer is material that takes fire from the point of ignition to another series of plant to create another point of ignition. It can also be viewed along a spectrum of simple to sophisticated.

The simplest trailer might be gasoline soaked towels laid together to form a line of fire. Liquid accelerant splashed on the floor would be another example. Black powder loosely trailed so that it would not explode but would create a flame path to another plant would be an excellent trailer.

More sophisticated trailer might be lengths of safety fuse or detonation cord as discussed earlier.

Burn Patterns

The movement of flame throughout a structure might indicate the nature of the fire's origin. The *rate of burn* may be ascertained visually. For example, slow burning, smoldering fire will show:

1. Uniform ceiling and wall damage, down to a line three or more feet below the ceiling
2. A baked appearance on painted or wood surfaces
3. Smoke stains around windows, doors, and on window glass

A more rapid burn will show:

1. Severe overhead damage
2. Severe charring on exposed wood surfaces
3. Sharp lines between burned and unburned areas, around windows and doors, and elements of crazed window glass

"V" Pattern. Normally, fire burns upward at rapid rates estimated to be 96 fps (about 65.5 miles per hour). The most common pattern associated with this upward movement is the "V" pattern, the apex of the "V" indicating the point of origin, with the two arms reaching toward the ceiling. Downward or lateral burning moves more slowly and occurs when the fuel source above the point of origin has been depleted. An unusual draft may seduce the flame, or a highly flammable material (trailer) might catch its attention. The breadth of the "V" will suggest the intensity of the fire and therefore the presence of accelerant. For example, a rapidly moving fire introduces a narrow "V" pattern, a slow less intense fire produces a wider "V" pattern. The former would be arson, the latter natural.

Flashover. In a confined room, about eight minutes into the burning, air molecules will become uniformly hot and ignite into a general scorch (flashover). Otherwise untouched materials and furnishings will break into fire. Because of the widespread destruction, this natural tendency might trick some investigators to think an arson has occurred.

Chimney Effect. Ventilation will cause the fire to move from its point of origin as it seeks out windows, doors, and stairways. Flame and heat have a natural tendency to travel upward. A part of the structure that might act as a chimney will direct the movement of the fire; this is called the chimney effect and it makes stairways, elevator shafts, laundry chutes, and dumbwaiters very dangerous places. Attics and cocklofts (small garrets) act the same way and can be viewed as horizontal chimneys.

Color of flame and smoke might be useful in determining the kind of combustible materials or fuels present. Of course, such observations need to be factored as to the time line of the fire. The best observation would be the earliest, that witness of the initial stage of the fire. Generally speaking the lighter the color of the flame or smoke the higher the temperature.

Flame Color and Temperature

Flame color	Temperature (°F)
Light red	900–1000
Dark red	1000–1100
Dark cherry	1100–1200
Medium cherry	1200–1300
Light cherry	1400–1500
Salmon	1600–1700
Orange	1700–1800
Lemon	1800–1900
Light yellow	1900–2100

White	2150–2250
Bright white	2500+

Smoke and Flame Colors Associated to Certain Fuels

Smoke Color	Flame Color	Fuel
Gray to Brown	Red to Yellow	Wood/Paper/ Cloth
Black	Red to White	Gasoline
White to Gray	Yellow to White	Benzine
Black to Brown	Yellow to White	Turpentine
Black	Dark Red to Orange-Yellow	Kerosene
Black	Blue White to White	Naphtha

Burn indicators are those signs and designs left on certain materials due to the presence of fire. Materials discussed here are common structural materials used in buildings: wood, glass, metal, and masonry.

- Wood takes on a particular appearance at various stages of burning called *alligatoring*. This is the appearance of blister-like marks on the wood. Large rolling blisters indicate rapid and intense heat suggesting arson. Smaller blisters indicate a longer, lower heat. In addition, smaller blisters might indicate the closeness to the point of origin of the fire. *Charring* of wood might be indicative as well. A sharp line of demarcation between charred and unburned areas of wood indicates a rapidly burning fire and suspicion of arson. A gradual change from charred and unburned wood indicates a slow burning fire. The depth of char might be revealing as well. For example, if an accelerant has been used the fire at the point of origin has probably sped away. On the other hand, if the char is deep it is probably the point of origin of a natural or non-arsonist fire.
- Glass is affected by fire in many ways. First there is *smoke staining* a process due to intensity of the heat near glass. High heat on the surface of glass causes increased molecular activity. The higher such activity the more difficult it is for soot stain to form. Therefore, the more and heavier the soot, the more likely the glass was relatively cool and further away from the flame. The less soot indicates closer proximity to the flames. *Crazing* is the cracking and breaking that occurs due to heat. Irregular and jagged breaks that create small pieces suggest rapid intense heat caused

by arson. Larger more regular and rounded smooth pieces suggest a slower fire. If incandescent light fixtures survive the fire, a *nippling* effect on the bulb will point towards the heat source. This does not apply to fluorescent bulbs.

- Metal, particularly those of smaller mass as opposed to structural steel, reflect heat through *sagging*. The nature of the metal and the amount of sagging that occurs can be suggestive of the intensity of the heat.
- Masonry, such as concrete, bricks, and cement, may be impacted in two ways, collectively called *spalling*. Spalling may appear as a discoloration due to accelerant splash. If heat is intense enough, pock marks and surface pitting may appear to the point of chipping of the materials.

Point of Origin of a fire is important to discover because it might have evidence as to the cause. Most likely it is going to be the area of greatest damage, but if sufficient trailer and accelerant had been used the fire might have raced out and away from the ignition place. Under normal circumstances a fire will stay longest at the place of origin because there is sufficient oxygen to feed it. Multiple points of origin immediately arouse suspicion.

However, *falldown fires* — those caused by falling burning material — can give the false impression of multiple causation. Generally, finding the lowest points of burning indicates place of origin. On burned flooring if the destruction is "V" shaped that means the fire was set on the floor. However, if the "V" is inverted in the floor it means the point of origin was in the basement or a floor below. Such an investigation, though dangerous because of the destruction and fragility of the scene, is necessary in discovering remains of incendiary devices and accelerant.

An *accelerant* is any substance that is used to stimulate and direct a fire. The most common forms of liquid accelerant are gasoline, lighter fluid, kerosene, and turpentine. Of course, accelerant may be used as plant and trailer as discussed above. When a liquid accelerant is used a burn pattern called *puddling* might result. This is when the accelerant seeps down in a hardwood floor or a tiled floor. Since only the fumes burn, the floor area is protected from burn and the accelerant leaves a stained but undestroyed section of the floor.

The detection of accelerant is important because its presence strongly suggests the work of arson. Frequently, since the fumes burn rather than the liquid, remnants of accelerant still might be found. Charred carpeting might contain residue; so might the cracks and joints in the flooring. Since no floor is perfectly flat, the baseboards and corners of the room might have elements of accelerant. Soils are absorbent and cool and might collect elements of accelerant splash or seepage from a house floor. Common means to detect the presence of an accelerant include human smell, technological devices, and canine detectives.

Human smell. If the burn site has not been overly soaked by the fire department, there is a chance that the aroma of the accelerant might still be present. However, odors might be masked by the general smoky aroma of the scene.

Technological devices. A number of mechanical detectors might be used to detect accelerants. Perhaps the most prominent is the catalytic combustion detector, commonly called the "Sniffer." This device takes vapor samples and reads the presence of accelerant. In the lab samples subjected to gas chromatographic analysis will detect the presence of hydrocarbons, the basis of most accelerant. Mass spectrometry is considered the state of the art in laboratory analysis of fire debris.

Canine detectives. Many of these hydrocarbon detectors are misleading, they simply miss many types of accelerant. Consequently, in the 1980s many arson squads introduced dogs as detectors. These animals were "imprinted" or specifically trained to detect a particular accelerant and have been found to be more successful than many mechanical devices.

Interviews. In any investigation of fire there are several people who need to be interviewed. These people include:

1. *Those who reported the fire.* Likely, they saw the smoke and flame at times that color and smell might be more revealing. In addition, they might have heard suspicious sounds.
2. *Fire fighters.* Although they have a different purpose for being on the scene, fire fighters do have an expertise, awareness, and history that can be of use in any information gathering strategy. Furthermore, the fire department might have arson investigators as part of their personnel.
3. *Regular users of the public space near the fire.* Police patrol officers, bus drivers, taxi drivers, and postal workers might have a familiarity and observations that might be useful.
4. *Owner of the property.* The owner might be a genuine victim of the fire and so any enemies, neighbors, former employees, etc., need to be discovered. Also, if the owner is thought to be part of the crime, his history and story needs to be known.
5. *Insurance companies.* Many of the larger insurance companies have arson prevention and detection components and have developed considerable expertise in this crime. They have a considerable interest in minimizing fraudulent claims.
6. *Informants.* Detectives may have to resort to underworld informants to learn of any movements of professional torches in the area.

Conclusions

The investigation of explosions and fire is a very difficult and dangerous job. Clearance rates remain low. Fragile and dirty crime scenes provide constant opportunity for injury. While the state of the art for detecting and preventing these crimes has increased, so has the ingenuity and passions of those who violate the law in this manner.

Chapter 13

Theft Investigation

General

For purposes of this chapter theft is defined as the fraudulent taking of personal property owned by another, against their will, with the intent of depriving them of it and converting it to personal benefit.

This chapter is divided into three parts, each constituting a subdivision of this definition of theft. First, robbery is presented; it is theft with the use of force or fear. Second, burglary is discussed; it is the breaking and entering (or some forceful entry) into the property of another to commit theft. Third, other sundry crimes are addressed: a large and wide-ranging body of theft consisting of fencing operations, auto theft, shoplifting, computer theft, and confidence games. This selection of topics is meant to be suggestive rather than comprehensive.

This body of crime is very important for the following reasons. First, it is very widespread. A look at any criminal statistics shows the most prevalent of crime categories is some form of theft. Second, it is costly and accounts for millions of dollars of loss per year. Not only are money and property lost, but when it occurs in the business sector, much of the cost is passed along to consumers in higher prices of goods. Many businesses and people spend enormous amounts of money in creating defensive or preventative security measures. Third, clearance for theft is low and rarely exceeds 20 percent. One study by John Eck for the Police Executive Research Forum (PERF) set forth some interesting conclusions. According to Eck's research, if a robbery or burglary is reported in progress the police have about a 33 percent chance of making the arrest. If the crime is reported one minute later the police have a 10 percent chance of making an arrest. If a crime is reported fifteen minutes after its commission the police have a 5 percent chance.[1] This demonstrates the difficulty of this crime category for the criminal justice system. Fourth, it illustrates the problem of victims and their victim-prone behavior. While it is not chic to blame the victim, many victims of theft have set themselves up to victimization by conducting their lives and businesses in ways to help the criminal commit his or her criminal acts. Fifth, theft crimes offer the police in general and

---

1. John Eck, Solving Crimes: The Investigation of Burglary and Robbery. Washington, DC: Police Executive Research Forum, 1979.

the investigator in particular a new role; that of an educator. Officers need to inform the public about the principles of defensible space and defensible strategy. These two ideas are based upon the notion that ordinary citizens, rather than the police, can be more successful in preventing crime. Appropriate lighting and landscaping around the home, greater security measures around the business, and alertness to dangers all around in individual lifestyles could make it more difficult for the criminal to commit his crime.

Theft gives us a look into the subculture of crime as well. As early as the 1930s the work of Edwin Sutherland, *The Professional Thief*, had a crook by the name of Chic Conwell set forth the attributes of professionalism. According to Conwell truly professional thieves:

1. Make a regular business of stealing.
2. Learn their skills from experienced thieves.
3. Develop skilled techniques, the most important being the manipulation of people.
4. Carefully plan their acts.
5. Look upon themselves as superior to amateur crooks.
6. Have a code of ethics used among other professionals.
7. Are sympathetic and congenial with other professionals.
8. View success and failure as a matter of luck.
9. Have developed a criminal slang and status system.
10. Rarely engage in only one specialty of crime.
11. Usually operate in partnerships, teams, or gangs.[2]

More modern research places emphasis on the importance learning to be a thief. In other words, it is important to be accepted by the criminal group or at least hangout with them and learn from their talk and actions. These more criminological notions are useful to the investigator. Knowing about the criminal subculture, its strengths and weaknesses, will inform investigators as they seek information in the areas where crimes most often occur and criminals reside.

Robbery

Robbery is the taking of property from a victim by force or threat of violence. As early as the thirteenth century Henry de Bracton, one of King Henry III's judges who helped to build the common law, defined robbery as aggravated theft. The model penal code in 1962 reaffirmed this notion

---

2. Edwin Sutherland, *The Professional Thief* (Chicago: University Chicago Press, 1937), pp. 2–42.

by defining robbery as doing or threatening physical harm during the commission of theft.

Robbery has a long and interesting history in Anglo-American criminal justice. For example, very early it was equated with the dissatisfactions of the lower classes. Poorer people were a threat to the upper classes. Periods of political oppression, economic dislocations, and social transformations spawned social bandits. Robin Hood was not only a robber, but he and his gang became folk heroes. Highwaymen in the sixteenth century were so prevalent and popular with the masses that a law, the Highwayman Act, was passed in 1692 to encourage citizens to help officials capture criminals by offering rewards. Pirates also touched this notion of noble robber when they attacked the enemies of the country. Even when they turned against the rich merchants of their own country, large numbers of ordinary citizens tolerated them. The streets and social circles of Charleston, South Carolina, and New Orleans were filled with such kept criminals. In America a host of robbers emerged after the Civil War to become equivalent social bandits. Names like the Younger brothers, the Dalton boys, Frank and Jesse James, Sam Bass, and Butch Cassidy crossed the line from villains to heroes.

From Robin Hood to Sundance Kid a mystique or myth emerged around these noble robbers. In fiction more than reality, this robber began his career as an honest person who became a victim of some injustice. He set out to right these personal and social wrongs. His attacks upon the elites inspired vicarious satisfaction and support from the oppressed. Robbing the rich to give to the poor became an important element. Killing, except in self-defense, was minimal. The noble robber was always true to his following, the gang, and the wider circle of supporters. He was admired and respected by large numbers of folk, and exaggerated stories of personal character and deeds emerged; he did for them what they seemed powerless to do themselves. He almost always died or was captured, but only because of betrayal. Shortly after his end a legend began to build and bestow qualities larger than life. In a curious twist, crook becomes hero and criminal justice personnel become villains. In times of social divisions and prevalence of legitimate violence, one might expect the surge of this form of violent theft.

Robbery continues to be the most widespread and costly crime today. Numerous studies present a picture of contemporary robbery and robbers in America and includes the following details:

1. Robbery most often occurs in the more populous cities of America.
2. Such crimes are generally committed by a male stranger.
3. Robbery offenders tend to be young males predominately between 15 and 25 years of age.

4. Robbery offenders are likely to be black males. Sixty- one percent of those arrested in 1992 were black and 38 percent were white. This in a country where the black population is estimated to be 12 percent.

5. Robbery victims are usually white males over 21. Robbery is more likely to be an intraracial crime than any other violent crime. However, since many black males in America are stereotyped as violent and dangerous, they cannot travel far from their home areas to commit crime without raising suspicions. That means a large number of black victims might be expected. White victims tend likely to have drifted into dangerous areas.

6. Robbery tends to take place on the streets. Around 55 percent of robberies take place in alleys, side streets, parking lots, and playgrounds.

7. The robber usually has a weapon. The most typical robbery is an armed robbery with knives or guns present.

8. Victims tend not to be injured or to be slightly injured. Studies indicate that seven out of ten victims of a robbery are not hurt.

9. However, some injury might occur if resistance is offered. When this occurs one in twelve robbery victims is seriously injured.

10. Physical harm is most likely to involve kicking, shoving, beating, or knocking the victim down.

11. Nearly a quarter of the nation's prisoners are convicted for robbery.

12. The average time spent in prison for robbery is three years, over twice the average for all other offenses.

13. Those who rob from institutions are likely to be prosecuted and serve longer prison terms than those who robbed from individuals.

14. The public has greater sympathy for those who steal from institutions than those who rob individuals.

In America, a discussion of robbery must address the issue of race. Black offenders make up a disproportionate number of offenders caught up in the criminal justice system. Besides historical racism and segregation, there are other reasons for this black factor in robbery. First, robbery is instrumental, it allows an unemployed, low-skilled individual to gain cash. Second, robbery is quick and easy; it does not take much skill beyond bravado. Third, it allows for fast money. In a society where success is equated with commercial goods a mugging provides cash to buy things. Fourth, robbery allows the powerless young black male to express his toughness and masculinity. Fifth, robbery by blacks on whites strikes fear in whites, the dominate culture. Such an event may be seen as payback time after hundreds of years of oppression. However, it must be remembered that many black robbers attack other blacks, and to interpret robbery by blacks on whites purely as revenge might be an over-simplification.

Motivation for Committing Robbery

Motivations for robbery can be placed into three large categories:

1. Desire for money is the largest (57 percent) reason for committing a robbery. Within this classification the largest item money is needed for is drugs (17 percent). Money needed for other specific items besides drugs (16 percent) and just a general desire to have more money (16 percent) are the next important reasons. Specific needs of food and shelter are other reasons (8 percent) for robbery.

2. Reasons other than money account for 24 percent of the motivation. Excitement of the event (6 percent), anger (6 percent), impressing friends (6 percent), and being drunk or on drugs (6 percent) make up this category. Willie Sutton, the famed bank robber of the 1920s and 1930s, when asked why he robbed banks, provided two answers. First, the more cryptic, humorous, and often-quoted statement: "That's where the money is" was probably not really his comment. Sutton's second answer was far more revealing. "Why did I rob banks?" he said. "Because I enjoyed it. I loved it. I was more alive when I was inside a bank, robbing it, than at any other time in my life."[3]

3. Nineteen percent of the perpetrators insist that they are not really robbers. Six percent claim that they were with a friend who actually started the robbery. Some were just recovering money owed them, they claimed (5 percent). A small number were actually engaging in burglary and it turned into robbery when interrupted in the act (4 percent). Another 4 percent were in a fight and it turned into a robbery.

Robbery Categories

For analytical purposes one may divide robbery into various categories:

1. *Visible Public Robbery.* This kind of robbery occurs in public space such as streets, parking lots, and alleys. The word "public" here should be thought of going beyond notions of the traffic of people. Public also means that the police patrol in its everyday activities could and should act as a deterrent. This kind of robbery becomes a criticism of police as a preventive force. Four out of ten robberies occur on the street, and there are three types: unarmed but violent, armed, and snatch-and-flee. All types

---

3. See Willie Sutton and Edward Linn, *Where the Money Was: The Memoirs of the World's Greatest Bank Robber* (New York: Ballantine Books, 1976).

depend on the element of surprise and speed. Generally they are done at dusk or after dark. These are opportunistic with vulnerable victims, such as women and elderly men, selected. This is likely to be a style most often used by the more amateur criminal and frequently more than one assailant is involved.

2. *Nonvisible Public Robbery.* These occur in public space too, but they are off the streets where the police might more easily prevent or protect the victim. For example, these might occur in the lobby or elevator of a residential building, or in a subway station or on a subway platform. More planning and less spontaneity characterize these types of robbery. While multiple assailants are likely, there is a greater likelihood of a single assailant. Women and elderly men are the favorite target for this type of robbery and weapons are usually present. More time is spent at the scene and violence is more likely because of the general hidden nature of the activity. These robbers seem to have graduated from the visible street crime category to this one.

3. *Commercial Robbery.* These robberies are committed against small businesses and chain stores. All night liquor stores and gas stations are commonly victimized. Favorite times are late on Wednesday, Thursday, and Friday nights. Weapons are commonly used and any resistance will result in injury or death. Older and more experienced and desperate robbers commit these crimes. Money for drugs is seen as the main cause of these robberies. Since these robberies are committed against small businesses, the amount of money taken is likely to be small.

Consequently, there has been an increase of another type of commercial victim. In the first half of the 1990s a new victim emerged dramatically as bank heists increased. For example, there was a record total bank robberies in 1990 of 7,837. Cities like Los Angeles went from 633 bank robberies in 1990 to 810 in 1991; Atlanta increased from 109 to 247 in the same period. Since there is so much money for the taking, a bank robbery is a high-risk venture. Historically this was the province of the professional thief, but today more amateurs seem to be involved, and the average take of a bank robbery seems to have gone down. In 1932, the average loss in bank robbery was $5,583, in 1991 it was $3,177.[4] It is estimated that three out of four bank robbers are caught, and they face up to 25 years in federal prison for the crime. The rash of bank heists in Los Angeles is connected to the development of branch banking, the small suburban bank connected to a larger downtown one, and the sprawl of the freeway road

---

4. Hugh Barlow, *Introduction to Criminology*, 7th ed. (New York: Harper Collins, 1996), p. 157.

system allowing quick access and retreat. These bank heists generally take one of two forms. First, there is the holdup in which a note or weapon is presented to the teller and money is demanded. Second, a "take over" in which hostages are taken and the robbers go for the vault and safe systems.

There has been some evidence that bands of Columbian Jewel thieves have been in operation. They operate in teams of four to ten members and their success depends on stealthiness and deception. For example, they will enter a retail jewelry store, a hotel lobby, or municipal airport, in small groups. Once inside the retail outlet, some of them distract store employees while others open valuable jewelry displays and remove the contents. The FBI monitors the activities of these thieves through a special rapid identification system called "Colgem." These crimes raise the issue of "defensible space." This principle sees that the environment—our lighting systems, architecture styles, landscaping decisions, and business practices—might actually help the robber to commit his crime. For example, a liquor store with all kinds of beer advertisements on the windows hinders the outside view of the interior of the store and actually helps the thief. Of course, only so much can be done to prevent robbery. For example, most banks have all kinds of technology, such as alarms and cameras, but the drive for drug money overcomes the thief and robberies are tried anyway.

4. *Vehicle Robbery*. This form of robber steals from a commercial driver such as delivery van or bus drivers. Auto theft itself will be covered later. Inner city taxi drivers have been particularly endangered by vehicle robbery. Some defensible strategies have been instituted, such as Plexiglas separations dividing drivers from passengers in cabs and exact change policies for buses. The recent flurry of carjacking can be placed in this category. In these cases, an automobile driver stopped at a traffic light is confronted and forced to relinquish the car to the thief. Data suggest that carjacking occurs more often in urban areas after dark, young people are victimized most often, young men are offenders, half of these crimes are carried out by black offenders, and most offenders are armed. Unlike ordinary robbery, carjacking results in considerable loss; the average loss has been put at $4,000, more than 100 times the value of a typical robbery.

5. *Residential Robbery*. This robber enters the home to commit robbery. It is different from burglary because the thief knows or finds humans inside. Historically, this was a common form of robbery with the perpetrator called the "second-story man." While the family was downstairs dining or visiting, this robber sneaked into the upstairs and stole items. There has been such a rise in this activity in the last decade that new laws —house invasion, housebreaking, or residential robbery laws—have been passed to increase the punishment for the crime. These robbers select a

target based on a knowledge of valuables inside. Other kinds of crime such as rape and murder might be connected to this type of robbery.

The Robbery

Managing of the mugging is a critical part of this crime. The time spent and the degree of effort expended depends upon where the robber falls along the spectrum of professionalism to amateurism. One way to see the distinctions is along a continuum of skill. For example, one style of robbery would be:

1. *The Ambush*. In this style of robbery the offender is opportunistic. There has been little formal planning in terms of site and victim selection. This should not be taken as the lack of premeditation. These offenders have thought out the crime and determined to commit it, but they have not formalized it into a concrete plan. This robber simply sees an opportunity and takes it. Most likely this type of robber is on the beginning or initial steps of a robbery career. The element of surprise is essential to the entire scenario. The managing of the event by this robber is likely to be more filled with anxiety at all stages of the encounter.
2. *The Selective Raid*. There is minimal planning connected to this robbery style. Choice sites, or "feeding grounds," and paths of exit have been selected. Most likely the planning has been determined with the aid of the environment, those places that allow the greatest cover due to lighting and building design. This kind of robber has made a more calculated career move, he has probably had some experience in the act of robbery.
3. *The Planned Operation*. These robbers have made greater commitments to the activity. There is much greater planning in terms of site and victim selection. Though still present, anxiety levels are lower among these criminals. These criminals commit larger "scores," getting away with more money and are less likely to be captured. Many of these robbers are single operators.

Another way to make distinctions is along the following three points. First, there is the amateur who is just beginning or flirting with this activity. Amateurs often begin this activity out of boredom and mischievous dare. They are young and just learning the trade. Because of their low skill level, they are frequently apprehended by the police.

Second, there is the habitual criminal, that robber who frequently commits crime but has other lines of work such as burglary, pimping, and hustling. Robbery is not the sole source of his income. Although habitual criminals are repeat robbers, they do not develop a sense of professionalism honing their skills and methods. Still, they want to associate with criminals and the criminal subculture. Largely, they are not trusted by other more professional robbers and will not be brought into partnerships or teams planning a crime. Habitual criminals frequently get caught.

Third, there is the professional robber. He engages in robbery almost exclusively and it is his main source of income. Willie Sutton, the famed robber of the 1920s and 1930s, claimed the professional was one who constantly thought and planned robberies.[5] These robbers are relatively small in number but they are responsible for most of the big scores. As one author has observed

> Professionalism means more than quasi membership in a criminal subculture. It means developing skills, talents, know-how, competence, viewpoints, a way-of-life, and assorted rationalizations and justifications. It means weighing risks, choosing among alternatives, planning, using caution, and subscribing to a code of conduct. Professionalism in robbery means that robbery is a part of one's life.[6]

With small degrees of difference the amateur, habitual, and professional robber must deal with the act of stealing. One may think of robbery occurring in three phases:

First, there is the pre-confrontation stage, or that interval before the robber comes upon the perspective victim. Several things have to be done in this stage. The robber, based upon his experience level, has considerable anxiety. Will the victim resist? Are there unexpected witnesses nearby? Will the police happen upon the scene? Will I fail or be captured? To minimize these fears several things might be done. First, there might be joining up with others, setting up a team. Second, there would be the level of planning done. More experienced and professional robbers would spend time in target selection. Role assignments for the job must be made; who is to be the lookout, the wheelman, the gunman, the voice? Primary cars need to be stolen and license plates removed for the get away. Secondary cars need to be parked at key areas or transfer points in the get away. Time and place for meeting and splitting up the money must be determined. Finally, and most important for the more professional robber, there is a need to study the target and rehearse the approach and exit from the site. In spite of these preparations, there is always the possibility of the unexpected arrival of the police or a witness. Robbery remains a high-risk activity filled with anxiety.

Second, the robber confronts and enjoins the victim in the event stage. At this time the robber must transfer his anxiety over to the victim. This

---

5. Willie Sutton and Edward Linn, *Where the Money Was: The Memoirs of the World's Greatest Bank Robber* (New York: Ballantine Books, 1977).

6. Hugh D. Barlow, *Introduction to Criminology*, 7th ed. (New York: Harper Collins, 1996), p.155.

victim management might be done in several ways. Surprise is essential to catch and keep the victim off guard. Of course, victim selection is critical; a weak or vulnerable victim (a woman or elderly man) will be less stressful for the robber. Robbers have a limited number of tools to maintain control. They are the voice commands, appearance, and the use of force. Intimidation by use of menacing words and weapons will help insure success. A hooded or masked appearance not only keeps identities secret but disguises any anxiety the robber might have. The robber may use preemptive force to maintain control. Not only must the robber maintain a level of tension for his control, but he must not let it get out of hand. A hysterical victim might be as disruptive to the event as a stubborn one. And, quickness of the action will guarantee victim confusion and compliance; a successful robbery should be finished in less than three minutes.

Third, there is the exit stage at which the victim is left behind and the retreat is carried out. This is the most important part of a robbery. As with the crime itself, the getaway should be as fast as possible. At this time any residual anxiety is alleviated, the event has been a success and the rewards gained. Victims too might become emboldened and provide a last minute threat. Avenues of egress might be dangerous as well. Police might be following, and since the criminal act has been carried out the robbers feel even greater pressure not to be captured. The sentences for robbery are quite different from those of just attempted robbery. It is during the getaway that violence between the robber and the police might erupt. But generally the robber experiences euphoria and may carelessly leave evidence behind. It is also in this stage, if the robbers are more professional, that strategies for separation and laying low for a period are carried out.

Investigations

Investigations of robbery are extremely difficult; they are fast, traumatic, and have little in the way of physical evidence. There are some essential activities to keep in mind.

1. *Interview the victim.* In such encounters the victim is likely to be the sole source of information. Of course, the event was likely to be so fast and frightening that victims will have little to offer. Various interview aids, as discussed in previous chapters, may be useful. Forensic artistry, be it a sketch, plastic overlays, or computer programs like Compusketch, might be used to help the remembering process of the victim.
2. *Interview internal sources.* Since robbery is so prevalent, other detectives might recognize the modus operandi of this particular

case. Existing departmental records of offenders, both active and inactive, might be of use. Interviewing patrol officers of the beat in which the event occurred would be very helpful. These officers likely were the first on the scene when the crime was committed and have a history with the area.

3. *Search for other witness.* Existing known witnesses and a canvass for other witnesses needs to be done.
4. *Assess physical evidence.* Avenues of entrance and exit from the scene need to be ascertained and a search for physical evidence carried out. Footprints and discarded items might be found.
5. *Interview informants.*
6. *Take the educative role.* In terms of public relations and education the officers should take the opportunity to instruct the victim and witnesses on the preventive measures that might be taken to avoid such victimization in the future. Such an activity would be essential in working on burglary.

Burglary

Burglary is the breaking and entering of a building to commit theft. The forceful entry may be dramatic with considerable or slight damage. Partial entrance, or the entrance of another object to snag and fetch objects, satisfies the law when determining burglary. Entry is breaking the boundary of expected privacy. This crime can be as frightening as robbery. Even though they might not be physically present at the crime, burglary victims feel personally violated to find their home or business ransacked and robbed. There were close to 3 million burglaries reported to the police in 1993, which account for about 20 percent of all index crimes. This crime is important beyond the personal real and sense of loss. It has given rise to a booming security business. J.P. Freeman & Company, a security research and consulting firm, says that the amount of money spent on installing and monitoring residential security systems increased 67 percent between 1988 and 1993, with $15 billion being spent during that period. One in six homes have some security system, it is claimed.[7] This does not account for security for businesses.

Historically, burglary has focused upon residential sites. Indeed, many people kept most of their valuables at home and the wealthy were victimized. The burglary menace was so great in Chicago in 1857 that the newspapers moaned that "Things are coming to a terrible pass in this city. Chicago seems to be delivered over into the keeping of thieves and house

---

7. *New York Times* (August 18, 1994).

breakers."[8] By the mid-19th century, larger amounts were guaranteed in the burglary of the commercial world. The first recorded bank burglary in America, for example, was in New York City on March 19, 1831, when thieves got away with $245,000 in cash. In particular, bank burglary was a common occurrence beginning in the last half of the nineteenth century. "Gentleman burglars" were known for their long and painstaking jobs that earned them profits in the thousands. This became such a problem that the Pinkerton National Detective Agency were retained by the American Bankers Association beginning in the 1880s to detect and deter these highly professional burglars. In addition, there appeared to be a race between the safe makers and the safe breakers. The former tried to create more burglar resistant vaults and the latter came up with ways to compromise them.

By the turn of the century a new burglar, the Yegg burglar, appeared on the scene. The Yegg used nitroglycerin as a way to break the safes and revolutionized bank burglary. Throughout the 20th century, banks became so security-conscious that burglary became very difficult. Other commercial and residential burglaries took their place. For example, in 1970 residential burglary accounted for 58 percent of the total number of burglaries. Of course, there are many more opportunities, more residences, than businesses so such an average might be misleading.

Residential Burglary

Of the various possible burglaries, residential burglary is the most fearsome as the sense of personal violation is greater. The chance of additional victimization is great. According to the Justice Department, three-fifths of all rapes in the home are committed by burglars. Violence of some sort occurs in 30 percent of burglaries in which someone is home during the break-in.[9] Victims of residential burglary are revealing. A burglary rate of victims in 1992 shows the following to be important:

1. *Ethnicity*. Whites had a rate of 46.4 per 1,000, blacks 68.4 per 1,000, and Hispanics are higher with 69.9.
2. *Household income*. People with incomes less than $7,500 had a rate of 71.3 per 1,000, from $7,500 to $9,999 were at 63.4, and those with incomes between $10,000-$14,999 were at 61.2. The rate diminished with every increasing income category. Those with $50,000 or more had a burglary rate of 43.6 per 1,000.

---

8. *Chicago Daily Tribune* (June 24, 1857).

9. Bureau of Justice Statistics, *Households Touched by Crime, 1987* (Washington, DC: U.S. Department of Justice, 1988).

3. *Residence.* Those living within the central city had a rate of 60.1 per 1,000, suburban dwellers were at 44.6, and non-metropolitan residences were at 41.7.

4. *Ownership.* Those who owned the home had a rate of 39.4 per 1,000, and those renting had a rate of 65.8.[10]

Clearly, the poor minority renting and living in central city are the most likely to be burgled.

The Burglar

On a simplistic level burglars come to their crimes with a variety of skills and sense of commitment. Consequently, a crude typology might be created along a spectrum of skill.

First, there is the professional. Actually, the professional might be seen along two lines. The old-fashioned "Gentleman Burglars" are rare today but they are useful as a type reference. These professionals commit only a few crimes per year. They like to plan deeply and go for a few "big scores." They have developed elaborate techniques, information systems, and fencing outlets. Since there is so much planning, and a sense of what they are looking for, these burglars may ransack to a lesser degree. They are likely to have wider predatory patterns, being national and even international in scope. They are arrested rarely, and when it happens, they have money for excellent legal representation. Aside from these old elites, there is a more numerous professional. These burglars may not have as developed of a style but they are habitual and use burglary as their sole source of income. Their numbers are greater and they are more confined in their predatory patterns.

Second, there is the amateur. They commit numerous crimes in rapid succession. These people are impulsive and planning is absent or minimal. Their skill levels are low and brute force is characteristic. They rely on personal observation or casual information sources. They tend to ransack and destroy the residency and may leave behind valuable objects because they narrowly define their quest to cash. They are local thieves, likely neighborhood crooks, with minimal outlets for their goods.

Other categories of burglars infrequently considered are acquaintance burglars, those people who know the victim beyond casual encounters. They have been in the residency on a social basis and know of the victim's possessions. Sometimes estranged husbands break into their former homes to take property they think should go to them. Some neighborly burglars like to think of themselves as "the good guys." They select their victims based upon neighborhood feelings. Troublesome neighbors will be select-

---

10. Bureau of Justice Statistics, *Criminal Victimizations in the United States, 1992* (Washington, DC: U.S. Department of Justice, 1994).

ed as targets, not so much for the goods but for the reputation they have. Then there is the possibility of fraudulence, when the victims, for a variety of reasons, claim a break-in and property loss when in fact no such thing happened. They may want publicity, insurance money, save face, or cheat the Internal Revenue Service.

For criminological and investigative purposes an in-depth study of the residential burglar may be useful. The work and analysis of two scholars, Wright and Decker, will shape the discussion.

Deciding to Commit a Burglary

We know that young and poor men largely commit burglary. What are the reasons compelling them to do so? Clearly there is the need of quick money. They want this money for three reasons. One reason is to "keep the party going," or to live high. They have been loitering around, drinking, smoking, visiting, and partying, when they find they are running short of money. Second, there is the desire to keep up appearances, owning status items. Clothes top the list of these items, followed by cars and car accessories. Then there are those who need to keep things together, they need money for daily subsistence such as food, shelter, and clothing for their children.

Another reason is the general aversion to legitimate work. First, most do not have faith or the skill level to make the amount of money they think is necessary for their lifestyle. Second, work would hamper their preferred lifestyle. Precise schedules, punctuality, and disciplined subordination to authority is far from their idea of the good life. One of Wright and Decker's burglars makes the point.

> I like it to where I can just run around. I don't got to get up at no certain time, just whenever I wake up. I ain't gotta go to bed a certain time to get up at a certain time. Go to bed around one o'clock or when I want, get up when I want. Ain't got to go to work and work eight hours. Just go in and do a five minute job, get that money, that's just basically it.[11]

Third, there are the psychic rewards. The thrill of violating a person's privacy, being in and a part of their most private space and property. In an otherwise dull and dreary world, the burglary is an adventure. Revenge might be present as well, especially when the burglar is black and the victim is white.

Furthermore, these burglars want the money or goods fast. They were coasting along when the need came upon them. They wanted to take care of the problem quickly. There was no desire to find long ranged solutions, the quick fix was all that was expected or desired.

---

11. Quoted in Richard T. Wright and Scott H. Decker, *Burglars on the Job: Streetlife and Residential Break- ins* (Boston: Northeastern University Press, 1994), p. 48.

Choosing the Target

Most often burglars have a prospective target in mind long before the immediate need arises to commit the burglary. They have considerable information already about the target. This information is gained in three ways.

1. *The burglars know the occupants.* One-fifth of the burglars interviewed by Wright and Decker knew the occupants as casual acquaintances. These potential victims were neighbors who the burglar encountered in his day-to-day activities. Other times the burglar has had legitimate access to the victim's house. They might have been employed by a home decorating or remodeling company. Others might have been delivery men.

2. *The burglars had received a tip.* Sometimes this information came from "tipsters," those people who pass on information for a fee. More often they pick up information from friends or other street acquaintances. The more high-level burglars often rely heavily upon information from inside sources.

3. *Burglars search for the target.* No matter the skill level, street people even casually committed to burglary are always on the watch for likely candidates. Two questions emerge at the outset.

First, where to search? Most low-level burglars are restricted to areas within walking distance. Also, those burglars from the minority populations can go only to those areas where they do not arouse suspicion. Furthermore, since the burglar wants to minimize detection he wants to be able to predict the preventive measures and the reactions of the victim; this is best done by stealing from those most like him. Consequently black offenders generally seek out targets in black areas and white offenders select white victims. When just sitting or standing out in public space, they have one eye on vulnerable places. In addition, police patrol activities would be noted by burglars. High-crime areas, such as drug dealing districts, draw a lot of police; these areas would be avoided by the more rational burglar.

Second, there is the task of choosing a specific target within the general area. Almost all burglars look for signs tipping off the likelihood for the crime. For example, the place had to suggest from the outside that there was "good stuff" inside. The best clue was the size of the residency with large homes favored over small ones. Condition of the property was another indicator; well-kept places suggest pride in ownership and the likelihood of valuables inside. The type of car parked in the drive way also gives clues. The more highly motivated and committed the burglar, the more likely some kind of surveillance of prospective targets is done to "clock" the comings and goings of the residence. Therefore, these burglars were less concerned about safety measures. In addition, the time of day was an issue of some burglars. For example, 46 percent favored the morning, that time when people were off to work or school and there was a natural traffic of delivery and utilities personnel about. Midday was favored by 18 percent. Afternoons and evenings each received 10 percent. Late night was favored by 16 percent of the burglars interviewed.

4. *Approaching the specific target.* By the time the burglar has got to this stage he is firmly committed to carrying out the burglary. An interesting problem arises. His surveillance has been done largely from a distance. With his closer approach other indicators focus in on the thief. Types of locks on the doors and decals in the window for the scaring off of burglars only now come into the picture. They become largely irrelevant. But there are some things that might emerge to alter plans. First, chief of which is occupancy. Most burglars would avoid entering a place that they know the residents are home. Some burglars will call the residency to double check for occupancy. A favorite thing is to call from a public phone leaving the phone off the hook. Then the thief goes to the house and if he hears the phone still ringing he knows the house is empty. This was a better tactic in the days before the answering machine. Some thieves even determine the work number of the residents and call them there to make sure they are not at home. Barking dogs are another form of occupancy they wish to avoid. Alarms may act as "occupancy proxies" as well. Second, burglars regard visibility as the next important risk factor. Trees, bushes, lack of lighting, corners, and hidden places become part of the calculation. Next to being seen would be the likelihood of being heard. The burglar would select a residency not too close to its neighbors. Third, the degree of force necessary to make the entry is of concern. Locks are of little concern. On the other hand security bars or storm windows seem to be a deterrent. Burglars just do not want to take the time and make the effort, especially if it means making a lot of noise.

Entering the Target

Many burglars go from public to private property by posing as a legitimate trespasser. They may don work clothes and pretend to be any number of workers who might have real reason to be there. Painters, delivery people, moving van, and utilities workers are favorite disguises. This is a stressful time for the burglar and he cannot show hesitation and caution because that can be seen and interpreted as suspicious by neighbors. Being seen is not the issue, it's being seen as suspicious that has to be avoided. Many others choose to use the cover of night.

Common Techniques to Gain Entry

Prying	Use of a jimmy, screwdriver, tire iron, pry bar, or knife to force a door, window, or lock. Tool impressions are likely to be left behind.
Picking	Use of a knife or locksmith's tools to open the lock.
Pulling	Using a tool, such as a dent puller from an auto body repair shop, to pull the lock cylinder out.
Smash and crash	Breaking glass to gain entry.
Cutting glass	Using a glass cutter and suction cup to cut a hole in the glass and then to reach in and unlock a window or door.
Loiding	Slipping a celluloid strip or credit card between the lock and door jamb.
Brute force	Kicking and physically forcing the door to open.
Window/door entry	Entering through an open window or door. Forty percent of residential burglaries are without any force.
Remove door or parts	Removing a panel or entire door out of the framework.
Key entry	Finding of a hidden key or copying a key to be used later.[12]

Entry was a critical step in the burglary. Some burglars felt, in the name of not appearing suspicious, they should just walk up, ring the front door bell, and enter the front door. For most the entry point needed to be one least visible from the street and the neighbors. Generally this meant at the back of the residency compromising the door or window. Those residencies with an attached garage were a favorite. The thief could easily gain entrance to the garage and take his time in the privacy of that place to get into the house. Security hardware might shift strategies, as most locks are easily broken. If there is a "dead bolt," which are quite difficult, the bur-

12. Harry O'Reilly, *Practical Burglary Investigation* (Chicago: Office of Security Programs, University of Illinois at Chicago, 1991).

glar will shift to a window. Because of the noise factor most burglars would like to avoid breaking a window. When this was done the noise had to be minimized. A newspaper or cloth up against the glass would muffle the sound. Any sign of an alarm might force a shift of targets.

Search and Discovery

Once inside the residency the burglar does a quick survey of all the rooms to make sure that indeed no one is at home. Quickness is an important part of the crime. Seventy percent of burglaries take less than 20 minutes. Twenty-three percent take 20 to 45 minutes. Only seven percent take longer than 45 minutes. Then one of two strategies are used to find the goods to be taken.

First, there is the brief search. The most important place to go is the master bedroom; it is there they believe that the cash, jewelry, and guns would most likely be kept. Four places in the bedroom are focused upon. First stop would be the dresser, dumping the contents of the drawers onto the floor, because there the likelihood of cash and jewelry is greatest. Next would be the bedside table where a handgun would most likely be found. Then the bed followed by the closets. Some then go into the bathroom, particularly the medicine cabinet, looking for drugs. The living room would be the last room searched before the departure. It is here that larger objects might be taken. Most burglars would prefer to concentrate on smaller items, but if previous searches uncovered little then televisions, videocassette recorders, and stereo units might be stolen. Of course, such searches go much faster if there is a team of burglars which is often the case.

The second style would be the more leisurely search. In this case the burglar knows that the residents are to be gone for a long period and they feel they can take their time. Not only do they more leisurely look for loot, but they do a lot of other things as well. For example, many burglars defile the residency by defecating or urinating on the floor, furniture, or furnishings. Some entertain themselves. They may even cook a meal. Some even browse through family photos. Of course, the longer and more active the burglar is in the residency the more likely there will be investigative evidence left behind.

Departure

Now the criminal has committed the crime so it is vital to escape. Burglars will want to leave the quickest and less conspicuous way. If they came in the front door they will likely leave the same way. If they broke in a window they will more likely leave by the door. The more amateur thief will experience a sense of euphoria as they leave. Of course, even the professional will experience such feelings but to a lesser degree. This can lead to carelessness and leaving evidence behind for the investigator.

Disposing

Money is the most prized item in any burglary because it can be immediately used. However, most times the loot from a burglary will be in goods that need to be translated into cash. There are four ways in which a burglar makes this happen. First, there is the professional fence. Most burglars do not use these criminals. Fences greatly deflate the value of the articles stole so as to maximize their profit margins. Connection to fences marks the difference between an amateur and a professional. Second, there is the pawnshop. Pawnshops give cash or loans for goods. They are legitimate and visible shops frequently on the list of any detective. They also deflate the value of the items. Third, a drug dealer. Many dealers have an abundance of cash that needs laundering. Taking burgled goods and then reselling in other areas might satisfy this need. Four, friends and acquaintances might be an outlet for goods. On rare occasion burglars will keep such items as guns and jewelry for themselves. As time passes and pressure to get rid of the goods and get cash increase, some burglars will even sell to strangers. Of course, they sell in areas that they think are safe to do so.

Commercial Burglary

Burglaries of commercial establishments are less common than residences, but this is largely because there are fewer businesses than homes. Of course, the favorite target for commercial burglary would be the bank, but these institutions have become so security conscious that it is very difficult to do so. Consequently, this discussion will be aimed at non-banking businesses. Although, there are many items in a business that might be stolen, such as furs, jewelry, guns, and appliances, the main interest of the burglar would be to get money. Most businesses deposit receipts over night so that means that the business has sloppy business procedures and left large amounts of money in the store or that the amount of money to be obtained will be relatively scant. Of course, the main place to expect to find money is in a safe.

For purposes of simplicity, safes come in two generic varieties. First, there are those that are basically fire-resistant, in which valuables are protected from theft and fire. In between the layers of steel, there is a fire-resistant material that, in a way, compromises the security of the safe. Geometrically, these safes might be identified because of their square or rectangular doors. Second, there are the money chests. They take on a more circular look and are more secure from theft, but less protective during fire.

There are several ways safes can be compromised. These can be arranged into two categories, simple and sophisticated. These categories are selected to suggest an interpretation of the skill level of the burglar.

Simple

The simple assault of a safe can be considered in several ways. First, the simplest attack is to carry away the safe and compromise it later at leisure. This is not often done because of the weight and volume of the safe. Several people might need to take part and a strong vehicle, such as a pick-up truck, needs to be used. The other method of attack is blasting. At first glance, this might not seem to be simple but the ease of acquiring explosive materials makes this a very simple tactic. Historically, blasting powder, TNT and dynamite were commonly used. Now nitroglycerin and a variety of plastic explosives are used. Third, the four P's fit into this category:

1. *Pulling.* This method relies upon placing a tool (similar to a wheel-pulling device) that pulls out the lock spindle and thus compromises the safe.
2. *Punching.* More popular than pulling, this method relies upon driving the locking spindle inward by heavy blows from a hammer or sledge hammer.
3. *Prying.* This method depends on hitting the safe to cause a gap and then using a jimmy-type device to pry open the door. It is considered to be the most amateurish of these types.
4. *Peeling.* As above, a gap has to be created generally in the upper left corner of the save door and then the door is peeled downward to expose the rivets connecting the frame. Then the rivets are popped.

Sophisticated

The knowledge about safe construction, facility with a number of special tools, and the expenditure of energy mark the sophisticated safe burglar. There are three types to consider. First, there is the old and honored skill of manipulation. This is probably rarely done today but it consists of opening the lock by feeling or listening for the tumblers of the combination to stumble upon the correct opening sequence. Second, there is drilling. Burglars use a high-torque drill with diamond or carbide tipped bits to penetrate the safe. Since the door is the strongest section of a safe, generally they will attack the sides. Multiple drills might be made, or a core drill, to obtain a large enough hole to reach in for the valuables. Third, there is burning. Initially, burning meant the use of an acetylene torch in which heat cut into the steel. This is a very popular method since so many small and easily accessible torches are available. The problem is that many safes have steel that is not easily compromised by a simple acetylene device. More useful and sophisticated is the thermal burning bar. This device is used in construction companies, shipyards, and demolition companies. It can generate heat and energy to burn through a 6-inch-thick piece of tempered steel in 15 seconds. It is a dangerous tool and few can use it; only the most sophisticated safe burglars will resort to the thermal burning bar.

Investigation of Burglary

The investigation of burglary is very difficult and clearance rates remain constantly low.

1. The crime scene is the most important source of evidence. Tool marks for entry, fingerprints as property is ransacked, types of things taken (and left behind), evidence of leisurely lingering, and pathways of exit all may have useful information.
2. Witnesses, such as nearby neighbors, may have heard and seen something out of the ordinary.
3. Modus operandi of other known burglars might be used for leads. Small time burglars usually commit their crime nearer home and the police might have knowledge of the method of operations of local crooks.
4. Informants in the area might have information on active burglars.
5. Crimes analysis and mapping will certainly show patterns of activity.
6. Finally, the investigator has the responsibility and opportunity to teach the victim, and — in a public relations gesture — the neighborhood about defensible space concepts. Residents and commercial establishments need to see how their environment and lifestyles might enable criminals to better do their crimes.

Other Thefts

The number of thefts besides robbery and burglary are legion. Only a few can be discussed here.

Fencing

Since burglars frequently obtain goods rather than cash, the fence is a critical part of the above crimes and a segway (or transition) to those that follow. The fence straddles two worlds. First, there are the criminals who need the fence to transform stolen articles into cash. Without the services of the fence the risks for the thief would increase. Second, the noncriminal world relies upon the fence to provide goods at a cheaper price than found in the legitimate market.

There are four elements to this crime. The property must have been:

1. stolen,
2. received or concealed,
3. accepted with knowledge that it was stolen, and
4. received with criminal intent.

There is a hierarchical status among fences. First, there are the master fences. They have the money, organization, and network to receive all kinds of merchandise in large amounts at a moment's notice. Frequently these fences have legitimate business such as an antique, salvage, pawn, or flea market connections. Their outlets might be national and even international. Second, there are the more numerous specialty fences. They focus on one or a few specialty items such as jewelry and credit cards. They tend to restrict their business to the specialty crooks as well. Third, are the larger number of neighborhood fences. Although networks are important to all fences they are more critical and personal at this level. Several networking methods can be seen at this level, including:

1. *Kinship networks*, in which members of the family are involved. Generally, younger members steal and older ones fence the items.
2. *Work-a-day relationships*, in which a fence has a legitimate business and employees earn extra by bringing in goods for fencing.
3. *Recreation networks*, in which the participants, the thief and fence, meet on social and recreational levels.

Investigation of fencing operations depends on several things:

1. *Informants*. Since many fences are disguised by legitimate business operations or long lines of networks, the work of developing informants is critical.
2. *Stings*. First used in the late 1970s, wired undercover police pose as customers or thieves to collect evidence on fencing operations.
3. *Operation Identification*. One way to prevent or curtail burglary is to jeopardize the fence. Operation Identification began in the 1970s by encouraging citizens to mark their valuables. Perhaps a fur piece would have a special mark burned into an inconspicuous part of the skin. Valuable jewelry might have a special identifying etch mark. Such procedures might not impact the thief, but they place the fence in precarious positions.

Automobile Theft

Vehicle theft, as far back in history when it was predominately horse and buggy robbery, continues to be a major crime problem and is even becoming one of the FBI's index indicators. Unlike many thefts a single occurrence immediately is costly; while a victim of a street robbery or burglary may lose several hundred to a thousand dollars, an auto theft immediately costs the victim several thousand dollars. The FBI has estimated that losses to victims total $8 billion a year. Bureau of Justice statistics estimate that in 1992 2 million offenses occurred, this being a rate of 13 vehicles stolen for every 1,000 on the road.[13]

The risk of being a victim is not spread evenly. For example, most likely victims will be blacks living in rental apartments in the central sections of the city. But the types of automobiles stolen might be categorized. Cars wanted for stripping were largely German-made vehicles with good audio equipment. Those stolen for temporary use were American-made performance cars. Those taken to be kept were less expensive foreign cars.

There are several types of automobile thieves. They are those who do it for:

1. *Joyriding.* Young people between the ages of 15 and 19 predominate here. They keep the car until the fuel and thrill are gone and then just dump it. Likelihood of recovery is good. At one time these youthful thefts predominated, but they have been challenged by another group recently.
2. *Transportation.* Transients, hitchhikers, and runaways passing through town might steal a car to help them get to their next destination. Although not as easily recovered due to further proximity these vehicles are likely to be recovered to their owner.
3. *Crime commission.* A vehicle might be stolen to be used in a bank robbery or kidnaping, an instrument of homicide, or a means to discard a body. On occasion, an owner might want to commit insurance fraud by claiming a car was stolen when in fact it was set up for theft or other disposal. Auto insurers estimate that 10 percent of claims for auto theft each year are fraudulent. Several schemes of fraud have been noted. For example, there is the duplicate title fraud in which a person sells a car, obtains a duplicate title, then reports the car stolen, then surrenders the title to the insurance company for payment. Another scheme is the paper vehicle fraud in which a fictitious car is

---

13. Federal Bureau of Investigation, *Crimes in the United States, 1993* (Washington, DC: US Department of Justice, 1994), p. 50.

registered and insured, then "stolen" so that the insurance can be claimed.

4. *Professional theft rings*. So many professional criminals have taken to car theft, that the chances of recovery has declined to little better than 50 percent. Some professionals specialize in reselling stolen vehicles in America or abroad. Others become involved in "chop shop" activity. The car is stolen then stripped of its parts which are resold. Others operate "salvage-switch" rings. They purchase at low cost a wrecked car or truck and its ownership papers. Then they steal an identical make and model, exchange the vehicle identification number plate, make minimal alterations, then they sell the stolen car on the legitimate market.

One study conducted in England, while not conclusive, it is at least suggestive, sets forth some additional data on vehicle thieves. For example:

1. Most thieves start in their mid-teens under the tutelage of an older, more experienced thief.
2. Influence of friends, boredom, and the excitement of theft seem to be the reasons for beginning this activity.
3. Over time money becomes the most important reason. Over one-third of those interviewed progressed to be professional vehicle thieves.
4. Over half referred to themselves as "specialists." No other theft was done except car stealing. These specialists were likely to have had a youthful obsession with cars.
5. Car alarms appeared to deter about one-third of the thieves.
6. They believed that car theft was morally wrong, but did not consider it a serious crime.
7. The excitement of the crime out weighed any deterrent value of punishment.[14]

Investigations of vehicle theft have been aided with the creation of the National Auto Theft Bureau (NATB), a non-profit organization based in Chicago and set up by a consortium of insurance companies. It maintains a national file on stolen vehicles. It keeps files on national car theft rings, and it helps train police officers in the investigation of vehicle theft.

The growing nature of this crime has given rise to specialized investigators. For example, the International Association of Auto Theft Investigators has over a thousand members. It conducts seminars in cooperation with universities and colleges, and with local, state, federal, and provincial

---

14. Claire Nee, "Car Theft: The Offender's Perspective," *Home Office Research Findings* (February 1993).

police agencies. Information on the extent and technology of investigations of this crime are shared at these seminars and a quarterly newsletter is sent to the membership.

In addition, the National Insurance Crime Bureau publishes annually a passenger Vehicle Identification Manual that deciphers VINs on automobiles.

Other investigative techniques include awareness of some indicators that a car may have been stolen. For example, a broken side or vent window or any other evidence of forced entry is suggestive. The condition of a license plate might be suspicious. A dirty plate on an otherwise clean car should arouse some doubts. Additionally, a variety of identification numbers need to be examined, such as the engine number, which is a manufacturer's number on the engine block. This number is hard to get rid of without leaving signs of tampering.

Vehicle Identification Numbers (VIN) generally on the left side of the dash or instrumental panel and visible through the windshield can be removed but signs of tampering might be evident. Beginning with the 1981 model year, the National Highway Traffic Safety Administration, Department of Transportation, required manufacturers selling over the road vehicles in the United States to produce the vehicles with a 17-character vehicle identification number. This standard establishes a fixed VIN format including a check digit and applies to all passenger cars, multi-purpose passenger vehicles, trucks, buses, trailers, incomplete vehicles, and motorcycles with a gross vehicle weight of 10,000 pounds or less. The first three characters of the VIN format are designated the WMI (World Manufacture Identification). The WMI identifies the nation of origin, manufacturer, make, and type of vehicle. The second section has five characters and has been designated the VDS (Vehicle Description Section). The VDS identifies the attributes of the vehicle such as model, body style, and engine. The third section of the VIN is located after the check digit. It is eight characters in length and is called the VIS (Vehicle Identification Section). The first character represents the vehicle model year; the second character represents the plant of manufacture; and the last six characters represent the sequential production number. Such information, especially if it is kept out of the working knowledge of the crooks, can be very useful in investigating vehicle theft.

Shoplifting

The stealing of goods from a retail business is an ancient crime, but it got a major impetus in the late nineteenth century rise of the department store. Goods were more accessible and tempting in their presentation. Customer and employee theft heats up during the Christmas season when a reported 20 percent increase occurs. Retailers call it "shrinkage," jargon for having more merchandise on the books than on the shelves or in the cash register. Pilfering employees call it the "five-finger discount." Police call it shoplifting. Losses are so bad that, it is estimated, 1 out of 3 small business bankruptcies are caused by shoplifting thefts. Losses and the cost of extra security boost the retail price 2 to 3 cents a dollar on average. Annual costs range to $4 billion per year. Shoplifting is such a problem that the National Coalition to Prevent Shoplifting was formed in 1979 to help set up anti-shoplifting campaigns.

Retailers have attempted to meet the challenge of this growing criminal problem in several ways. First, going back over one hundred years, there has been the hiring of private security people to patrol and watch the valuables in the stores. At first, this was done by outside agencies such as Pinkertons or Burns. Later many stores set up their own security mechanism within the business organization. Second, there was the requirement that all sales personnel and other workers watch out for shoplifters. This placed sales people in an embarrassing situation. In those stores where there was some animosity between workers and management such a strategy was not carried out with any enthusiasm. Modern technology has produced a variety of devices to prevent theft. In fact modern retailers judge security devices in a new way. For example, the percentage of security devices judged effective by retailers is thus:

Electronic Tags	60%
Guards	17%
Point-of-sale computers	15%
Observation booths	13%
Visible tv monitors	13%
Mirrors	2%[15]

There are several types of shoplifters. The professional shoplifter accounts for a small number of criminals, but their organization and skill accounts for considerable damage. They travel across country in well-organized tours of theft. They are likely to use special devices. For example, historically they used a dress, coat, or pants with larger than normal pockets to secret things away. These "booster" clothes gave rise to the label for professional shoplifters as "booster gangs." While this is partially true of all shoplifters, the professional will be even more focused on the goods taken. For example, according to leaders in the retail department store industry, such items as higher-priced women's clothing was a favorite. In addition, electronic gadgets, gold jewelry, and small appliances were favored.

---

15. *Chicago Tribune* (December 11, 1985).

The Amateur shoplifter predominates in this crime. Shoplifting became such a problem in the early years of the department store that thieving women were defined as kleptomaniac rather than criminal so as to avoid the problems of prosecutions. The following is suggestive when considering the amateur shoplifter:

1. Sex

Female	55%
Male	45%

2. Age

16-20	26%
21-30	38%
31-60	31%
60 +	5%

3. Methods Used

Concealed in clothing	37%
Put in shopping bag	36%
Put in purse	19%
Put in briefcase	7%
Switch price tags	1%[16]

Dishonest employees form a significant part of this crime. "Fiddling," as this activity has been labeled, is quite extensive and ranges across a wide spectrum of types which includes shoplifting. Any number of reasons might motivate these criminals. First, they have extensive opportunity being legitimately around the goods or valuables. Second, they may feel inadequate in terms of pay and benefits; their theft is a means to compensate for perceived shortcomings in the worker-manager relationship. Third, the victim may be easily depersonalized. A vast corporation is easier to steal from than an individual. If the definitions of the victim are ambiguous so might the act of stealing from that victim.

Besides shoplifting, defined here in its broadest terms, these criminals come in a variety of styles. For example, there are the:

1. *Hawks,* or those working in environments that stress individuality and autonomy. Independent sales people and academics might be two examples. They frequently manipulate time and work performance. A favorite activity is to pad expense accounts and charge for work not done.

---

16. Taken from statistics by Woodward & Lothrop Department Store study as reported in *U.S. News & World Report* (December 3, 1979).

2. *Donkeys* are in jobs that provide some isolation but places rigid constraints. Retail sales people and assembly line workers might characterize this group. They take small change or goods to compensate for feelings of isolation and job inadequacy.

3. *Wolves* operate in groups and depend upon a clique solidarity. Prison guards and police officers might be placed here.

4. *Vultures* have jobs that give over all autonomy and freedom but are subject to a larger bureaucracy. Traveling sales people and postal workers are examples.[17]

The investigation of shoplifting and employee theft is a difficult task for several reasons. First, the crime takes place on private property that is open to large numbers of public. The police are not responsible for patrolling such places to act as a deterrent. Second, many stores have hired private security firms or created loss prevention units within their business organization. Sometimes these agencies are too aggressive and embarrassing in their procedures. Third, historically the store owner has wanted to downplay this crime. It places them in awkward positions they would rather avoid. Even if people are caught, retailers fear accusations of false arrest and possible adverse notoriety. Consequently, most stores have a policy of leniency. Forth, while the police might be quite knowledgeable about the professionals, so much of this activity is done by amateurs against whom traditional investigative procedures are less effective.

Computer Crime

In the last twenty years computers have grown at a remarkable rate. Commercial, governmental, and military activities rely upon computers at ever growing rates. One trillion dollars is moved electronically each week. For many people personal reliance is great as well. Over 4.7 million personal computers were sold in 1988; and that number has increased ever since. The kinds of computer criminals vary due to opportunity and skill levels. But all computer criminals seem to do it for one of several reasons:

1. Personal or financial gain,
2. Entertainment,
3. Revenge,
4. Personal favor,
5. Beat the System, the Challenge,

---

17. Gerald Mars, *Cheats at Work: An Anthropology of Workplace Crime* (London: Unwin Paperbacks, 1982).

6. Accident,
7. Vandalism.

One student of this crime has described computer crime metaphorically. For example, the computer may be seen as the:

1. *Playpen*, in which the abuser sees the computer as a toy.
2. *Fairyland*, in which the computer is an unreal world and real wrong cannot be done.
3. *Land of Opportunity*, in which there is nothing wrong going after a vulnerable system.
4. *Tool box*, in which the computer is just a way to get other things.
5. *Cookie jar*, in which the computer is a place to go to "borrow" a little now and then.
6. *War game*, in which hostile feelings are vented against a machine rather than people.[18]

There are several levels and types of computer criminality. These include internal computer crimes, telecommunications crimes, computer manipulation crimes, and hardware and software thefts.

1. *Internal computer crimes.* These crimes are those that alter programs resulting in the performance of unauthorized functions within the computer system. At the *simplest* level there is "data diddling," probably the most common crime, which changes information at the entry level. For example, changing one number or decimal point might change a person's payroll benefits. Benefit payments may be rounded down a few cents and these funds, which can amount to a lot in the aggregate, diverted to a fraudulent account; this is called the "Salami Technique" because the slice taken is so small so as not to be missed. This form of computer crime requires little skill and the number of suspects could be quite large. Another type of criminality might be "browsing," or the looking into the files of others to find private information that might be exploited in other ways.

At more *sophisticated* levels there are a series of activities by programmers who change an existing program so that it appears to act normally but in fact performs unwanted functions. For example, a "Trojan horse" is a program with useful functions but in addition has a hidden function so that when the logic conditions have been met, the program exploits the security features of the system. "Trap doors" and "logic bombs" do similar things. "Viruses" are sets of instructions that not only perform unauthorized functions but attach themselves to other programs and spread widely. A "Worm" can do the same thing but it does not need an existing

18. Larry Coutourie. "The Computer Criminal: An Investigative Assessment," *FBI Law Enforcement Bulletin* 58 (1989), pp. 18–22.

program to duplicate itself. In 1988 Robert Morris planted a worm through an independent program that penetrated computers on the network and replicated itself, thus rapidly overloading computers by first making them sluggish and then causing them to crash. Finally, there is "superzapping," or a set of instructions that bypasses all system controls and is designed to be used in time of an emergency. This master key allows the offender to access the computer at any time for any purpose.[19]

2. *Telecommunications crimes* involve illegal use of computer systems over telephone lines. "Hacking" attempts to find valid access codes for a computer system by continually calling the system with randomly generated codes. Once the valid code is stumbled upon, the computer system is invaded and compromised. "Phreaking" is a fraud done by an electronic device that sends out a sound to the phone company that mimics the sound that signals a normal long-distance call. It tricks the company into thinking a legal transaction is being made when actually it is not. A person doing this can ring up thousands of dollars in calls without being charged. Illegal bulletin boards, such as when a pedophile shares information with other like minded, are also set up on the information highway.

3. *Computer manipulation* crimes involve using the technology to help in the performance of another crime, such as embezzlement of a financial institution in which funds are diverted into a false account. Computers might be used to support other criminal activities such as prostitution rings and drug cartels.

4. *Hardware and software thefts* include "piracy," or the illegal copying of a software propriety package. Some may do so just for a personal copy but others might make many copies for criminal sale and profit. There may be theft of microcomputer chips and other elements of the system.[20]

Investigating Computer Crime

Only in the last two decades has law enforcement met standards to fight this crime; several details are important to know.

1. *Statutes.* The first state computer crime statute was enacted in Florida in 1978. Since that time every state has addressed this form of theft through statute. Most have made a law specifically aimed at computer crime. Others have amended existing theft law inserting computer theft as part of the general theft crime.[21]

---

19. Prevention Committee, President's Council on Integrity and Efficiency, *Computers: Crime, Clues and Controls: A Management Guide* (March 1986).

20. J. Thomas McEwen, *Dedicated Computer Crime Units* (Washington, DC: Department of Justice, 1989).

21. Richard C. Hollinger and Lonn Lanza-Kaduce, "The Process of Criminalization: The Case of Computer Crime Laws," *Criminology* 26 (1988), p. 101.

2. *Types of crooks.* Generally, the computer crook is not the precocious hacker who compromises major systems. More likely the crook is an employee who is a legitimate and nontechnical end user of the system. Seventy-five percent of computer crimes are done by employees, and the average age of the criminals tends to be 29. They hold managerial or professional positions. According to one study 88 percent thought of their activity as a game, a challenge, rather than a crime. When criminality was a possible thought, these criminals felt they were Robin Hoods robbing from the rich and oppressive.[22]

3. *Types of theft* have been estimated as:

Use of computer for money theft	45%
Theft of Information	16%
Damage to Software	16%
Alteration of Data	12%
Theft of Services	10%
Trespass	2%[23]

4. *Nature of investigations.* It is estimated that 11 percent of computer crime is reported. Most police investigators do not have the technical skills to investigate this crime. The FBI and larger cities might have a few people who are knowledgeable but resources have come late and slight. The FBI has established a Computer Analysis and Response Team (CART) to help federal and local law enforcement investigate this activity. The team is available for those agencies who have met the guidelines for submission of forensic evidence for examination.[24] Consequently the important thing is to have officers who recognize that indeed a crime has occurred and then go to those who possess the necessary skills for advice.

5. *Clues to abuse* include:

Missing computer supplies,
Missing software,
Unauthorized use of computer time;
Unauthorized possession of computer disks or printouts;
Sloppy or nonexistent security measures;
Practice of passwords being public knowledge;
Evidence of numerous attempts to log on with invalid passwords.

---

22. Larry Coutourie, "The Computer Criminal: An Investigative Assessment," *FBI Law Enforcement Bulletin* 58 (1989), pp. 18–22.

23. National Center for Computer Crime Data, Los Angeles, California.

24. Michael G. Noblett, "The Computer: High-Tech Instrument of Crime," *FBI Law Enforcement Bulletin* 62 (1993), pp. 7–9.

6. *Guidelines for investigation*:

On-site information sources, such as interviews, need to be used;
Computer needs to be protected from further, intentional and
unintentional, tampering;
Support software needs to be seized;
Entire system may need to be seized.

Confidence Games

Swindlers have been around for a long time. The variety of "games" or
"cons" are numerous. These crimes are important because they are by guile
rather than force. They show the skill of the "grifter" because they create a
trust. The term confidence man was probably first coined by New York City
newspapers in 1849 when the swindler, William Thompson, would strike
up a conversation with a person and then ask, "Do you have confidence in
me to let me borrow your watch?" He would then disappear with the watch.
Since then hundreds of ways have been found to fleece the naive. The successful con artist must accomplish several things, making the victim or "mark":

1. Trust the con artist,
2. See that there is profit for him,
3. Part with his money to a stranger, and
4. Not report the incident to the police.

Con artists may be divided into two large categories, simple and sophisticated.

Simple

Most simple swindles are *short cons* or *bunco*. They rely upon a quick
turn around. Perhaps the simplest and longest lasting of these is the "drop."
A ring drop consists of placing a piece of worthless jewelry on the sidewalk
near a stranger (the "mark") by one member of the gang called the roper.
Another member of the team (the inside man) rushes forward to pick up
the item. He shows it to the mark and agrees to share the proceeds if it
can be sold. The mark is convinced to put up some money as a token of
good faith. The grifter leaves with the money and the mark has the worthless jewelry. A "purse drop" is similar except it is a found wallet or purse.
The "pigeon drop" is a little more elaborate but has the same general features. In this case, the victim in a pigeon drop is invited to share some
money that has supposedly been found by one member of the confidence
team. In order to qualify for that share, however, the mark must put up
some good faith money. This money is supposedly mixed with the found

money but in fact is switched and the victim ends up with a bag of worthless paper. Variations of the "green goods" scam fit here too. In the old days it was money, but today a mark is asked to buy some goods, such as liquor or TV's, at a much-reduced cost. They get home with their box of goods to see that they are very inferior or worthless. Another is the "lotto scam." In this case a foreigner comes up to the mark with a winning lottery ticket and a story that he cannot collect on it because he is not a citizen. He will share half the ticket prize with you if you cash it in. Simply he has found the winning numbers of the previous day and put them down on a new ticket but disguises the date. You give to the con artist half the value then attempt to collect on the ticket. Meanwhile the con is over and the grifter is gone with your money. Other confidence games include:

1. Carpet cleaning scams;
2. Phony charity/religious solicitations;
3. Contest winner promotions;
4. Magazine subscriptions;
5. 900 number solicitations;
6. Travel club offers.

Sophisticated

A little more sophisticated swindle would be the bank examiner con. In this swindle the mark is asked to help test the honesty of a bank clerk by withdrawing some money from his account. When the victim returns home with the money the examiner shows up to take the money for laboratory analysis or some other official reason. Official documents are left with the mark but they are worthless and the money disappears.

Another example would be a variety of home improvement and repair scams. The contractor comes into the home and offers repairs at a greatly reduced price, but he needs some money up front to buy materials. Then, he either disappears with this money doing no work or stays around to partially do the job before disappearing. Some grifters form traveling gangs of these repair teams and have been referred to as the "Irish Travelers."

Finally there is the infamous Ponzi or pyramid scheme. This scam is based upon the referral system in which a mark buys into a company and obtains the right to sell others the right to sell the product. Profits are made on a commission fee of those brought into the scheme. In actuality there is no product, just a pyramid of people selling to an ever growing number of other people the right to hire even more people. Profits at the top of the pyramid can be great.

It is difficult to investigate these crimes, however:

1. Most of these cons are well known and modus operandi of the more professional grifters are identified.
2. Many larger police departments have set up specialized bunco squads to investigate these crimes.
3. The type of victim generally selected for the con is known and can be targeted for education, such as white, unmarried or living alone females between the ages of 65 and 79. When these victims were asked why they succumbed to these criminals they commonly referred to friendliness and the appearance of wealth of the con artist.[25]

Conclusions

Theft is the single largest criminal activity in the world. It includes a wide variety of types of activities, ranging from personally violent to stealth craftiness. A culture of criminality is in place with a number of professionals and an even larger number of amateurs. The police in general and investigators in particular have had only mixed results in combating this problem. Clearance rates remain low. Public awareness of the problem and the limited ability of the police to do much about it remains a major challenge. The public, particularly those most vulnerable, need to be aware and use defensible strategies to challenge this criminality.

25. Monroe Friedman, "Confidence Swindles of Older Consumers," *Journal of Consumer Affairs* 26 (1992), pp. 20–46.

Index